Dear Reader:

The book you are about to read is the latest bestseller from the St. Martin's True Crime Library, the imprint the *New York Times* calls "the leader in true crime!" Each month, we offer you a fascinating account of the latest, most sensational crime that has captured the national attention. St. Martin's is the publisher of perennial bestselling true crime author Jack Olsen, whose SALT OF THE EARTH is the true story of one woman's triumph over life-shattering violence; Joseph Wambaugh called it "powerful and absorbing." Fannie Weinstein and Melinda Wilson tell the story of a beautiful honors student who was lured into the dark world of sex for hire in THE COED CALL GIRL MURDER. St. Martin's is also proud to publish two-time Edgar Award-winning author Carlton Stowers, whose TO THE LAST BREATH recounts a two-year-old girl's mysterious death, and the dogged investigation that led loved ones to the most unlikely murderer: her own father. In the book you now hold, "IF I DIE . . .", Michael Fleeman explores an unusual case in which the victim's will leaves a tantalizing clue . . .

St. Martin's True Crime Library gives you the stories *behind* the headlines. Our authors take you right to the scene of the crime and into the minds of the most notorious murderers to show you what really makes them tick. St. Martin's True Crime Library paperbacks are better than the most terrifying thriller, because it's all true! The next time you want a crackling good read, make sure it's got the St. Martin's True Crime Library logo on the spine—you'll be up all night!

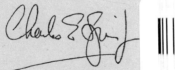

Charles E. Spicer, Jr.
Executive Editor, St. Martin's True Crime Library

On the night of January 21, 1995, all was quiet and cool up in Eldorado Canyon. A gentle rain began to fall. The fish weren't biting. It was so dark the four fishermen couldn't see the jagged mountains on the Arizona side of the lake. By 1 a.m.—now Saturday—they were tired and cold. They packed up their gear and headed for home. The trek back proved to be tougher than the hike down. The four men walked in a tight, single-file line, with one of them holding a flashlight. They stumbled and slipped on the steep, loose ground, basically stones and gravel on top of solid rock. They couldn't find the trail they took down, so they headed up a ravine.

They were about halfway up the ravine when they spotted it. Steven didn't even see it at first, focused as he was on the terrain in front of him. But the flashlight beam from behind him had caught it, just off to the right.

"There's a human skull!" one of the men behind Steven shouted . . .

"IF I DIE..."

MICHAEL FLEEMAN

St. Martin's Paperbacks

This is a work of nonfiction. Dialogue has been recreated from public records, trial and grand jury testimony and interviews by the author. All of the names are real except for these pseudonyms: Maria Aquino, Ed, Peter, and Sara.

"IF I DIE . . ."

Copyright © 2002 by Michael Fleeman.

Cover photograph courtesy AP/Wide World Photos.

ISBN: 0-312-98046-9

Printed in the United States of America

St. Martin's Paperbacks edition/January 2002

10 9 8 7 6 5 4 3 2 1

About 1874, the richest gold in Eldorado Canyon was found in the Techatticup, 300 feet down. It assayed at $33,000 per ton and was called the bridal chamber because you could see the gold stringing through the white quartz vein. Of the three partners that owned the mine, two were strychnine poisoned within a week of the discovery.

— CARD POSTED IN A LITTLE MUSEUM IN
MODERN-DAY ELDORADO CANYON, NEVADA

"IF I DIE..."

1

ELDORADO CANYON

A car came to a stop on a lonely turnout above Lake Mohave, a long narrow reservoir straddling the Nevada–Arizona border. In the cold winter moonlight, Steven Vermilya and three companions piled out of the car after the ninety-minute drive from Las Vegas, unloading their tackle boxes and poles for a long night of fishing for striped bass and catfish. They would have this part of the lake to themselves. The nearest settlement was Nelson's Landing, some five miles to the west, deep in Eldorado Canyon, where the bullet-riddled "No Trespassing" signs nearly outnumbered the hardy inhabitants.

Carrying their gear, the fishermen stumbled down the rocky slope until they reached a cliff that dropped off into nothing but darkness. They backtracked and found a loose gravel path that led them to an old boat launch area that had been washed out by floodwaters in the 1970s. They had nothing but a single flashlight and the moonlight to guide them—Steven acknowledged that the trip wasn't well thought out—and by the time they reached water's edge even the moonlight began to fade behind gathering clouds.

They fished for about four hours at the landing, where a century earlier steamers had unloaded men and supplies for the gold and silver mines up the canyon. Eldorado was a boomtown in those days, larger, richer and meaner than the dusty stopover on the desert floor that the Spanish explorers had named Las Vegas—*The Meadows*—for its oases. The notorious Indian outlaw Queho had lived and died in this wild canyon. His mummified body would be found in a cliff-side cave, the leathery remains lying next to the watchman's badge belonging to one of the 20 people he was said to have murdered.

But this night, January 21, 1995, all was quiet and cool. A gentle rain began to fall. The fish weren't biting. It was so dark the men couldn't see the jagged mountains on the Arizona side of the lake. By 1 a.m.—now Saturday—they were tired and cold. They packed up their gear and headed for home. The trek back proved to be tougher than the hike down. The four men walked in a tight, single-file line, with Vermilya at the front, and a buddy behind him holding the flashlight. They stumbled and slipped on the steep, loose ground, basically stones and gravel on top of solid rock. They couldn't find the trail they took down, so they headed up a ravine.

They were about halfway up the ravine when they spotted it. Steven didn't even see it at first, focused as he was on the terrain in front of him. But the flashlight beam from behind him had caught it, just off to the right.

"There's a human skull!" one of the men behind Steven shouted.

He thought they were teasing him. By now, the men were so uncomfortable that grim humor had set in. But this was no joke. There lay a skull on the rocky ground, resting on what would have been its left cheek. Clearly visible were the fillings in the teeth and what looked like cartilage holding the jaw to the rest of the skull.

Steven and two of the other men were trained military policemen, from Nellis Air Force Base north of Las Vegas. They knew enough not to touch it.

The plan was to get home to Las Vegas and call the police. They scampered up the ravine to their car, threw their gear inside and drove out of the overlook parking area, up the narrow road that wound through Eldorado Canyon.

They never seriously considered stopping in Nelson's Landing to use a phone. There were no gas stations or stores, only the little houses and mobile homes, which didn't look inviting. On the way to the lake, they had seen a sign on a building that read: "Do Not Stop Here."

"After we found the skull," Steven recalled, "the sign kind of took on a new meaning."

By daybreak, they'd return to Eldorado Canyon, where riches and death have long been intertwined like the gold running through the quartz in a glory hole that turned out to be a deadly bridal chamber.

Detective Phil Ramos got the phone call at home about noon on Saturday, January 21, 1995. It was his supervisor, Sgt. Bill Keeton. "Guess what?" Keeton prodded him.

Ramos didn't have to guess. He and Vaccaro weren't the on-call detectives that weekend—that was Mike Franks and partner Brent Becker—so Keeton could only be calling about one thing. There was a break in the biggest case of their careers.

Ramos and Vaccaro arranged to drive separately to Nelson's Landing, where they would meet Franks and Becker, who had been there for hours. It was a glorious afternoon, the kind of crisp, clean day that could only follow a rain, El Niño taking a breather. As they traveled across the desert, the road through Eldorado Canyon became narrow and winding after the little settlement of Nelson's Landing, the center stripe disappearing altogether as the neglected pavement turned bumpy. All along the road, past the abandoned mines where the locals insisted there was still plenty of gold and silver left for anybody with the grit to go after it, one sign after another issued warnings and prohibitions: "No Shooting Area. Loaded Weapons Prohibited." Others warned, "Watch Downhill Speed," "No Dumping," "No Trespassing," "Road Narrows." Many of them were aerated by shotgun blasts; the no-shooting admonition obviously carried little weight in this remote canyon.

Ramos and Vaccaro arrived at the parking area overlooking Lake Mohave. Much of the crime scene had been processed by the time Ramos and Vaccaro got there. The detectives were given the basics: Four fishermen had stumbled onto a skull in a rocky ravine the night before.

Three of them had returned to Nelson's Landing to point out the skull—the fourth had had to work that morning. They were interviewed and let go.

The scene was being processed by analyst Sheree Norman, who had been called to Nelson's Landing at 11 that morning. She made a diagram of the area and had photos taken. The skull was located about 70 yards away from the roadway, down the steep embankment, in a gully carved out by rainwater running down toward the lake, another couple hundred yards away. The skull was remarkably well preserved; the jaw was still attached, the ligaments having survived the elements. The skull had a small blackened area, as if the head had been exposed to fire. In the back of the skull were three small holes—very possibly bullet holes.

As the police were being led to the skull by the fishermen earlier that morning, they found what could have been the source of the charring. A fire pit was located just a few yards up the hill from the skull. There were small bone fragments in the pit. Norman recalled that the area was "not unlike what you found in a barbecue pit." Only this appeared to be a human barbecue. On a bluff above, Norman saw more bone fragments next to bird droppings. "We speculate there was a lot of animal activity helping themselves to what was left in the fire pit," she said.

If this was the remains of a human, the fire had consumed any traces of clothing or shoes. There was not so much as a zipper or metal button. But amid the bones were some other things: metal bands, two hasps, a lock assembly—in the locked position—pieces of fire-blackened wood and remnants of a floral-design lining paper that had escaped the flames. Norman knew immediately where these had come from. They were what was left of an antique humpback chest, like the one Norman's mother, an antique collector, had given her when she was growing up in New Jersey. From the metal straps, she could tell that the trunk was about standard size, 20 inches by 36 inches at the base. She had no way of telling how high it was, because the straps only went around the base of the trunk. The wood that would have made up the sides was nothing but little burned scraps.

Some effort was likely exerted to get the trunk to this spot, suggesting that the body had been in it. A rough gravel trail led down the hill, but passed well away from the burned area. From the trail, etched in the gravel, were what Norman suspected to be parallel drag marks, about 20 inches apart, leading toward the fire pit, but stopping far short of it.

After the coroner's technician had removed the human remains, Norman had scooped up some of the burned dirt and rocks, the wood and the paper, and placed them in clean metal paint cans for testing in the police lab. She plucked out the hasps and the lock and put them in bags. She put the big metal strips in a large box. She also found a number of old-fashioned, square-shafted nails, which she collected.

From the fire pit, she measured the distance down the steep ravine to where the skull lay on its left side against three rocks, the eye sockets peering downhill. It was 35 feet away. She suspected it may have rolled down to the spot, but she couldn't be sure.

One more piece of evidence would be found—explaining why Ramos and Vaccaro were called out on their day off. Located about 13 feet from the burn area draped over a rock, was a bracelet, badly tarnished, on which little jewels spelled out the name RON.

2

RRR-1

Read the history of Las Vegas, and it's a common theme: A man with a vision looks at what others would consider a vast wasteland and sees only promise. Ronald J. Rudin would join their ranks in his own modest way with everybody from turn-of-the-century real estate speculator William Clark (the Clark in Clark County, Nevada) to mobster and casino builder Benjamin "Bugsy" Siegel.

In the early 1960s, Ron was primed for change. He was a 30-year-old Korean War vet, and his home state of Illinois held no future for him. His plans to expand a Chicago manufacturing plant were stymied by his business partner. Out here in the West, he could do it alone.

The Las Vegas of four decades ago bore little resemblance to the corporate-run Disneyland for adults of today. It was a smaller, more intimate, perhaps more dangerous town, where the doormen addressed the high rollers by name and where it wouldn't be unusual to see a member of the Rat Pack, including Frank himself, at the tables, blowing off some steam after wowing them with a boozy show at the Desert Inn.

But the more carnal aspects of Las Vegas held no appeal for Ron. He would place his bets far away from the casinos, in the thriving real estate market. "After the Korean War, he was looking for ways to make money but not just with a job," explained his cousin Robert Riley, who grew up with Ron. "He wasn't going to just work for somebody. He was going to do something that had great potential, he felt. I think he looked at Las Vegas as that kind of place. He looked at Las Vegas as having potential for tremendous growth."

*　　　*　　　*

Born on November 14, 1930, Ron Rudin grew up in Joliet, Illinois, a middle-class suburban steel town on the Des Plaines River, 40 miles southwest of Chicago. Although it was the depths of the Depression, the Rudin family did not struggle. Ron's father, the tough, bigger-than-life Roy Rudin, earned a good salary working for a chemical company. His job took him to far-off exotic places where the company looked for raw materials. A snapshot from 1943 showed Roy Rudin in British Guyana, a cigarette in one hand and a pith helmet in the other. An avid hunter, his prey once included a huge snake in the jungles of South America.

By all indications Ron both loved and feared his father. When Roy Rudin spoke, people tended to snap to attention. Ron was an only child, and his mother Stella doted on him. He in turn worshipped his mother. Stella was also described by several of Ron's cousins as their favorite aunt, a generous, warm-hearted woman who, if she had any flaw, it was that she was a terrible driver.

Though his father was often away, Ron appeared to have had a rich and happy childhood. He spent summers on the southern Illinois farm owned by his maternal grandparents, playing with his cousins, and hunting birds and squirrels with a single-shot .22 rifle, which he was allowed to use when he was as young as six. Ron had inherited not only his father's love of hunting, but some of his strong personality as well. He would be the leader of whatever little pack of cousins was there at the time—often to his financial benefit. "Let's just say Ron was good at marbles and things like that," recalled his cousin Riley, who said the two were as close as brothers when they were kids. "He would be tighter than a bark on a tree. He knew every penny that he had—and tried to figure out how to get yours if you let him."

But it wasn't all Norman Rockwell for the Rudin family. During a visit to the farm, tragedy struck. His father was found slumped over in a chair. He had died of a heart attack. Ron was young; family members couldn't remember exactly how old, though they thought he was about ten. Ron never talked about it much, one of many things he would internalize over his life, but relatives could tell he took it hard. It drew Ron even closer to his mother.

When not on the farm, Ron lived up north in Joliet, attending schools in the public system: Moran Elementary, (later renamed Cunningham Elementary) junior high at Farragut School, and then Joliet High School where he was a member of the ROTC. A snapshot from his 1948 graduation is pure Americana: a handsome young man, standing in cap and gown in front of a brick house with a white picket fence. As he got older, in the 1950s, he grew sideburns and kept his wavy hair long on top.

After graduating from high school, Ron enlisted in the Illinois Army National Guard. He would later tell a friend that he did this to avoid service in the Korean War, but it didn't work. He graduated from Joliet Junior College in 1950, then was shipped overseas, writing frequently to family members and enclosing black-and-white photos of the Army camps where he was stationed. In the pictures he cut a dashing figure—tall, slender, his hair cut only a little shorter for Army regulations, a rifle slung over his shoulder. His letters focused on the headaches of camp life; people knew he saw action in Korea, but he would never talk about it, in his letters or in conversations when he returned. Like his father's death, it was something he refused to discuss.

After the war, Ron worked in a small soldering-supplies manufacturing company in Chicago that his mother had purchased with a partner, and he developed an interest in flying, taking lessons that he paid for under the GI Bill. A fellow student, John Reuther, who owned a radiator repair business in Chicago—and who had co-incidentally bought soldering supplies from Ron's business—found Ron friendly enough, but very tight-lipped, difficult to draw out. Talk of the war was off-limits.

One day, in about 1958, Reuther and some friends invited Ron to go skeet-shooting on property that Reuther owned. Ron agreed, and Reuther, not knowing about Ron's experiences shooting on his grandparents' farm, said, "He put us all to shame." Reuther noticed something else about Ron: While the other men were shooting, Ron would be picking up the spent shotgun shells. He would bring them home and reload them rather than waste money buying new ones.

Ron excelled in his flying classes, quickly got his license and either purchased or leased a plane, a Howard, that was left over from the war. An eager Ron wanted to fly it to California, even though he was still inexperienced on the notoriously tricky aircraft. One day he set off for the West.

"He decided to take off at 4 in the afternoon," recalled Reuther. "I said, 'You've been waiting months to leave, what's the rush now? Wait 'til morning.' Well, he didn't want to wait. They took off from Lockport and they got down to Champaign, at the University of Illinois airfield. He was landing in the sun. He had flown our airplane, but no two airplanes are the same. The Howard's one of the hardest planes ever to land."

As Ron approached the runway, "It got away from him," Reuther said. "It come down hard. The gear went up, ruptured the belly tank. And they had 100-octane fuel. They went sideways down the concrete runway. Fortunately, there wasn't a spark. The three of them walked away, and, to my knowledge, Ron didn't get back into another airplane, except on the airline."

With flying behind him and work at the soldering materials plant unsatisfying, Ron went on a hunting trip to Wyoming. He had taken a detour through Las Vegas on his way home, where he fell in love with the wide-open spaces. He started earning money doing light construction work, saved up enough to run his own company, then began investing in real estate, mainly houses that had been foreclosed. He fixed them up and sold them for a profit. Business was great. The population of Las Vegas was soaring. He called his friends and relatives and tried to get them to join him.

He was quoted as telling Reuther, the radiator man, "They're coming from California for the weekend and they gotta go home Sunday night, and they're blowing up radiators as fast as they could get across the desert." Reuther declined, but did visit often and invested—well, as it turned out—in real estate at Ron's urging.

As the money flowed in, Ron bought a low-mileage used '62 Cadillac, a convertible and *the* prestige car of the era. He affixed it with personalized plates: RRR-1. He had actually wanted RR-1, but the owner of the Red Rock Theater across the street from his offices had taken that one. From that time on, Ron never drove anything but a Cadillac.

In 1963, he purchased his first and only home: a modest two-bedroom, two-bathroom single-story house that had been built in 1955 on nearly half an acre of land on Alpine Place west of downtown. The property resembled a small fortress, surrounded by a cinder block wall topped in razor wire. While it sorely lacked what people in Ron's business called curb appeal, it was located exactly where he wanted it: right behind the shopping mall on Charleston Boulevard, the busy street where Ron Rudin Realty was located. Only an alley separated the two. In time, Ron would buy the mall, as well.

He joined the usual business groups, from the Junior Chamber of Commerce to the local real estate board. He sponsored a softball team that often made the finals against the team from the police department, where he would find many friends who shared his love of guns and hunting. His Cadillac would sport a sticker reading, "Support Your Sheriff." He would often go on hunting trips with police friends to northern Nevada, and he would take at least two African safaris.

When he wasn't playing hard he was working hard, putting in punishing days, then enjoying himself at night. Although Ron was not known to have had even a single girlfriend in Chicago—spending his time with guns and airplanes—he more than made up for the lack in Las Vegas. Two years after arriving there, Ron married Donna L. Brinkmeyer on December 26, 1962, in a large ceremony attended by many of his aunts, uncles, cousins and, of course, his mother. Donna, like many of Ron's women, worked for him in the real estate office, as a secretary. Ron paid her $200 a month. Ron at the time was making about $600 a month.

In what would become an ongoing pattern for Ron, the marriage didn't last. This one was particularly short—less than one year. On July 7, 1963, Donna filed for divorce, seeking community property and a 1960 Cadillac. Donna, the plaintiff in the action, stated her grounds for divorce from Ron, the defendant, in blunt terms: "Since the marriage, the defendant has treated the plaintiff with extreme cruelty, mental and physical in character, and has caused her great and grievous mental and physical suffering and pain without provocation."

Ron denied the allegations. On September 12, 1963, a judge granted Donna the divorce, giving her the car and half the proceeds from the sale of another house on Shadow Lane.

Ron would remain single for eight years, his longest span without a spouse while in Nevada. As the real estate business chugged along, he expanded his gun collecting hobby into a full-fledged business, Vegas Gun Traders, stockpiling large amounts of weapons in a small room in his house. He would obtain special licenses to deal in fully automatic machine guns and handguns with silencers. He also got a permit to carry a concealed weapon. He often would be packing two or three handguns. His Cadillac had a shotgun in the trunk and another handgun in an armrest.

His love of guns was matched only by his love of women. Now single again, Ron was a relentless flirt. He could put on a sexy voice and use flattery to his advantage. He would lavish gifts on women, take them out to nice restaurants, invite them traveling. The fact that he was rich and handsome didn't hurt his chances, either. He would be juggling two or more girlfriends at times, sometimes dating his own employees. His love life would get so complicated that if he had a girlfriend working in the office, he'd sneak across the hall to the barbershop to call another girlfriend.

But the most important woman in his life was Stella, his widowed mother, still living back in the cold climate of Chicago. After years of Ron's pestering, she finally agreed to move out to Las Vegas, arriving in about 1967. He bought her a Cadillac like his and a home down the street near the house of Ron's friend Jerry Stump, who had a barber shop across the hall from Ron's offices. Ron and his mother would frequently have dinner together at the Las Vegas Country Club, where Ron was a member.

"Stella was a sounding board for him," said Stump. "He would always call her up and talk about his problems, mainly women problems."

Ron had another problem he didn't talk to his mother about, a problem that may have contributed to his divorce: his drinking. He usually drank when problems arose in the business—when a deal fell through or he couldn't sell a property for as much as he wanted. He borrowed money to buy his fixer-upper homes, and he often found himself with cash flow problems. His books at times were a mess. There would be indications that the Internal Revenue Service wasn't getting all that it should. His drinking changed his personality from friendly to somber, gruff even.

By 1971, Ron was ready to settle down again, this time with Caralynne Holland, an attractive blond insurance agent. They married on April 17, 1971, and the couple, along with Caralynne's daughter from a previous marriage, moved into the house on Alpine. During the marriage, Caralynne would get a real estate license and work with Ron, establishing a professional relationship that would long outlast the personal one. "He was a delightful man," she would say later. "He was my very good friend and business associate."

Not that life with Ron was perfect. She found that Ron had a preoccupation with personal security. Living in the Alpine home was like living in a mini–Fort Knox. Ron did have a virtual armory in the house, everything from hunting rifles to vintage Tommy guns. Still, it could all be seen as a bit much. He had hired Alarmco Inc. to install a top-of-the-line security system at the house. Activated by punching a five-digit code, the system had motion detectors on the doors and windows of the master bedroom, living room and dining room. Any movement would trigger a deafening bell outside the house and a horn inside. The alarm was turned on night and day, and it was wired to Ron's office, so he could hear it at work.

About a dozen times a year the system went off accidentally, usually when Ron returned home late from work and forgot to disarm it.

Security cameras also had their eyes on the property, one posted inside the front gate of the driveway, another in a parking lot next to the house. In addition to the alarm system, Ron also had his four Llewellyn setter hunting dogs that roamed the edges of the back yard and barked at the slightest noise.

If the fixation on security had at least some basis in reason, Ron's sense of style was completely perplexing. He would go for long stretches wearing only black clothes, a curious choice in the desert where the blistering summer heat and punishing glare of the sun suggested light colors as a better alternative. But Ron liked this Johnny Cash look, despite Caralynne's protestations. "I tried to change him, but I wasn't successful," she said. At the peak of his black period, he had as many as 35 pairs of black slacks and black shirts, along with black sweaters and black cowboy boots.

The color scheme extended to his Cadillacs, which were also always black. Once the only Cadillac he could find in the model he wanted was white; he drove it to the shop and had it painted black. His Cadillacs were always his pride and joy, and he treated them like the babies he would never have. Ron kept his cars spotless. If he was in the mountains inspecting investment properties, he'd call ahead to his office to have somebody ready to wipe the dust off when he got back.

One thing that Caralynne had no trouble with was Ron's love of jewelry. He bought a lot of it for her, as he did for all the women in his life, and he liked to wear it himself. He wore a distinctive ring on his left hand. It had three marquis-cut diamonds totaling about six carats set in white gold. "They certainly made a statement, but even though it sounds very flashy and maybe gauche, it wasn't, because of the way they were set. It really was very masculine-looking and very elegant-looking," she said.

On their second anniversary, in 1973, she gave him a bracelet made of white gold, with RON spelled out in little diamonds. As long as she knew him, he never took off that bracelet.

Overall, Caralynne found Ron charming, a "snazzy dresser," handsome and kind. But there was something that Caralynne never could adjust to, what she called Ron's "one problem." She said that when he was drinking he was a quiet drunk, sometimes perhaps a little silly. He would drink, then he would fall asleep. "His drinking never affected anyone but himself," she would later tell a jury. "He was never abusive, he was never unkind."

How much his drinking contributed to problems in their marriage, Caralynne wouldn't say. But there were problems, deeper ones than the alarm systems, the dogs and the black clothes. And after four years, the couple separated. The divorce complaint was filed in December of 1975, but the details of the proceeding are unknown. The papers were sealed. It was, Caralynne would acknowledge, a "sad divorce" but also a "very amicable agreement." They would remain friends and business associates for the next 20 years, and Caralynne never took off her wedding ring from Ron, even after she remarried.

Those close to Ron said they couldn't be sure why the couple had split, but they could spot the trouble signs in this and Ron's other relationships.

"He probably was not the easiest person to live with," said Ron's longtime bookkeeper, Sharon Melton. "He was an only child and he had that Only Child Syndrome. He wanted his women to devote their lives to him. He had wives who were outgoing and vivacious. They wanted to socialize and he didn't. He liked to work and go home and have dinner and watch TV and go to bed, then get up and go to work the next day."

Ron also had a jealous streak. "Ron's problem was that he was possessive," said his barber friend Jerry Stump. "He wanted to be Number One. He once got a new secretary. I went out for coffee with her. Ron found out and said to me, 'Jerry, you're not screwing my secretary, are you?' I guess he was joking, but you didn't know." Sometimes Stump would purposely make small talk to a new female hire of Ron's "to keep Ron honest."

Ron's inability to stay in a relationship weighed on him. He once told his friend John Reuther, who had a long and happy marriage, "John, I wish I could be so lucky like you are to find somebody like your wife."

But it caused more grief for Ron's mother, Stella, who desperately wanted her only child to settle down and give her some grandchildren. This was a common lament to her siblings and their children, who all kept in close touch with Stella, if not with Ron. Family members would visit Las Vegas frequently, though they'd usually stay with Stella. Ron always seemed too busy with his real estate business to do much socializing. It seemed that each trip meant the introduction of a new wife or girlfriend of Ron's, and after awhile the women all started to blur together. They were usually pretty, usually blond. Stella remained the link between Ron and his family, the source of the best information about Ron's latest romantic escapade. It was Stella who would send Christmas and birthday cards to relatives, signed "Stella and Ron."

Every few months, a cousin or two would come to Las Vegas for a visit. If Ron had time he'd show them the sights, though he didn't know many too well himself. Casinos were alien to him. "He thought that people that played the slot machines and gambled were stupid," said cousin Robert Riley. "He would say, 'They sure didn't build these big buildings by letting people take all the winnings away.' To my knowledge he never put a quarter in a machine. He was really an avid person along those lines. He was against gambling, not morally, but financially."

Ron did pick up a few of Las Vegas' customs, though. When his cousin Karen Pitcher and her husband visited Stella in the early 1970s, Ron got them tickets to see Elvis Presley. He advised them that the tickets weren't enough; they had to tip the man at the door so they could get better seats.

Although Stella Rudin worried that her son would never find the right woman, it wasn't for lack of trying. By the late 1970s, not long after his divorce from Caralynne, Ron's perpetually wandering eye caught the face of a pretty blond hairdresser named Peggy June Randolph, a divorced mother of three—two boys and a girl—originally from New Mexico. From the very beginning, people knew that Peggy was just Ron's type.

"She was young, beautiful, full of life, always laughing," recalled Peggy's aunt, Frances Starr. "We would go on vacation to Las Vegas and see her and the kids. She was a hairdresser at one time, and one summer that we were there she dyed our hair, cut it, fixed it up. It made us look like glamour girls—or prostitutes, depending on how you looked at it."

Ron and Peggy got married on April 15, 1977, in Las Vegas. Ron was 46 years old, and Peggy was 31. "She was always saying that he was good for her," said Frances Starr, whose husband, Chris, was the brother of Peggy's mother. "He bought her anything she wanted. I don't know if he gave her an allowance or what. But she bought some furniture for her mom and had her mom's house painted."

Peggy's appeal to Ron extended far beyond her looks and style. She had something else none of the other women in his life ever did: Peggy could handle a gun. Like Ron, she was an avid hunter, and had no problem trekking over rocky terrain in the desert of the Southwest stalking game, large and small. She was so skilled that one of her hunting conquests made the local paper. The *Review-Journal* photo captured a smartly dressed woman in a sport coat, her hair puffed up in a fancy 'do. She knelt next to what the caption called a "trophy prize oryx"—an animal with long straight horns that shoot out in a V-formation. The caption said she'd bagged the beast during a December 1978 hunt on the White Sands Missile Proving Grounds in New Mexico. It noted that Peggy was "the only person to draw both special permits for the African animal and the Persian ibex." She shot the second largest oryx in New Mexico history on December 16, with horns measuring 39-2/16 inches, with a 30.06 rifle. "She also shot two antelope during the hunting season."

But the breathless account in the paper contrasted with Peggy's private pain. Behind the scenes, she was dealing with severe depression, family members would report. "She was in bad shape mentally," recalled John Reuther, who during one of his visits to Las Vegas had dinner with Ron a couple of times, while Peggy stayed home. She once joined them for breakfast, but didn't say anything during the entire meal.

But Reuther had no idea just how bad things were. According to police reports, on December 20, 1978, just four days after returning from that hunting trip, Peggy called one of her daughters. "Mrs. Rudin was very depressed and at completion of call advised her daughter not to worry about her any more," the police report said.

That same day, another relative of Peggy's called Ron's office and asked an employee there to check on Peggy in the house in back. This relative had also spoken with Peggy and was worried about her. One employee tried getting into the house, but it was locked. She called over to Ron's maintenance man, Ollie Grinfelds, to try to get inside. But just as Ollie arrived, Ron pulled into the driveway.

Ron walked into the house to find the door to the bedroom locked. He forced open the door and found Peggy lying on her back. She was wearing a colorful bathrobe and slippers. A large pool of blood formed around her head. The top of her skull was missing. On the side of the bed was a Colt .357 Magnum handgun. Ron picked it up and put it on a dresser. Realizing he shouldn't have touched the gun, he says he put it back on the floor near where he found it.

He first tried calling a friend and hunting buddy, Jack Ruggles, a detective with Metro. Unable to reach him, he then called a friend and attorney, David Goldwater, who contacted police.

The investigation was headed by Detective Dave Hatch, who in his report described the crime scene in great detail, including the ravaged body. He noted that the bedroom was in "immaculate condition" with the exception of the shooting scene. He also spotted two short-barreled shotguns—riot guns—leaning against the wall next to the door to the bedroom. He took the statements of Ron and his attorney.

Based on the severity of the wound, and the powder burns on Peggy's right hand, the detective concluded that Peggy—who was left-handed—had held the butt of the gun with her left hand and the barrel with her right, up against her head, and fired.

"It was ascertained by Investigating Officers that the deceased, due to her despondent condition, had refused to return to work and had remained in her residence since their recent hunting trip," the report said. "The time of death was established to be possibly between 2 p.m. and 3 p.m. this date 12/20/78, this death being an apparent suicide."

An autopsy was conducted. A toxicology test found traces of the sedative diasepam, or Valium, in her blood. The coroner agreed with the detective: Thirty-six-year-old Peggy Rudin had died by her own hand.

Ron had told friends that Peggy's young son had died years earlier—the exact date and circumstances weren't known—but it was said to have been around Christmas, making December a difficult month for her.

But for years afterwards, there would always be the suggestion that this was no suicide at all, that police glossed over the investigation for their friend Ron, whose fingerprints, after all, were on the gun.

What's more, there was the matter of the apparent suicide note, a handwritten letter on lined yellow paper, folded on the nightstand. The letter was written in what appeared to be two different styles of handwriting.

The first part of the letter, in neat letters, sloping evenly to the right, read:

Ron—

All the jewelry you gave me is in the white envelope.

The rest of my personal belongings please give to my mother and Michelle—it isn't much but it's all I have to leave them.

My one request is that there be no funeral service of any kind and that this be kept out of the papers to protect you and my family from humiliation.

Then, in a different handwriting, with the capital letters sloping the opposite direction, to the left, there was this addition:

Please put my body @ Palm Mortuary where my son is buried.

Thanks
Peg.

Years later, when the suicide note was released to the public, there would be speculation that Ron made this addition himself. The "Ps" in "Please" and "Peg" looked very similar to the large, looping "Rs" that Ron used in his signature. Why he would do this would never be known, and police made no reference to the two distinctive handwritings in the note.

Despite her final request, there was a funeral for Peggy, two days before Christmas on December 23, 1978. It was there the suspicions about Ron erupted into the confrontation between Ron and Peggy's uncle Chris Starr, a mechanic for the railroads in Colorado. It happened just after Starr and his wife walked in.

Chris' wife Frances recalled seeing two beefy men with guns visible under their jackets. She asked them if the guns were real. "Absolutely," they said. This being Las Vegas, she assumed the men were mobsters. She found out later they were Ron's Metro police friends.

Chris, shaken by his beloved niece's death, walked up to Ron and called him a "son-of-a-bitch" or a "dirty bastard," Frances couldn't remember which. He spoke so loudly that one of Ron's police friends and hunting partners, Officer Jack Ruggles, could hear the whole thing, and would later put the matter into an official report.

"You killed her, didn't you?" steamed Chris.

"What do you mean?" Ron shot back.

"I will get you for this, you'll see," Chris said.

"If you feel that way, then let's go down the street and you can try," Ron said.

"Oh, no," said Chris, "I'll find you in a bar or someplace when you least expect it and put something on you that you can't handle. I really mean it, you'll see."

Frances tried to calm her husband. "Chris, this is not the time to start an argument!" she snapped. "We're here out of respect for Peggy."

And that was how it was left. Chris and Frances Starr went back to their home in Colorado, where Chris brooded about his niece's death until the day he died 18 years later. Frances insists her late husband had no reason to accuse Ron except out of grief and anger. "Chris couldn't kill a spider even if he wanted to," she said. "But he was a little mouthy." It was the first and last time Chris had seen Ron Rudin.

No charges were ever filed against Ron, but he was never the same afterwards. Despite his macho stance at the funeral, Ron struggled to recover from both Peggy's death and the confrontation. Some say he never recovered.

"Ron was really, really upset," recalled Jerry Stump. "He used to have this Christmas party every year at the office. He'd put a tree up in the office. After that, no trees, no Christmas parties at the office. After that, he hated the holidays."

For the next year, he put flowers on Peggy's grave every day. He also began a spiritual quest. He started attending the Church of Religious Science. There were about 600 members of the church, though attendance varied from Sunday to Sunday. "It's the type of church where not everyone comes every Sunday. You're not going to go to Hell because you were not at church," said the Reverend Raymond Cobb, who was the pastor at the time. Ron was no exception. He attended services on Sunday, though not all the time, and he would go to the events that followed, lunch and coffee socials.

Ron also went to Cobb for counseling. The pastor wouldn't say what he helped Ron with—"That wouldn't be ethical," he said—but noted that the counseling for members generally focused on the usual problems and changes people faced in life. Cobb also recalled that over the years Ron explored other religions, including, he believed, Scientology.

Ron plunged himself into work. Always one to put in long hours, he embarked on his most ambitious project. From 1980 to 1981 he began developing land in the Cold Creek area of Mount Charleston, part of a mountain range 45 miles northwest of Las Vegas. He subdivided the land in half-acre lots and sold them, holding the mortgages himself. The buyers then built their own structures. It was a major undertaking, requiring the arrangement of everything from the permits to the overseeing of the development of the wild land into usable parcels. Ron worked 14-hour days, often spending the night in the mountains in a trailer.

By all accounts, the project was a great financial success, providing Ron with a steady flow of cash. But as with the suicide of Peggy, there were whispers about Cold Creek. There were allegations of shady business deals, of disgruntled buyers. He would occasionally clash with environmentalists, whom he hated, and constantly had problems with various planning boards, subcontractors, banks and title agencies. Again, no action was ever taken against him. The money was rolling in and, at age 51, Ron could have retired comfortably.

But Cold Creek just whetted his appetite. He developed a much grander plan for his other property on Mount Charleston, in the Lee Canyon area. He called his old friend John Reuther and told him about it.

"What do you keep struggling for?" Reuther asked him. "My God, don't you have enough out of what you got with Cold Creek?"

"Well," Ron said, "I've got to do something."

That's when Ron launched his Lee Canyon resort project with all the salesmanship he could muster.

Tom Dye, at the time the business editor of the *Review-Journal*, recalled when Rudin burst into the newsroom one summer day in 1984, full of energy and self-confidence. Ron told Dye that he had a vision. He said that Las Vegas had plenty to offer for the tourists, but what do you do if you're *from* Las Vegas? Where do the locals go to get away?

The answer was 50 miles distant in the pine-covered coolness of Mount Charleston, where Ron owned 82 acres abutting the Toiyabe National Forest at the 7,200-foot level. Rudin's plan was to build what he called a "country club in the mountains"—a $12 million playground designed to give the stressed-out Las Vegas dweller a weekend escape. The resort in the Lee Canyon area would feature a 170-room lodge with underground parking, indoor and outdoor swimming pools, racquet ball courts, ice skating rink, health club, sauna, hiking trails and a 240-space RV park.

Dye wrote a story that ran July 29, 1984, under the headline, "A new resort for Mt. Charleston," which quoted Rudin as saying, "we have needed something like this around here for a long time."

Above the story, the paper ran a photo of Rudin, looking intently over a large map of Lee Canyon. He was nattily dressed in a tie and blue shirt, the sleeves rolled halfway up his forearm—ready for business. He had apparently taken a breather from his black wardrobe period. He was shot in profile, his angular features as defined as the jagged mountain range behind him. The photo captured Ron Rudin at the top of his game: rich, handsome, ambitious.

And that was also the problem. Rudin was too confident, talked too big. The description that came to Dye's mind was "a little squirrely."

"I couldn't quite put my finger on it," Dye would recall years later, "but he made me a little nervous."

Ron had been purchasing various parcels in Lee Canyon in the early 80s. One parcel he purchased in a deal involving Caralynne, who represented the seller. Ron bought the property but put it in the name of a relative, who didn't know anything about the deal. He used other names for other parcels. Caralynne would later insist there was nothing wrong with his dealings; that these were simply "nominee" names—not an unheard of practice in real estate—and that Ron made no secret of the fact he owned the land, thus his promotional efforts. And he even asked Robert Riley if he could use his cousin's name on one of the parcel purchases.

"He did say, 'Do you mind buying or being a party to this?' And I said, 'No, as long as there's no tax consequences, you can do whatever you want. Just don't get me in jail,'" said Riley. "I really don't think Ron would steal and do anything significantly illegal. He may stretch the truth and have me buy something without the end result being known by someone else. But I think he was just a very, very astute businessman."

His bookkeeper Sharon Melton had once noticed that Ron's business records showed promissory notes for property held in the names of three men who either didn't exist or didn't know their names were being used. The effect would be to make it look to the IRS as though Ron was carrying more debt—and thus required to pay less in taxes—than in fact he was. Sharon confronted Ron, and she claimed that he quickly fixed the situation.

As he pushed his real estate business into high gear, Ron was also getting his love life back in order. That following spring after unveiling the Lee Canyon project to the local paper, he married Karen Carmany on April 20, 1985, another attractive woman with an outgoing personality. He lavished her with jewelry, furs and charm.

But she soon found that Ron could be two different people, one when he was sober, quite another when he was drinking. She would later say that when he was throwing back the vodka he would change "from a nice gentleman who smiled into a man who didn't smile and had a mean, gruff voice and a mean-looking face." He would put her down, call her stupid, accuse her of not caring about him, of not loving him. The drinking was accompanied by Ron's growing paranoia. He wouldn't go out after dark and would be in bed by 9 p.m. every night. "He was afraid, afraid of what I don't know," she said.

His personality changes would often be triggered by problems at work. And those problems were mounting. Ron would find that getting in the front door of the local newspaper office was much easier than getting a major mountain resort off the ground. More than a year later, the project was still just a dream.

Outwardly, he continued to be bullish on the project,

telling Dye in a story published August 4, 1985, that the resort was the answer to Las Vegans' dreams. "This is a high-stress town," Rudin said. "People need to have some place to get away. I think the people here really relate to the outdoors and recreation."

Behind the scenes, Ron knew all about stress. He told his wife that at times he was on the brink of bankruptcy. The stress led to the drinking, and the drinking led to the verbal abuse. Their marriage—his fourth—was falling apart. In June 1987, he filed for divorce. The court papers said that the couple were "unable to live together in marital harmony." In the divorce agreement, Ron kept all the real estate, from the house on Alpine to all interest in what he was then calling the Lee Canyon Nevada RV Park development. Karen got to keep the gifts, including a mink stole, a mink collar, a Rolex watch, a gold and diamond necklace, a gold wedding ring, gold earrings and a 1983 Mazda RX-7 sports car.

Later that year, in October 1987, Rudin announced a scaled-down version of the project. Gone were the lodge and the swimming pools and racquetball courts. The resort now consisted of the RV park and a primitive campground. The lodge was scaled back from 170 rooms to 21. He said he had won government approval to sell limited partnerships.

It took him a year to raise enough money to begin low-level construction. In 1988, he dug a well, put in water storage tanks and graded primitive roads. He continued to push the project as a local getaway: "Family recreation is a biggie."

That was as far as he got. "The financing went south, and he didn't have enough money of his own to do that," said his friend John Reuther. Ron continued to hold out hope of developing Lee Canyon, but he would never see it. He still had his residential real estate business, buying and rehabbing and selling houses and condos. The money still came in from the Cold Creek subdivision.

His love life didn't suffer either. By 1987, at age 56,

he had fallen for somebody new, a pretty 44-year-old red-head with a soft Southern-flavored voice who had recently started attending the Church of Religious Science. She, too, had been married four times before.

3

MARGARET

Margaret was always a prolific writer, keeping journals, diaries, logs. It helped her sort things out, put everything in perspective, cope with heartaches. But in many of her writings, she would put a certain distance between herself and the events that swirled around her. She was, it seemed, like an actor playing Margaret, rather than a real person in a real world. In 1987 she wrote in her diary:

> My life has always been unique, exciting, full of change, challenges and stimulus and full of an interesting cast of characters. And that is OK. It just is, and I accept that for my past. But I know that by programming my mind I can now redirect any future stage plays and pick my own screenplay and cast, because I am the producer, director and star of any and all new plays on my stage called life. I've always vaguely known these facts and lived my life accordingly, but I never realized what control I could have over every segment of this onetime stage production called Margaret's Life.

The curtain rose on the story of Margaret's life on May 31, 1943, in Memphis, Tennessee. Margaret Frost was the first of three daughters born to Horris, a barber, and Eloise, a store manager. Sisters Barbara and Dona would follow. Margaret was always closest to Barbara. Her relationship with Dona was more complicated, the women sometimes going years without speaking. Margaret would later tell interviewers that her family struggled as she grew up. Despite a booming post-war economy, financial problems kept the family on the move. "I lived in 15 different states before I graduated high school," she would tell the

Las Vegas Review-Journal. That's all she would tell, keeping many details of her younger years to herself.

The family finally settled in northern Illinois, in the Chicago suburbs. Less than a year after graduating from high school, Margaret married Gerald W. Mason, on February 2, 1962, in Winthrop Harbor, Illinois, just north of Zion. Margaret was 18 years old. They moved to Chicago, and two years later, their son Michael was born. Their daughter Kristina was born three years after that, in 1967. Margaret would fondly recall the early years of her marriage. A family photo shows her as a pretty, dark-haired woman with horn-rimmed glasses. "He was a carpenter," she later told Court TV. "We were just starting out. I can remember that when we were our happiest, he was making just $75 a week."

The happy times didn't last. After 10 years of marriage, they split. In 1973, Margaret filed for divorce on the grounds of emotional cruelty. "Over the years it got worse," she testified at a divorce hearing. "We started arguing constantly. He didn't approve of anything I did. He didn't like my friends, my dress. He wouldn't allow me to work. I became very nervous and upset."

Asked if he was "cold and indifferent" to her, she answered yes. She also said that he told her he no longer loved her. It began to affect her physically. "I became very edgy, nervous with the kids, short-tempered," Margaret testified.

Her sister, then going by her married name of Barbara Stavrou, testified that Margaret had been "very good" toward her husband, and that his conduct was "rather cold." It left Margaret "very unhappy, depressed," yet still fit to have custody of the children, then ages 6 and 9.

On the basis of this testimony, the judge found that Gerald Mason was "guilty of extreme and repeated mental cruelty," and granted Margaret's request for a divorce. The couple then entered into an agreement, citing "irreconcilable differences," and giving Margaret custody of the children, $40 a week in child support, and ownership of their 1969 Ford and all household furniture.

Marriage and divorce would come to dominate Margaret's life over the next 15 years, as her hopes of finding security for herself and her children would always fail. Margaret would later say that she quickly remarried, in 1974, but details of that marriage aren't known. Police had received tips that she'd married a man in Kentucky, perhaps a horse trainer, but they could never confirm it. Margaret herself would never say anything about that husband. She did tell one interviewer that the marriage ended when she filed for divorce in 1976.

Again, Margaret didn't stay single for long. When she was 36 years old, with two children and two marriages in her past, she began seeing Philip N. Brown, a 46-year-old widower from Wadsworth, Illinois, who ran a company that made and installed kitchen cabinets. During a trip to Las Vegas, while visiting some of Margaret's girlfriends, they impulsively married at the Candlelight Wedding Chapel in the heat of the summer, on August 27, 1978. Margaret and her two children returned to northern Illinois and moved into Brown's eight-acre horse ranch. The couple had a second marriage ceremony—this time in the jurisdiction of Lake County, Illinois, two months later, on October 21, 1978.

This marriage lasted less than a year. In his June 1979 action, Brown claimed emotional cruelty, though there was no dramatic problem. Starting in January 1979, just four months into their marriage, Margaret told him she wished she had stayed in Las Vegas. The couple were having trouble simply getting along. Brown gave Margaret $10,000 in exchange for her agreement to drop any claims for alimony or a share of his business. She also got no share of the ranch or of an investment property. He agreed to pay her medical costs for a recent surgery that wasn't specified. After the divorce, she walked away with her children, and Brown would never again speak to his bride of 10 months.

Two years later, in 1981, after what Margaret told one

interviewer was a particularly brutal winter in the Chicago area, she made her way back to Las Vegas, where her sister Barbara and her new husband, lawyer Robert Le-Pome, lived. After three marriages, Margaret was no better off financially than she had been when she was an 18-year-old daughter of a barber. She had two children to support and little money. Then came reason for hope.

Her sister set Margaret up with a wealthy Las Vegas man named Richard N. Krafve. A businessman and gun dealer, Krafve recieved money from a trust fund established by his father, Richard E. Krafve, the onetime Ford Motor Company special products division general manager who oversaw the ill-fated introduction of the Edsel in the late 1950s. The Edsel went down as one of the biggest flops in automotive history, but the elder Krafve ended up doing well enough to leave his son a generous trust.

The two of them hit it off. On April 3, 1982, Margaret married Richard in a ceremony before the Reverend Rex J. McCulley, a minister of the Salvation Army. Margaret's sister, Barbara, was a witness. Margaret's fourth marriage would be the longest since she and her first husband stayed together for a decade. Krafve built a massive $800,000 home that they lived in and Margaret, after a lifetime of struggle, got her first taste of living well. But Krafve was careful about his money; he had Margaret sign a prenuptial agreement.

As had happened three times before, problems arose in the marriage. Margaret would later tell an interviewer that her daughter Kristina, then 15, struggled to adjust to Las Vegas. Margaret returned to Illinois for a time to allow her to finish high school.

By late 1985, after less than four years of marriage, the couple separated. Or, as Krafve related it in court papers, Margaret up and left him. He claimed that he went on a hunting trip at the end of December, and when he returned on January 9, 1986, he "immediately discovered that [Margaret] had removed approximately two-thirds of the furniture . . . as well as numerous items of personal property." But she didn't stop there. Krafve went to his safety deposit box and found that it, too, had been relieved of "certain items of jewelry and other valuable property."

Margaret went to court first, filing for divorce with the help of one of the best attorneys in town, Stewart Bell, a well-connected former public defender with a thriving private practice. Margaret would claim years later that she'd wanted a smooth, amicable divorce, with just a few demands on Krafve, who would counter-file. But she said that when Bell found out that Margaret hadn't been represented by her own attorney while signing the prenuptial agreement, he got excited—and litigious. The case started looking even better when Margaret told Bell that during her marriage—but after signing the prenup—Richard built that big house, a portion of which Margaret may have been entitled to under community property laws.

In court papers, Margaret wrote: "Mr. Bell became excited and said this was not going to be a nice quiet divorce because my husband had deceived me about Nevada common property laws and how prenuptial agreements weren't worth the paper they were written on if they didn't disclose all assets prior to being signed—therefore, it wasn't valid and he [Mr. Bell] could break it." She said that Bell "went on and on" about how Krafve was taking advantage of her ignorance of Nevada laws. "He said for me to trust his experience in such things and he'd make Dick Krafve pay for causing me such grief and unequitable division of assets rightly mine," she wrote.

On January 16, 1986, the divorce got ugly. Margaret filed for a temporary restraining order against Krafve, barring him from "threatening or actually committing physical or emotional harm" upon Margaret at her home or work. "During the term of the marriage, [Krafve] has threatened physical harm and has been verbally abusive," Margaret said in an affidavit. Further, Margaret said she "genuinely believes that upon service of the [divorce] complaint on file herein that the defendant will carry out his threats and become physically violent."

By the end of the divorce case, however, Margaret seemed more unhappy with her attorney than with her estranged husband. She said the get-tough strategy caused stress and problems she had not anticipated. "It was made more difficult because of my father's worsening health problems, not to mention delayed court filings," Margaret alleged years later in an affidavit. "Mr. Bell was not available to discuss motions and hearings with me prior to court appearances and he would not let me be a part of his decision making process."

In the end, she said in court papers: "The more time went by the more the stress and family dissention took it's [sic] toll. Mr. Bell billed me double what his original quote for the divorce would be, and there was no end in sight." Margaret called another attorney, her sister's husband Robert LePome, who worked out what she called a "reasonable" settlement.

"I had to fire Stewart Bell and wrote a letter to him complaining about his service and his bill and for making my divorce far more difficult than I wanted," she said.

On May 28, 1987, Margaret's divorce from Richard Krafve was finalized. It was a tough year all around for Margaret. She found herself in a familiar position: divorced, financially insecure. She was 44 years old. She didn't get any of Krafve's millions. The divorce left her with just $11,000 of the Krafve family's Ford fortune, and even that was spread out over four months and didn't count the cost of lawyers. The year 1987 also brought the death of her father. Margaret had a hysterectomy. Her daughter was suffering unspecified problems. Her children were now grown and starting their own lives, and for the first time, Margaret was alone.

She had joined the Science of Mind Church of Religious Science, a Los Angeles–based church that combined science, philosophy and religion. Margaret would later insist she had no intention of getting into another relationship so soon after her fourth divorce. But she was at a vulnerable place in her life.

It was after a Sunday service, during the social gathering, that she met a tall, smooth talker in cowboy boots named Ronald Rudin.

4

FIFTH TIME AROUND

He sat right behind her in church, introduced himself after the service, then invited her to join him for lunch at the Las Vegas Country Club. Soon, he was asking for more than a date. "He started immediately with the 'Let's get married, let's get married,' " Margaret would tell the *Review-Journal*. "I didn't understand the push. I didn't realize until later that this was the kind of normal operating procedure for someone who wants to hide things." At first, though, the sense that something lay hidden beneath Ron's charming exterior intrigued Margaret. "I liked his strengths, his weaknesses, his sense of humor. He was mysterious. You didn't know what he was going to do next," she told the newspaper.

Plus, he had those cowboy boots. "He seemed very charming, very much at ease with women," she would later tell Court TV. "Good-looking, rather low-key, self-assured and macho. I happen to like macho and I was teasing one of my friends before I met him that the next man had to wear cowboy boots because so many in Las Vegas do."

Ron could be secretive about many things—his business, his war experiences—but he was open about Margaret, introducing her to his family at the eighty-fifth birthday party for his mother Stella, by now in badly declining health.

"They were not married yet. They were sitting on the sofa, holding hands, and being very lovey-dovey, as lovers do," recalled Ron's cousin, Karen Pitcher. "We thought Margaret was very, very nice. They met in church and she was an Illinois girl. Those two pieces of information came from Aunt Stella, and she seemed happy about Margaret. Stella was very ill at the time. I think she was of the opinion that Ron would get married and this would be the right girl for him. We were so happy to hear they were married after that."

The family thought Margaret was beautiful, well-dressed, classy. She spoke softly and put on no airs. A couple of the relatives at the party were in the shoe sales business and they immediately recognized Margaret's footwear. The shoes were Italian.

Margaret would later insist that she wasn't going after Ron's money. Had cash been the issue, she said, she would have stayed with Krafve. Margaret would also contend that she didn't go into this marriage without at least hearing some warnings about Ron. "I remember talking to a couple of different people that said, 'Don't do it, don't get involved with him, you don't know what he's like, you don't know. He has a bad business history, he is a womanizer,' " she told Court TV. "They were trying to advise me not to do it, and I just refused to listen."

But the fear of loneliness can be a powerful force. It was, she would admit, "sort of a rebound thing for both of us."

"My biggest problem has always been that . . . I had never been alone. Never," she told Court TV. "All my life, if I was single, I had the children. They were my focus. Or I had a man."

On September 11, 1987, Ron and Margaret were married at Mission of the Bells, a small chapel on Las Vegas Boulevard. The service was conducted by Raymond Cobb of the Church of Religious Science, though he couldn't remember anything about it. "I've done so many," he said. But he said that if the marriage was at the Mission of the Bells as the marriage certificate with his signature on it attests, then it was probably your typical fast Las Vegas hookup. "You pay the chapel fee at the chapel and most of the time you've got about 15 minutes for the whole wedding before you're on your way out," he said.

Although Ron had introduced Margaret to his relatives before the wedding, he waited a little longer to break the news to the people at work. Bookkeeper Sharon Melton said she was in the office one day when she heard another employee announce, "There's a Mrs. Rudin on the phone."

Sharon looked at her boss and asked, "Is there something you want to tell us?"

"Oh, I got married," he said.

Jerry Stump recalled: "He had just come back from their honeymoon or something. He came into the barbershop and introduced her. I had never seen her or anything. It was a complete surprise."

In more ways than one. After 30 years of observing Ron's amorous adventures, Jerry thought he knew about Ron's tastes. Ron's four previous wives were all blondes. Margaret was a redhead. Jerry shared this observation with the new Mrs. Rudin.

"The next day," Stump said, "her hair was blond."

The newly bleached Margaret moved into Ron's house on Alpine Place, and Ron and Margaret remained active in the church, going on church-sponsored trips to Zion National Park in Utah and Death Valley in California.

Ron's family members, who had watched Ron's long, spotty romantic history, were as relieved as they were happy. "I was very impressed with her," recalled Ron's cousin Doris Cowan. "We thought: Finally, Ron's found someone and that it will last. They'll have a good marriage and we're happy for him. We wished them nothing but the best."

But within months trouble simmered. Margaret began to learn about Ron's other side: the booze, the guns, the security systems, his wildly swinging moods, which seemed to get worse around the holidays, when Peggy had died. "I had bought him and his mother lots of presents because he had said that Xmas '85 had been bad for him," she wrote in her diary, which would be obtained by prosecutors. "I'd make food for an office party for his staff and invited some of his business connections but no one came—he really has no friends. I had tried so hard to include Ron in all the plans and activities so he could feel part of a family."

On January 24, 1988, she wrote, she and Ron had attended a weekend self-improvement seminar. "I felt a big, black empty feeling when Dr. Robertson said our Higher Consciousness would lift the veil between us and the one we love and let us know what is to be between us. I felt fear afterwards because all I saw was a void. He and I are always on a high (of love) or a low (of dissolution) and it's draining."

The problems reached a breaking point.

A few days later, on February 2, 1988, they would have the fight in which Ron got his feelings hurt. "Ron was looking for an excuse to get drunk again," Margaret wrote in her diary. "All I said was one of his friends was good looking and he made a big deal of it, in spite of the fact I apologized and told him several times I'd said it in a kidding manner."

Margaret was fixing dinner so he would have something to eat while she went out later to a church meeting. As she did this, she saw one of the lights on the phone go on. Ron was on the phone in the other room. "[I] knew he was talking to a woman," Margaret wrote. "When I picked up the phone he was and he was so drunk he didn't even know I was listening.

"He was asking her how good she was in bed and implying he did not make love often enough at home (wonder how she would have reacted if I'd told her the truth—once and sometimes twice a day is not enough for him and he'll make love even if he's late for an appointment or keeping his secretary locked out of the office)."

Margaret said the woman asked Ron, "Are her kids giving you a hard time again?"

Devastated, Margaret observed, "I knew he'd talked to her before and he was complaining and he projected a crybaby–weak attitude to a person that now had an opinion of me and my kids that wasn't even true," Margaret put in her diary. "My heart was pounding so hard I'm surprised it didn't break as he played his macho role to the hilt."

Then, Margaret wrote, after the phone call Ron "had nerve enough to walk over to me and tell me how I was his purpose for living and how he loved me more than anyone.

"I said, 'Is that right? Tell me how much you love me again while that woman you were just talking to tells you she is a number nine in bed and you are degrading me and my love by lying about me?' "

That's when Margaret pulled a gun.

The confrontation took place in their bedroom. Ron and Margaret struggled over the gun. Ron grabbed the weapon and it went off. The bullet harmlessly struck an oil painting of a lake scene, piercing the canvas, hitting the wall, and ricocheting back out of the picture without hitting either one of them.

Ron got the gun away from her and fired off another round into the headboard of the bed.

Margaret packed her things as Ron begged her to stay. "You don't have to do this. Don't go. Please stay with me," she quoted Ron as saying.

Margaret didn't go, this time. As she told her diary, "Like a fool, I believed none of this wouldn't have happened if he hadn't been drunk so I should forget that he flips out emotionally even when he is not drunk."

The next day, she wrote, "I am numb at this point and don't know why I've been treated this way by Ron and why I can not just leave him."

A day later, she wrote: "Ron professes his undying love again. When do we get off this roller coaster? (Please God!)."

Ron's problem, Margaret would later tell a newspaper reporter, was exactly what Sharon Melton and others had seen: a controlling nature. "He wanted someone who would work in his office, who would be his wife, a cook, a housekeeper," Margaret told the paper. "I was looking for some relief." At the same time, Margaret, it would be alleged, was as much a control freak as her husband, perhaps even more so. This wouldn't be the first time she listened in on her husband's phone calls, it would be alleged. With these two strong personalities clashing, at least once in an argument that could have been lethal, something had to give.

It happened on September 23, 1988, just 12 days after their first anniversary. Ron Rudin filed for divorce. It was a boilerplate filing, stating that Ron lived in the jurisdiction of the court, that the couple were married in the state of Nevada and that there were no minor children at issue. It also said there was no community property or any community debts for the court to deal with.

"Wherefore," the complaint stated, Ron Rudin asked the court that "the bonds of matrimony now and heretofore existing between Plaintiff and Defendant be dissolved, set aside and forever held for naught, and that the parties hereto, and each of them, be restored to their single, unmarried status."

It summed up the basis for the divorce as this: "The parties are incompatible in marriage."

In the turbulent weeks surrounding the divorce filing, Margaret would move out of the Alpine Place house, taking boxes of her belongings with her. These were confusing times, and Ron, normally a very careful businessman, found himself losing track of things.

For instance, normally he carefully stored and protected the weapons in the little room in the house, not just because he liked to do it that way, but because it was the law. The U.S. Bureau of Alcohol, Tobacco and Firearms required careful accounting of certain kinds of weapons, particularly machine guns and pistols with silencers, both of which required licenses and both of which Ron stored at his home.

In October of 1988, in the days after Ron filed for divorce, the ATF inspected Ron's gun collection and found one item missing: a .22-caliber Ruger pistol with a silencer. "Unable to locate in inventory," the ATF inspector wrote in the report. "Mr. Rudin said he still has it, but can't find it. Will notify ATF if actually lost."

In a follow-up letter to the ATF that month, Ron suggested the gun fell through cracks during his marital upheaval:

"During a recent back compliance inspection, I discovered that a Ruger .22 semi-automatic with suppressor was missing. I was aware of this fact several weeks before the inspection, but thought I had misplaced the weapon. At inspection time it was still missing. I was advised to contact your office to report. I have a suspicion the gun was packed away or taken by person or persons unknown during my wife's packing her furniture and personal belongings for storage at that or about that time due to a separation and pending divorce proceedings after a marriage of one year. If by chance the weapon turns up, I will notify your office immediately."

Within months of the breakup, however, Ron and Margaret were working on a reconciliation, the roller-coaster relationship heading back toward a high. By May 3, 1989, just shy of eight months of the divorce filing, Ron withdrew the petition. Margaret would move back in.

Ron was at a difficult point in his life. His beloved mother's health was deteriorating rapidly, and on July 2, 1989, she died at age 87. Ron lost the most important woman in his life.

Life with Margaret, meanwhile, never got easier. They would fight, make up, then fight again. Each always seemed to be playing mind games with the other. "She used to come over the barbershop and be real friendly with us," recalled Jerry Stump. "I think she was doing that to bug Ron. I think it did." At the same time, Ron would keep Margaret in the dark about his business dealings and outside friendships, something he knew irritated her more than anything.

He also played the money card. Margaret would work at a nearby antique store, dreamed of running her own business. But she never had the money. Ron didn't let her have access to his bank accounts. He put her on an allowance, ensuring that he would always have money to hold over her. Margaret would complain repeatedly that Ron was too cheap, that she didn't have enough money, and that at times she would have to sell jewelry for spending cash.

Back and forth it went, the couple's arguments seemingly getting worse each time. One fight was so bad that the police came out and hauled them both away in patrol cars, much to Margaret's annoyance. She claimed Ron hit her. "I was the one who was bleeding, I was the one who called police, yet they said, 'We are going to take both of you to jail,' " she would tell a reporter. She blamed Ron's drinking for triggering his violence. "He would throw things, a vase or a book."

Afterward, Ron tried to make light of it. He told bookkeeper Sharon Melton in a phone call: "You'll never guess where I spent the night—in jail," he said, then burst out laughing.

Ron would tell his co-workers that Margaret once offered to get a divorce for $50,000. When things got dicey between them, his co-workers would joke, "You should have given her the 50 grand."

"I know, I know," he'd say.

But that was a front—his macho side as Margaret would call it. Deep down, Ron was hurting. He confided as much to his old friend John Reuther and Reuther's wife Susan, during a chat in the realty office when they were out for a vacation.

"I don't know how long it will last," he told them.

He sought out his family for advice.

"I knew they were not getting along," recalled his cousin Karen Pitcher. "Ron had called me a time or two, saying, 'How do you do it?' My husband and I have never been separated or anything. Being a woman, I think it's always the man's fault. I said, Ron, you have to give up a little, it has to be a 50–50 thing. You have to meet her halfway."

Over time, Ron's friends and relatives, who had generally liked Margaret—and who knew full well how difficult Ron could be—stopped giving Margaret the benefit of the doubt. Harold Boscutti, a real estate broker who was Ron's friend and business partner for 30 years, recalled that after marrying Margaret, Ron's social life seemed to suddenly cut off. For years, Ron and his close friends would get together for Christmas at Ron's house, "And when he married Margaret, that was the end of all that," Boscutti said. "No more socializing with Ron involved."

Any time he wanted to see his old friend, it would have to be away from the house or office. "Ron and I would get together and do man talk and stuff or go to lunch, but even that shut way down," Boscutti said. "Our communication was mainly either by phone or I'd go in his office and I'd talk."

Margaret, it seemed to those watching the relationship, was trying to turn Ron away from his friends and family. Ron's cousin Doris Cowan said that Margaret had started redirecting Ron's mail. "Margaret sent the whole family a little note saying, We're having trouble getting our mail at the Charleston address. From now on send letters to this other address," Doris recalled. "That cut Ron off from his family. He got no Christmas cards, no birthday cards, nothing, for several years. I sent everything to that new address. Once I wrote him a letter about the old farm because he had inherited it. He never answered me."

Margaret also allegedly continued to monitor Ron's phone calls by listening in on the extension at home. Ron apparently didn't know she was doing this, but suspected that she was snooping in some manner. He started telling her to stay away from the office, but Margaret could get around that edict. "She would call the minute she knew he was not in the office," Sharon Melton said. "She would call just to harass us. She could see when he was not in the office. The house was right there."

In the spring of 1991, Ron recounted his worries about

Margaret to his financial lawyer, Patricia Brown. In her notes from a meeting with him, Brown said Ron was "quite distressed about his wife." Ron felt that Margaret was suffering from some sort of dual personality disorder and was undergoing counseling, according to Brown's notes. "At one point, she can be a lovely wife, but her schizophrenic personality turns her into a vicious and violent individual under her other personality." Ron told Brown that his wife once took a shot at him.

Ron's friends and business associates began to worry about him. He asked his secretary to check his phones for taps. The secretary elicited the help of one of the members of the Moose Lodge in the mini-mall. The lodge man worked for the phone company, and he inspected the phones but didn't find anything. Ron wasn't taking any chances. He changed the phone system, disconnecting the office line that went to the house.

What Ron didn't know was that pulling the plug on the phone line wouldn't stop Margaret from probing into his affairs. She would soon have a new, and more effective tool, authorities would allege.

5

SPY GAMES

The Spy Factory was a San Antonio, Texas–based chain of about 20 stores nationwide that sold a wide range of products for a clientele that ranged from the nervous to the just plain crazy. Its stock included surveillance and counter-surveillance devices, personal protection items and some cheap novelties. An advertising flier posted around town read, "Be Prepared. There's no better investment than a personal protection device."

In the spring of 1991, Margaret Rudin and her younger sister, Dona Cantrel, went to a Spy Factory outlet in a little shopping center on the corner of Paradise Road and Sahara Avenue at the north end of The Strip near the Sahara Hotel and Casino. Margaret had a long discussion with the sales clerk before settling on her purchases: two transmitters, a receiver and a tape recorder.

The transmitters would be used as hidden microphones to pick up conversations, then send a voice signal to the receiver, which would be hooked up to a voice-activated tape recorder. Margaret bought top-of-the-line gear.

The transmitters were disguised to look like regular ivory-colored three-plug wall adaptors, those little devices that go into a single plug and make it into three outlets. In fact, the transmitters were working three-plug adaptors, but the backs had been taken off and the secret electronics installed. The transmitters were plugged into the outlet and ran off electricity. The microphone was sensitive enough to pick up voices within five or ten feet. The transmitter had a range of a half-block or more, depending on the atmospheric conditions. Margaret bought two transmitters.

The receiver that would pick up the voice signals from the adaptor was a small black box slightly larger than a cigarette pack with a one-inch antenna. It ran off a special six-volt lithium battery that would need to be changed as frequently as once a week with heavy use. The tape recorder was just an ordinary model that would turn on every time it detected a sound and turn off with silence.

The bill came to $1,500.

At the time, the purchase was legal in the state of Nevada, though there were strict legal limits on how the devices could be used. Authorities claim it was illegal, for instance, to use the device without the knowledge of the person being listened in on—in other words, to put it to its intended sneaky purpose. Spy Factory workers were in the habit of not asking too many questions of their customers, who often paid in cash and didn't reveal their names.

According to Dona, Margaret snuck into Ron's office and plugged in two of the transmitter devices—one in Ron's private office, the other under the desk of Sharon Melton, who had an office down the hall near the back door. Margaret stashed the receiver and tape recorder in the middle drawer of an antique desk in her home, Dona said.

The system wasn't perfect. Margaret soon found that the lithium battery didn't last very long. Late one night, she needed a new one. The Spy Factory was only open from 10 a.m. to 6 p.m., Monday through Saturday. She still had the business card of the 20-year-old manager, Richard Aker III. Because his customers could sometimes be a little loopy, Richard didn't list his home phone number in the directory. But his father, Richard Aker, Jr., was in the book.

Margaret called and, to the son's annoyance, the father gave Margaret the younger Aker's unlisted home number. The manager had never been called at home before by a customer, and so when Margaret Rudin reached him late that evening after his wife had already gone to bed, he was surprised. After identifying herself, Margaret said she needed new batteries for her receiver. Aker recognized her voice; she had been in the store a half-dozen times with questions about the equipment. He politely told her there was nothing she could do at that hour but to go to the store the next day. Within a week, she picked up new batteries.

According to authorities, for the next three years, from the privacy of her home, Margaret sat with headphones to her ears and monitored the activities of her husband, Sharon Melton and anyone else who got near those two transmitters disguised as electrical adaptors. Many of the conversations were captured by the voice-activated tape recorder, authorities allege, with the tapes labeled and stashed in a suitcase.

Margaret was then in a position to hear everything that went on in Ron's office—his meetings, his end of phone conversations, any private musings to himself—as well as everything that happened in the workspace at Sharon Melton, who would emerge as a strong foe of Margaret's.

(* The Spy Factory chain has since been closed by the federal government for illegally selling wiretapping and bugging devices. The Las Vegas store was closed in 1994. In 1997, executives pleaded guilty to charges including smuggling and illegally selling wiretapping and bugging equipment and conspiracy, and agreed to forfeit more than $2.3 million in sales proceeds from 1989 to 1995. Richard Aker III was never implicated in any wrongdoing.)

As the years progressed, the marriage continued on its up-and-down course, though the downs seemed to be more frequent. Margaret for a time considered divorcing Ron, according to her sister. All she was waiting for was some money from an insurance settlement, stemming from injuries she had suffered in a car accident.

Ron was also unhappy—and scared. In 1993, he met his financial adviser Patricia Brown for year-end planning. He told her that he had seen a doctor in Utah and wanted to see another one in Arizona. Brown later recalled: "He felt that he was being—well, I believe . . . poisoned is what he had said. And so he was looking at a chemical imbalance in his body, as I recall the conversation."

And who did he think was doing this?

"His wife," Brown said.

The following year, 1994, Ron's family, which had held such high hopes for the marriage, knew that things weren't working out. Ron and Margaret joined about 15 of his relatives for a family reunion at an aunt's house in Colorado that year. "We weren't there in the house very long before Margaret pulled us aside, my sister and myself and the other girl cousins, and she started bad-mouthing Ron," cousin Doris Cowan said. "It was odd. I wouldn't have done it, especially at a family reunion. It was just getting started. We wanted to have a good time. But that kind of put a wall between us and Ron during that whole thing. All we could think of was all the terrible things he did to poor Margaret."

In May of 1994, John Reuther and his wife Susan visited Ron in Las Vegas. It was obvious to the Reuthers that Ron's marriage was in trouble. Reuther remembered that one night he and his wife arranged to meet Ron for dinner at a restaurant called Port Tack on Sahara.

"I don't think Margaret will make it this evening," Ron told them.

"Why?" Reuther asked, though he knew full well why. He could tell by the tone of Ron's voice that Ron and Margaret were going at each other.

"I'll meet you," Ron said.

John and Susan arrived at the restaurant first, and they were surprised to see Ron walk in with Margaret. The entire evening, Margaret didn't want to leave Ron's side, not even to go to the bathroom.

The next day, when John and his wife were at the airport in Las Vegas awaiting their flight home to Illinois, John called Ron at his office from a pay phone. Ron wasn't happy.

"John, I couldn't talk last night," he told Reuther. "This one's got me worried," he said of Margaret.

"What do you mean?"

"I found a paper in the house where she has diagramed out how she's going to split up my money with her relatives."

"Ron, you'd better watch your back."

"I've already talked to the lawyers."

Whether Margaret overheard this conversation isn't known.

Despite Ron's concerns—or perhaps because of them—finally helped Margaret open that antique shop she had wanted for so many years. The store was to be located in the end unit of Ron's mini-mall, replacing the Moose Lodge, which was relocating. It proved to be an expensive endeavor for a man who had hated to part with money since he was a young boy. He would complain that he pumped as much as $100,000 into Margaret's business.

He didn't give Margaret everything she wanted. She complained to her sister Dona that, while Ron gave her the seed money to renovate the Moose Lodge space, he made her pay rent like the other tenants. This became a "source of conflict," Dona would later say. Margaret, according to her sister, "wasn't willing to do that."

But she had few choices. Dona would claim that Margaret desperately needed Ron's money. "She had told me she was in arrears on her charge cards, her Nieman Marcus, and had made some sort of repayment agreement," Dona said. Margaret couldn't live up to the store's terms. "She was having conversations with me that they had more stringent requirements than other stores," Dona said. "If she couldn't keep the original agreement, [she said] how did they expect her to keep the repayment agreement?"

Dona had reminded her sister that she once spoke of divorcing Ron in 1992. The sisters had a falling-out that year and did not speak again until 1994. By then, Dona said, "She indicated that he was not in good health. . . . She thought she would wait."

Indeed, Ron did start complaining of heart ailments, for which he took medicine, and he told friends he was worried he might have prostate cancer. He was by now more than two decades older than his father was when he died of a heart attack, and Ron fixated on his health. He had stopped the drinking and started a health food regimen. Some days he felt better than others. But diet didn't seem to be his health problem.

Jerry Stump said he too once flat-out warned Ron that Margaret was going to kill him some day. "I remember me telling him one night: I wouldn't spend another night with that crazy lady," said Stump. "Ron would just laugh it off."

It got to the point where people Ron didn't even know started to worry about him. One was Bruce Hornabach, a "picker" in the antique trade, who scoured the antique stores and secondhand shops for bargains to resell to dealers. He had been finding antiques for Margaret to build on inventory for her soon-to-open store.

They'd handle the transactions at his house, where he operated his business. Since they spoke two or three times a week, he got to know a little bit about her—and her troubled marriage. She would complain to Bruce that Ron wouldn't give her enough money to buy antiques, and that she'd have to sell some of her jewelry to raise cash. But Margaret said she didn't plan to divorce Ron. She had other ideas.

"I don't how many times she told me the only reason she was staying with him was because he would die," Bruce would recall. "She would stay with him strictly because he was going to die. She wasn't going to get any money if she divorced him."

When he heard Margaret say these things, Bruce just kept quiet. He didn't know what to say. Then one day, Margaret told him her plan wasn't going to work. Ron's health situation wasn't as dire as she had been led to believe. "She didn't know what to do," Bruce said. "She thought he was going to die, and now he wasn't going to die."

Bruce didn't know Ron Rudin. But Bruce knew he had

to do something. He went to another of his clients, Sharon Melton, whom he knew worked as Ron's bookkeeper and who had operated her own antique store on the side stocked with some of Bruce's finds. He told Sharon that he was concerned about Ron's safety. Bruce made up his mind.

In late August or early September of 1994, he arranged a meeting with Ron at Ron's real estate offices. When he got there, Bruce was nervous. "I didn't know if he was going to beat me up or throw me out," he said.

They exchanged pleasantries. Bruce told Ron from the outset how uncomfortable he was about what he had to say. He then told Ron that he was concerned for his safety because of the things that Margaret had said. Then he went over his conversations with Margaret about the money and Ron's health and her hopes that he would die.

Ron didn't beat up Bruce and he didn't throw him out. He didn't show much emotion at all.

"He was just very reflective," recalled Bruce, "and not the least bit surprised."

6
THE LETTER

It was about 10 a.m., a spectacular Saturday morning on December 17, 1994: sunny, cool, a gentle breeze blowing across the desert floor. Ron drove his black 1993 Cadillac across town from his home on the west side toward the neighborhood around the Las Vegas Country Club, just east of the The Strip.

He pulled the car up to 367 Pecos Way, a fixer-upper condominium that Ron had purchased a few months earlier to rehabilitate and then resell. As usual, Ron was armed. There was a shotgun in the trunk, a pistol in the armrest next to the driver's seat. He had a concealed weapons permit in his wallet and was known to carry as many as three pistols, two in holsters, one tucked in his boot.

Sue Lyles was waiting for him. She was a brunette, bespectacled, middle-aged woman, a little heavy-set, with two children and a bad marriage. Sue had once worked part-time for Ron on weekends from 1989 to 1991. Her paycheck from her full-time job as a tax auditor for the IRS didn't pay all the bills, what with her husband out of work. At Ron Rudin Realty she answered phones, filed, did data entry. She liked Ron as a boss. She liked Ron's wife, too—at first: Margaret, the attractive, soft-spoken woman whose voice had a hint of a Southern accent. The women would sometimes lunch together, Sue boasting about her children, Margaret boasting about her grandchildren.

Sue would get a promotion to revenue agent at the IRS, and her husband would return to work, so she didn't need to stay in Ron's employ, but she remained friendly with him. Not so with Margaret, who had developed a habit of complaining about Ron, calling him a drunkard, cheap.

Sue didn't see that side of him. Sue prided herself on being a good listener, and with Ron there was plenty to hear, mostly about Margaret and the grief she caused him. Occasionally, Sue would stop by the real estate office to say hello to Ron or to his bookkeeper, Sharon Melton, whom she liked.

Over the next two years, the visits would become more frequent. So would the phone calls. By early 1994, a change set in between Ron and Sue. She started calling him more frequently, but more carefully, after his secretary left at 5:30 p.m. If his secretary happened to still be there and answer, Sue would identify herself as "Sue from National Title." He would call her IRS voice mail after the others left her office at 5:15 p.m.

They began to meet, secretly, at his investment properties. They always made the arrangements by phone, never in person. She began to care deeply for Ron. Those were her words: care deeply. She wouldn't say love, even years later when so much had happened.

She sensed that he felt the same way. Then she was sure. November of 1994 was an emotional month for Ron, his 64th birthday. He said he had come home to an empty house, no party, no presents. He was at the end of his rope with Margaret. In a heartfelt phone call, he confessed his feelings for Sue. He cared deeply.

They had been here before, at the Pecos Way condominium, on the corner of Desert Inn, for one of their secret encounters. But this time it would be different. They weren't there for intimacy. They were there to solve a mystery.

About a week earlier, Sue had received two letters at home, one addressed to Rich Lyles, her 25-year-old son who lived nearby, and the other to a Melissa Lyles. There was no Melissa Lyles in the family but Rich's wife's name was Michelle. Sue assumed it was meant for her. The letters were unsigned and undated, but postmarked

December 8, 1994, from Las Vegas. They had been mailed in envelopes with prepaid postage.

Her son, who had recently finished graduate school, had come to visit and was going through his mail when he saw the letter addressed to him. He read just enough, before he asked his mother incredulously, "What is this?"

Typewritten all in capital letters and filled with misspellings and typographical errors, it read:

> YOUR MOTHER HAS BEEN SCREWING RONALD RUNIN THE REALTER FOR OVER A YEAR. SHE MEETS HIM AT VACANT HOUSES HE OWNS — DURING HER WORK TIME — AND SHE SCREWS HIM ON DIRTY CARPET FLOORS. HE BRAGS TO HIS FRIENDS AND LAUGHS AT HER BECAUSE HE TELLS EVERYONE HE DOES NOT HAVE TO GET A MOTEL ROOM AND HE DOES NOT HAVE TO BUY HER A LUNCH EVEN TO GET TO EAT HER PUSSY AS MUCH AS HE WANTS BECAUSE SHE WILL SREW HIM ANYWHERE AS LONG AS HE WANTS AND AS MANY TIMES AS HE WANTS AND KEEP THE SECRET FROM HIS WIFE AND HER HUSBAND.
>
> YOU ARE BEING TOLD NOW BECAUSE THE TIME IS NOW TO BE PREPAREED FOR A BIG SCANDLE. SIX MONTHS AGO THE WASHINGTON DC AND THE LAS VEGAS SECTION OF THE IRS INVESTIGATIONS WAS TOLD AND SUPPLIED WITH DATES, TIMES, PICTURES AND PROVEN TO THEM YOUR MOTHER WAS SREWING AROUND ON GOVERNMENT TAXPAPER EXPENSE TIME. TO PROVE THE POIT DUPLICATES WERE SENT TO THE TV STATION THAT DOES THE OF PUBLIC INTEREST EXPOSURES. TO DATE THEY HAVE UNDERTAKEN THE FOLLOWUP ON THEIR OWN BECAUSE THEY INVESTIGATION SINSATIONAL TYUPE EXPOSES AND WITH THE VIDEOTAPES THEY HAVE MADE OF YOUR MOTHER AND OTHER GOVERNMENTAL EMPLOYEES THAT THIS SCANDLE IS READY TO SPOTLIGHT YOU WILL NEED TO WARN YOUR FATHER TOO OF WHAT TO EXPECT.

Sue told Ron about the letters on Tuesday, December 13, when they met briefly in a parking lot of the library's West Charleston branch. That's when they arranged to get together the following Saturday at the condo.

Ron and Sue talked for more than an hour. They tried to sort things out, tried to answer some questions. They couldn't figure out how they had been discovered. They were so careful. It was as if somebody had been listening in on their private phone calls.

At first they thought the letters could have been sent by Sharon Melton just to cause a little trouble. A strong-willed woman known to stand up to Ron, Sharon had been unhappy with him lately. He had provided a space in his shopping center to wife Margaret so she could run an antiques store. That would put Margaret's store in the same mall as the real estate office. Sharon loathed Margaret, felt she was conniving, dangerous, out to get Ron and his money. She couldn't understand why Ron would want her anywhere near him during business hours. Sharon also ran her own antiques store on the side, though she would deny that her antipathy toward Margaret stemmed from jealousy or competitive concerns.

But as Sue and Ron discussed it further, they concluded that the letters hadn't come from Sharon. She could be mouthy with the boss, but she would never do something like this. Nothing this crass, nothing this cruel.

Sue knew who could.

Sue recalled, from her days working for Ron, that Margaret had an odd habit. When Sue and Margaret would chat about their families, Margaret was never able to remember the name of Sue's daughter, Natalie. Margaret always called her Melissa. Sue never knew why—there were no other Melissas in Sue's family nor any in the office as far as she knew. But it was a harmless enough mistake. She let it slide.

It all came back when Sue saw the letters. The one for Sue's son had his name correctly written on the envelope, but the one to her daughter was addressed to Melissa

Lyles. This wasn't intended for Sue's daughter-in-law. This letter was sent to Sue's 12-year-old daughter.

Sue was upset, confused, uncertain how to deal with the situation. She looked at Ron. She knew he was seething. He told her he knew just why Margaret would do this. She wanted his money. Margaret was looking for leverage—the kind of leverage she couldn't get just by divorcing him. She must have known his cash and real estate holdings were tied up in a trust.

"It's Lee Canyon," Ron told Sue. "She wants it."

It was worth millions, but he was holding on to it to develop into a resort. The letters had to be part of a strange plot by Margaret to get that land. Ron asked Sue if he should confront Margaret. Sue left it up to him. She said that he knew Margaret best and would know what to do.

Ron said he would talk to Sue after the weekend, on Monday. They ended their meeting with an embrace.

From the condo, Ron made his way to the mini-mall, where his company and Margaret's antiques shop were located. At 1 p.m., he walked through the glass front door of Antique Merchants. The grand opening celebration was in full swing. Invitations had gone out. Refreshments were being served to family—Margaret's family—and friends. Her sister Dona Cantrell helped out. The store was well stocked with furniture, knickknacks and an antique humpback trunk in the back, its lid open and little pillows tucked inside.

Ron had sunk thousands into this place, giving Margaret everything she wanted—or so he thought—as well as giving himself what he wanted: Keeping Margaret on a tight leash. Despite the happy atmosphere in the store, Ron was in no mood for celebration. He didn't even look at Margaret. Instead, he kept his attention on Dona. They exchanged smiles. At first, Margaret didn't even know he had come in. She swung around and saw him there, chatting up her sister.

Dona could feel the tension when Ron came into the store.

Then, as quickly as he arrived, he left.

The next day, Sunday, Ron was out and about again, headed for another antiques store, Antique Palace, on Tropicana and Jones, which was operated by Sharon the bookkeeper. She worked for him three days a week, the rest of the time in the shop. He rarely showed up unannounced. He had come by the store many times in the past, but he always called first. Ron had helped get the store up and running, having loaned Sharon $15,000.

When she saw him drive up in his Cadillac and park, it struck her as unusual. He came inside and poked around, looking at the antiques. He asked her how she was doing. They chatted about his real estate business. Sharon had been meeting with Ron's bankers the week before and knew that Ron had payments due on the revolving line of credit from Pioneer Bank. He told her he would make the payments the next day, Monday. Sharon would cut the checks.

As he browsed, Ron complained about Margaret, which was not unusual for him, and in Sharon he always had an attentive listener. He said Margaret's latest thing was that she had suddenly stopped doing the grocery shopping. He told Sharon that he was going to have to go out and buy some food if he was going to eat.

After about half an hour, Ron left the store, telling Sharon—as he had told Sue Lyles the day before—that he would see her on Monday.

Ron went to the market. From there that he called his business associate Harold Boscutti, who was in his own office, on Spring Mountain Road, typing up an offer somebody had made on a piece of real estate.

When Ron called that Sunday, he said he was on his cell phone in the aisle of a health food store looking for rice and potatoes, part of his new wholesome living kick, with what his perplexed friends called his "nuts and berries diet."

Ron had spoken briefly to Harold that morning before going to the store. But Harold had been busy and asked to speak with Ron later. In the second call, at about 1:30 p.m., they talked mostly business. Ron had just purchased some houses and they were discussing how they would fix them up—what colors of paint and carpeting they would choose. Ron also told Harold he had a big meeting that next day, on Monday, concerning the Lee Canyon property, the same property that Ron told Sue he suspected Margaret was trying to get. Ron didn't go into the details about the meeting. He didn't say whether he actually had a sale ready for the land, which was worth $5 million to $8 million. But Harold could sense Ron's enthusiasm. It was the most excited Ron had been in years. He seemed upbeat. Business was going well for him.

That evening, Ron was where he always was at that time of day—at home, in his modest two-bedroom house on Alpine Place, right around the corner from the real estate office.

At 8:10 p.m. the phone rang. It was Dorothea Flint, one of Margaret's friends. The women both used to live in Illinois—not far from Ron's hometown, although he didn't know them in his pre–Las Vegas days. Dorothea—or Dottie—asked to speak to Margaret. Ron said she wasn't there.

7

A LATE-NIGHT VISITOR

At about 1 a.m. Monday, Dec. 19, 1994, Carol Kawazoe was at the tail end of another punishing 20-hour day at C&C Taxes, a service that prepared tax returns. She would soon get a little more sleep, then resume a work-week that never really ended until the last forms were filed on April 15. Her husband Chris, who worked in a casino, stopped by the business. They chatted awhile.

Then they heard a knock. It was a strange time to get a visitor.

Outside, the temperatures hovered around freezing—a cool, dry winter night. The occasional car ventured down West Charleston Boulevard. The parking lot was empty. The Red Rock Theater movie multiplex across the street had shown its final Sunday night feature much earlier. No other business in the mini-mall—the barbershop, the gun shop, the real estate office owned by her landlord—was occupied.

Through the glass, they could see an attractive middle-aged woman smartly dressed in a blazer and either slacks or a skirt, Carol couldn't remember which. Chris recognized her first. It was Margaret Rudin, the wife of Carol's landlord, Ron Rudin. They let Margaret in and exchanged greetings, the couple wondering what this woman was up to. Margaret explained, in her soft voice, that she had seen the lights on in the office. She asked them if they wanted any coffee from a Winchell's donut shop nearby which was open all night.

"No, thank you," said Carol, and she mentioned that she had a coffee maker in the office. She asked if Margaret wanted a fresh cup. Although she had just offered to get coffee, Margaret declined with a polite: "No, thank you."

Just what Margaret did want wasn't immediately apparent. She seemed to have little purpose in stopping by except to chat. Margaret told them about the antique business she had just started at the far end of the mini-mall in a space that had previously been used by the Moose Lodge. She called her store Antique Merchants and it had celebrated its grand opening that weekend. She had split the space in two, operating half the store herself and subletting the other half to another antique dealer.

Margaret then started telling Carol and Chris about her personal life. She told them that her husband Ron wanted her home at night, that he didn't like her working late. It was for this reason, Margaret told them, that Ron had made the space in his mini-mall available to her. He wanted Margaret working close to the house, close to him.

All this went on for about a half-hour. Carol recalled that Margaret was calm, cordial, but in all the time she spoke to them never sat down. The subject of coffee never resurfaced. Margaret Rudin finally left. Carol and Chris could only shake their heads.

It was about 2 a.m.

8
WHERE'S RON?

Shortly before 8 o'clock on Monday morning, Jerry Stump pulled his car into the parking lot behind the shopping mall on West Charleston. Stump ran a throwback barbershop there, just across the hall from the landlord's real estate business. He had a loyal customer base, many of them older men who would sit in any of the three chairs for hours, paying as much for the conversation as the trim.

This was the beginning of the work week and traffic had already picked up on Charleston, commuters going to the business offices and government buildings downtown or to the casinos, hotels and restaurants on Fremont Street and The Strip. Normally Jerry had this day off. His West Hill Barbershop was closed on Sundays and Mondays. But on this Monday morning Jerry had a special customer, an invalid who was too weak to get to the shop. Jerry would stop in just long enough to get his barber tools, then leave for a house call.

He stepped up to the glass door to the mall and punched the secret code into the key pad that would turn off the alarm system to the main building. His friend Ron worried constantly about security. Ron was known to keep some of his gun stock in the real estate office along with thousands of dollars in cash in a desk drawer. Jerry picked up his tools and walked out the back door. Although he knew about Ron's security worries, Jerry didn't reactivate the alarm. It was nearly 8 a.m. by now. He figured Ron would arrive any minute, and left a little note on the alarm box telling him that the alarm was off but not to worry—that he had just been there. He left for his morning haircutting job.

In the next half-hour, employees started arriving at work at Ron Rudin Realty. The first were Ron's secretary,

Jill, who had been on the job for only a few months—
Ron tended to go through secretaries—and an older
woman named Lilly Grinfelds whose husband, Roman
"Ollie" Grinfelds, had worked for Ron for years. Ollie did
odd jobs—ran errands, kept the Cadillac clean—but Ron
mostly valued his company. Ollie was a confidant, something of a father figure, filling the gap left when Ron's
real father had died when he was a boy. Lilly didn't technically work for Ron but had come to the office anyway.
Ollie had been ill lately. His wife had come to see if she
could handle some of his duties.

When the women got to the mini-mall the doors were
locked and nobody was inside that they could see. They
were perplexed. Ron should have been there by now. His
Cadillac with the RRR-1 plates wasn't parked in its usual
place by the back glass door, and Ron was nowhere to be
seen. Neither of the women had keys to the building. All
they could do was stand around in the parking lot, waiting.

At about 9:10 a.m. Sharon Melton arrived. She was
surprised to see Jill and Lilly standing outside and Ron's
parking space empty. Sharon had spoken with Ron just
the day before at her antique shop and knew he had important business this morning. Ron never missed a loan
payment. He was so careful he often hand-delivered the
check.

"What's wrong?" Sharon asked Jill as she got out of
her car.

"Ron's not here," the secretary said.

Sharon Melton shuddered. This was not like Ron.

Ron had his drawbacks as a boss—he could be hard-
driving, cranky, brusque—but he was conscientious to the
point of obsession about keeping his employees aware of
his every move. If he was out inspecting a property in the
Cold Creek or Lee Canyon sections of Mount Charleston
or even going to a meeting at a title company or bank
nearby, he'd call the office several times to check in.
When he went on his hunting safaris to Africa, or big-

game shoots in Northern Nevada or New Mexico with his cop friends, he'd leave Sharon an itinerary. While traveling, he'd call from the airport while changing planes to check on business. When he took an Alaskan cruise he contacted her over the ship-to-shore radio five times a day. Ron was even known to stop by an employee's desk to give some instructions on the way to an appointment, then call from his cell phone with more instructions before he even reached his car in the parking lot.

It was now 9:30 a.m. It wasn't like he could be stuck in traffic, which in recent years was choking Las Vegas freeways as the city struggled to cope with its explosive growth. Ron lived almost literally a stone's throw from his office. Every morning he would pull his Cadillac out of his semi-circular driveway through one of the wrought-iron gates and go around the corner and into the back parking lot of the mini-mall, where these three women were now standing, a commute of a couple of hundred yards.

"Something's wrong," Lilly said again. "Something's drastically wrong."

Sharon gave Jill her cellular phone and asked to call Ron's private line at home. Nobody answered, not Ron, not his wife Margaret. Instead the answering machine picked up.

"This is Jill," the secretary said after the greeting. "Sharon and I and Lilly are waiting out here for you." She told Ron to call Sharon's cellular phone.

After about another half-hour, they grew tired of waiting. Sharon had a key to the building but worried that she didn't know the correct alarm code and would set it off. She didn't see the note that the barber had left saying he had already deactivated the alarm.

As Sharon pondered what to do, Jill walked to Winchell's across the street to get coffee for herself and the other women. Sharon and Lilly then went around the back of the office into the alley that separated the strip mall from Ron's house. They wanted to see if anyone was home, but they weren't tall enough to peek over the six-foot wall. Lilly called her taller son-in-law to ask if he could come down.

It was about then that Sharon heard the noises: a series of sharp sounds similar to gunshots—eight, maybe nine. Sharon would later describe the noises as a boom-boom-boom-boom in rapid succession.

"Get in the car! Let's get out of here!" Sharon told Lilly. "She will shoot us."

Sharon thought Margaret had flipped. Sharon and Lilly drove over to the Winchells' to meet up with Jill. Soon, Lilly's son-in-law came by and told them he couldn't see anything over the wall in the back yard but he did go around the front and looked through the wrought-iron gate. In the driveway was a large light-colored car, a Lincoln or Cadillac, he wasn't sure which. Margaret drove a large, light-green Lincoln Town Car. She must have been home. Why wasn't she returning their call? The son-in-law didn't see Ron's black Cadillac.

The women dispersed. Sharon drove to the office of a friend, David Meyer, who knew Ron. Shaken, she needed a cup of coffee to calm down. Once recovered, Sharon asked another friend there, Meyer's employee Holly Quinn, to call Margaret to see if she was at home. At about 10:30 a.m. Holly dialed the house. This time no answering machine. A soft voice answered.

"Hi, is this Margaret?" asked Holly, not really sure what to say.

"Yes it is. What is this about?"

"This is a floral delivery. I just wanted to make sure you'd be there."

Margaret hung up.

Sharon now knew that Margaret was home but hadn't returned the call from the women in the parking lot. What was Margaret up to? And what were those noises?

From there Sharon drove back to the mini-mall to see if Ron's car was there yet. It wasn't. She drove around to the nearby shopping centers looking for any sign of the

Cadillac. Eventually, she made her way to her own antique store, calling around town for Ron, worrying. She must have called his cell phone 100 times.

Ron would not be heard from all day. Sharon began to panic. That evening, Ronald Danner, a handyman who did work on Ron's investment properties, called Sharon at home.

"Where's Ron!" he shouted into the phone.

"Thank God you called me because I have not seen him all day," Sharon said. "I have not heard from him and I was hoping you had."

He hadn't.

"Should we call the police?" Sharon asked.

Until now, Sharon and the others had taken things into their own hands. Not even hearing the sounds she thought might be gunshots was enough to convince her to call 911, a lack of action she would have to answer for later. At the time, Sharon felt it was best not to involve the police immediately. Sharon worried what Ron would say. Ron was a private man, as obsessive about that as he was about security. She feared he would explode if she called the police only to find out it was a big mix-up. She started telling herself that those noises weren't gunshots. Maybe car backfires.

And yet . . . it didn't seem right. She discussed it with Danner. They decided that Danner would talk to Margaret the next morning.

The next day, he did just that. Danner, according to a statement he'd later give to police, got to the front door of Ron's house. He could see that the shutters to Ron's bedroom were closed. Danner had been to the house countless times and never knew Ron to close the bedroom shutters. There was also a vehicle at the house he didn't recognize, a blue van. Margaret answered the door. She wouldn't let him inside. She told him she didn't know where Ron was. Danner would later say that she didn't sound overly concerned.

Danner reported this to Sharon that Tuesday morning.

"I am going to the police," she said. "You can come with me or not, but I'm going."

At about 11 a.m., Sharon and Danner walked into the southwest substation of the Las Vegas Metropolitan Police Department, on Spring Mountain Road, not far from the real estate office. The front desk of the substation was staffed by Sandra Wassall, an Office Assistant II, whose duties entailed registering guns and helping people file reports. Sharon and Danner told the clerk that they wanted to file a missing persons report for their boss, who ran Ron Rudin Realty on West Charleston.

Wassall had handled missing persons reports before, but never had a person been reported missing by anybody but a spouse or close relative.

"Is he married?" Wassall asked.

"Yes," Sharon said, "but . . . I don't think she's going to file a report."

Wassall felt that before she took the report from Sharon and Ronald, she should talk to this wife, whom the pair identified as Margaret Rudin. But the clerk didn't know if that was the proper procedure. She called the detectives at the missing persons division for instructions, but got only voice mail. She left a message.

While awaiting a call back, Wassall pressed Sharon and Danner on why they thought there was a problem. Sharon went through the previous day's events, leaving out the loud noises; and explained how careful Ron was to always notify somebody if he was going to be late.

Wassall tried the detectives again, but still couldn't reach them.

Finally, she called Margaret, on a number provided by Sharon.

A woman answered.

"Is this Margaret?" she asked.

"Yes," came a gentle voice.

The clerk identified herself, explained that she had information that nobody had seen her husband for more than

24 hours. Margaret said she hadn't seen him, either.

"Are you going to file a missing persons report?" the clerk asked.

"I probably will."

Probably?

"When are you going to?" the clerk asked, stunned.

"I'm not sure."

What kind of wife didn't worry about a husband missing now for more than a day? Las Vegas didn't have a policy requiring a 48-hour wait before reporting a missing person. Wassall told Margaret that Sharon and Danner were in the substation and prepared to file the report if she didn't want to. Margaret changed her tune. She said that she would go to police.

"When?" Wassall asked.

"Soon," said Margaret, but she wanted to do it at another police substation, the one on Jones Street near the freeway, closer to downtown.

Wassall hung up, puzzled. Margaret Rudin's husband was missing and she didn't seem concerned. She seemed so . . . the word Wassall kept thinking was *lackadaisical*.

The detectives had still not called her back, so Wassall took a statement from Sharon and Danner. The statement would be attached to the formal report that Margaret said she would file. If Margaret didn't file a formal report by 4 p.m. the statement would become the official report. Just to cover all bases, the clerk also called the other substation to let them know that a Margaret Rudin was coming in to report that her husband was missing. The clerk felt strongly that somebody should take a report in this case, that it shouldn't fall through the cracks.

A little after 1:30 p.m., Sharon and Ronald Danner signed the statement and left the southwest substation.

Within a half-hour, Margaret Rudin did in fact show up at the northwest substation with Ronald Danner. Police clerk Iris Meccia took the report, typing into the computer Ron's name, address, and physical description: 6 feet tall,

220 pounds. She put in that he was last seen wearing a black shirt, black pants and black cowboy boots and that he drove a 1993 black Cadillac four-door with the license plate RRR-1. The vehicle was also missing. There was a description of the jewelry he usually wore, including two rings, a watch and an ID bracelet with the name "RON" written in diamonds.

In the boxes asking if the case was gang-related or involved substance abuse, the clerk typed in "No." The clerk then typed in the narrative portion of the report, based on her interviews with Danner and Margaret. Margaret is referred to as "PR," or Person Reporting:

> Ronald Danner stated that he talked to the missing person on Sunday night at approximately 18:30 hours. The missing person stated that he would see him Monday morning. Ronald Danner stated that it is not like the missing person to not show up for any of his important meetings that he had on Monday.
>
> Missing person has a CCW [a concealed weapons permit] and always carries his gun with him. The missing person is a gun dealer. He always carries at least $2000.00 with him at all times.
>
> Missing person has a heart problem and needs medication. The medication is at home.
>
> Missing person had a car cellular # 376-2508. They have tried to call him several times but it's always out of range.
>
> PR states that she saw him at approximately 1800 hours. PR stated that he has been depressed lately.

Getting this much out of the two of them wasn't easy. Meccia would ask Margaret a question and Danner would interrupt. She asked him to please let Margaret answer, but Danner kept interrupting. Finally, the clerk got the report done. She closed the file in the computer, which automatically time-stamped it at 13:58 hours, 1:58 p.m.

Wassall entered the report into the police department's

computer system, accessible by detectives and supervisors.

Ron's disappearance would get prompt attention at the police department—Sharon made sure of that. Sharon knew that Ron had friends at Metro, and the day after she gave her statement, she called Ron's office. Jill, the secretary who had been able to get into the building because the barber had deactivated the alarm, answered. She had called Ron's car phone constantly, but never gotten an answer. Sharon told Jill to call Jerry Keller, the newly elected sheriff who oversaw the Las Vegas Metro Police Department.

That evening, detectives from the missing persons division contacted Jill to inquire about Ron Rudin, the missing millionaire, about whom everybody was worried—everybody except his wife Margaret.

9

THE WORRIED SISTER

Dona Cantrell and Margaret Rudin had had their differences over the years. But by December 1994 they were on good terms. When Margaret was getting her antique shop up and running, she had hired Dona's teen-age son to do odd jobs. When the store finally opened, Dona was there to help out. They made plans for Dona to continue working afterwards.

But Dona could sense a strange undercurrent in their relationship. On the Saturday of the grand opening, December 17, 1994, there was that tense, wordless encounter between Ron and Margaret. Then, that night, Margaret called and left a message on Dona's machine. She thanked Dona for attending the grand opening, saying, "It was wonderful and perfect for you to be there." This wasn't the Margaret Dona knew in good or bad times. She was a little too effusive.

The next night, Sunday, at about 8:30 p.m., Margaret left another message on Dona's machine: "Just calling to see how you're doing. Miss you, love you."

There was no message the next day, Monday, December 19, 1994, the day that Ron had shocked his employees by failing to show up for work. Word had gotten to Dona, via her other sister Barbara, that Ron was missing. At about noon, Dona called Margaret to find out what was going on.

"Has he ever done this before?" she asked.

"Overnight, but not like this," said Margaret. Her tone was calm, matter-of-fact.

"Do you have any idea where he might have gone?" asked Dona. "Because I heard a mention of a hunting trip he had coming up within the next several months. Do you think he might be there, that he might have gone there?"

"I wouldn't think so. He was upset with them."

"That's really strange. That's really odd. What do you think?" asked Dona. "Have you checked for his luggage?"

There was a long pause, then Margaret said, "I haven't thought to do that."

"Have you gone to the police?"

Margaret, still calm, answered, "I guess I'll do that now."

In the coming days Dona would call several times to get updates on Ron. And each time, Margaret would say, "I don't want to talk about it." The more Dona pressed— "Has Ron come home?", "Have you heard anything?", "What do you think?"—the more forceful Margaret became.

"I don't want to talk about it."

10

THE MISSING MONEY

Ron Rudin often acted as though his business couldn't run without him. Now it had to. It was Wednesday, December 21, 1994, and nobody had seen or heard from him since the previous weekend. As concerned as his employees were about his welfare, they also had to worry about the business. By now, there were bills to be paid, contractors to oversee, supplies to order. Several deals were in limbo. Money coming in from the Cold Creek subdivision had to be deposited to keep the cash flowing. That big payment on the revolving line of credit that Ron was going to make Monday still had to be delivered, or Ron risked ruining his credit rating.

So even though her boss was nowhere to be found, Sharon Melton went to work as she usually did on Wednesdays, trying to keep the business going as best she could. At one point during the day, Harold Boscutti stopped by the office. He hadn't heard from Ron for a couple of days, and he was surprised to see Sharon there by herself. She looked sad. He asked her what the problem was, and she said that Ron was missing. Boscutti returned to his office, deeply concerned. This was not like Ron. The last time Boscutti had spoken to him, Ron was excited, had a big deal in the works with Lee Canyon.

Without Ron there, Sharon could only do so much with the finances. She wrote out the bills, but he had always signed the checks. There was a very real risk of a cash crunch if something didn't happen soon. Sharon did know where she could get her hands on some money. As long as she'd known him, Ron had always kept large amounts of cash in his office. Sharon, Jill and Ron Danner decided it would be best to go into the office after it. Sharon had a secondary motive for entering the office. It had suddenly occurred to her that nobody had checked it since Ron disappeared. The office was locked, protected by a separate alarm system. It was Ron's sanctuary. Could he be in there, dead from a heart attack?

At about 12:30 p.m. they entered Ron's office. There was no grim surprise, just Ron's messy desk, with so much paper piled on it that you couldn't see the top. Danner quickly found the money in one of the drawers. Together, they counted it out: $12,361. It was mostly in hundreds and fifties. To protect themselves against any claim that they had stolen the money, Sharon wrote down the amount and the denominations, and they all signed the paper. Danner added a note that he was the one who had opened the drawer.

Sharon felt that the money should go somewhere safe. She also felt that somebody had better start making some decisions about the business. That night, she called an attorney named Patricia Brown, whom she knew handled Ron's living trust, which he had set up in 1979 to protect his assets from tax liabilities and other problems if he died. Sharon was familiar with the trust because Ron had once asked her if she would be one of the trustees. In the phone call, Brown told her that, in fact, Sharon and one of Ron's business associates, real estate broker Harold Boscutti, were the trustees. They arranged for a meeting the next day at Brown's office to discuss what to do until Ron turned up.

While it took Margaret more than a day to report her husband missing, she wasted little time reporting to police what she believed was a break-in at his office and the theft of about $15,000. It turned out that when the employees went into Ron's office, the alarm had gone off. The alarm company contacted Margaret, who got in touch with police and filled out a statement to Officer Tim Vaughn. In her own handwriting, Margaret (listing her occupation as "antique shop") implicated Sharon Melton and Ron Danner.

The report made only a passing reference to Ron's absence. She noted that this statement "is in addition to the missing person report I put in on my husband yesterday." The theft report, however, was considerably more detailed than the bare-bones report she had made about her husband.

Margaret wrote:

Alarmco Security called me at home at 12:37 p.m. and said someone was in my husband's inner office and had set off the motion detector and asked who had permission to be here. I said "no one" and asked her to wait while I called his scy—I did and asked Jill who was in Ron's office and she said Danner and Sharon and I said Alarmco is on the other phone and they should not be in there, tell them to exit Ron's room because I had told Danner earlier that I would be opening Ron's office later this afternoon and if they wanted anything out of there that we could move it out there and I got back to Alarmco and asked what to do and she told me how they would take care of reset.

I made apt. to meet one of their Alarmco's alarm runners (Don Grubbs) at 5 p.m.—he was early so we entered at 4:32 p.m. and inspected Ron's office to see if money, gun inventory etc. was still there and we found the $15,000 in cash that Ron keeps in his middle and right desk drawers to be totally gone. The guns appear to be all there.

I asked Jill to please stay until Metro could take a report. She became very nervous and made many phone calls while Don and I were waiting together that I didn't notice her but he said she really seemed aggitated [sic] and nervous and worried and kept making phone calls. She left her phone # and address and said Metro could call her and she left.

The barber shop employees and owner left and he (Jerry) asked me if I'd turn on the hall alarm when I left and I will. Fred from Alarmco stayed with the

Metro officer and me until 6:50 when we finished this report.

Sharon Melton owes Ron close to $20,000. Danner owes Ron close to $10,000.

Margaret signed the bottom of the statement.

She also called Harold and told him that $15,000 was missing from Ron's office. Then she started bad-mouthing Ron, saying that she had hired a private detective to follow him and that he was having an affair. Harold didn't know Margaret well, but he got a bad sense of her over the phone. She spoke, he would later say, like Scarlett O'Hara, in a "little girl voice," all helpless and confused. Harold had been a salesman all his life and prided himself on reading people, particularly when they were trying to get something out of him. "I think she was kind of angling for something," he recalled. Just what, he couldn't be sure.

11

MARGARET SPEAKS

When Detective Patrick Barry, of the Missing Persons Detail of the Las Vegas Metropolitan Police Department, called Margaret Rudin the morning of Thursday, December 22, 1994, he tried to keep the conversation short. He didn't want her to get too emotional before they even had a chance to meet. Her husband had been missing for more than three days, and police had no idea where he was. In the short conversation, Barry arranged to meet with Margaret later that morning.

Up until this point, Barry and partner Frank Janise had handled the case in routine fashion. After they were assigned the case by their sergeant, they got a copy of the original missing persons report taken by Iris Meccia at the northwest station. He looked it over and found nothing startling. No red flag, save for the missing person's age—at 64 he was older than the usual—and the fact that he was a prominent businessman. The sergeant characterized the case to Barry as a little more important than the usual one, but nothing monumental. Despite Ron Rudin's links to Metro, Barry insisted that he got no pressure from police brass.

The detectives put out an ATL—Attempt To Locate—Metro's equivalent of the APB. Patrol officers were provided with the information on Rudin before their shifts. It would be broadcast over the police radios every few hours to remind officers to keep a lookout for the 6-foot-tall, 220-pound white male possibly wearing all black, or his black Cadillac, license plate RRR-1. Teletypes with the same information went out to police departments in Southwestern states. And the police entered Ron's description into the FBI's National Crime Information Center computer, accessible by police agencies throughout the nation.

They contacted Las Vegas' two airports, McCarran International and the smaller North Las Vegas Air Terminal, to see if any of the police officers or security guards had spotted Rudin or the Cadillac. They contacted a police officer who happened to live at Mt. Charleston, where Ron's properties were located, to check the lodges and other places.

At 11:30 a.m. that Thursday, Barry and Janise arrived as scheduled at Antique Merchants, in the end unit of a shopping center on Charleston. They went inside, and Margaret was there; so, too, was her sister, Dona Cantrell. Barry scanned the shop. He didn't notice any customers.

The detectives asked Margaret if she would be willing to give a formal, taped statement to assist police in figuring out what had happened to her husband. At first she balked. She wanted to talk to her attorney. The detectives explained that all they wanted to do was help her. Margaret agreed to talk without a lawyer.

Barry set down his tape recorder and turned it on. He would be gentle with her, trying to establish rapport with someone who could very well turn out to be an anxiety-ridden wife. Janise would hardly utter a word.

Barry said into the microphone: "Details: Today is the twenty-second of December, 1145 hours, and we're conducting an interview at 5100 West Charleston Boulevard regarding a missing report on Ronald Rudin under Event Number 941220-0973. We are interviewing the missing person's wife, Margaret."

Then he turned to Margaret.

"Mrs. Rudin, I just—again, on tape so it's mentioned—this is a taped interview solely for the purpose of it picks up better than I write. And we get it much more accurate when it's transcripted. Do you have any objections to the tape being on?"

"No, sir," Margaret answered softly.

"If you can, lean in a little," Barry told her. "It helps

a little bit, so it will be easier to be transcribed." He asked her to give her name and birth date.

"Margaret Rudin, May 31, 1943."

He asked her to spell her last name, which she did. He then told her, "Mrs. Rudin, we are investigating the whereabouts of your husband, which was reported to us on the twentieth [sic], which would be Monday. When was the last time that you had contact with Ronald?"

"Uh, Sunday evening, and I'm not sure of that. I saw him about 6:30," she said. "Then I left for a couple of hours and then called him."

She couldn't pinpoint a time of the call.

"I'm not sure if I called around, you know, 8:30 or if it was 9:00 or 9:30. But somewhere in that, you know, time frame," she said. "I talked to him on the telephone from the cellular," she said. "And I saw him right after work on Sunday, 'cause I had worked all day. And he had come in and out of the shop several different times.

"When I got off work, he'd wanted to go to a movie. And when I got off from work I went over and I said, 'Did you find a movie you want to go to?' And he said, 'No, there's none of them any good.'

"And so I, you know, waited around the house for a little bit and said, you know, 'Can I fix you anything to eat?' and so forth. And he said . . ."

Margaret stumbled for the words.

"He . . . a mental . . . uh . . . depressed," she said. "He's been real depressed lately."

She quoted Ron as telling her, "There's nothing good on TV. There's no good movies or nothing."

Margaret said she told him, "If you don't object, then I'll go back to work."

To this, Ron replied with what Margaret said was his usual inside joke.

"He . . . He . . . He's kidding because he says this a lot," said Margaret. "He said, um, 'No, you can go back to work 'cause I've got somebody else to go with me to a movie anyway.' "

According to Margaret, Ron joked that somebody had answered his personal ad in the paper and that he would go with her to the movie.

Margaret told the detective, "He's always making comments about, you know, 'I have a personal ad.' So I just left and said, 'OK, I hope she likes your kind of movie.' And I left."

Barry asked Margaret where she worked.

"Here," she told him, and he asked for the name and address, which she provided: Antique Merchants, 5100 West Charleston.

Margaret then returned to talking about that last night she saw Ron.

"And I was here because it was our grand opening sale that Saturday and Sunday."

Barry asked: "So then you went back to work, that was the last time that you had seen him? He was at home?"

"He was at home, uh, he's uh, watching television. He was reading the newspaper. He had the newspaper."

Barry nodded. Margaret continued, "He seemed OK. He wasn't, you know, upset. He wasn't," Margaret said, but then she said he probably was upset. "He had been a little peeved at me over the weekend because I had to work all the time," she said. "That's why I'm sure he made the comment about, you know, get somebody else to go to the movie with me. But he was fine. And everything was fine with us."

Barry nodded.

"And the last words he said to me was, 'I love you.' " she said.

The following day, she said, that Monday, Ron's co-workers were in a tizzy over his failure to show up to work, but she wasn't overly concerned.

"I thought: Well, he just was, you know, trying to make a point, or he did, you know, go out for a while or something. So I wasn't worried about it."

At this point, Barry had her back up, trying to pin her down a little more on exactly when she'd last seen her husband. The detective said: "Are you getting a little bit ahead? I want to know when you were back to the store, about what time did you go home?"

"OK, OK," she said. "Uh, I came um, I took—I had a computer part that one of my friends wanted to borrow. And so I took the computer to him. He was going to use the printer, and he was going to fix the hard drive in the computer. I stayed there for a couple of hours 'cause he and I are working on a book together."

"Now who is he?" asked Barry.

"A friend of mine. His name is Jack Carpenter."

"And he works here also?"

"No, he's just working on my book."

Barry didn't ask about the book. He nodded and let Margaret continue.

"And, uh, then I left there," she said. "I went by the grocery store and got a few things. Um, I thought, 'I'll call Ron and see if he's changed his mind.' If he'd like to go do anything. And I called and he was real short. It was a real short conversation. And I just said, 'How are you doing? You OK? Do you want—?' And he said, 'No, everything's fine, I love you.'"

"About what time was this?" asked Barry.

"I think it was about 9:00," she said.

"About 9:00 p.m.?"

"So I came back to work," she said. "And I stayed here and did all kinds of things because of the sale until about, I think, it was 1 o'clock or 1:15 or something like that. And I thought and I just worked better at night. I do that a lot. I stay a lot at night."

"It would be about 1:15 a.m.?" asked Barry.

"Right," she said. "And then I went—there is some new people down at the end that have a CPA office," she said, referring to Carole Kawazoe. She said she met with those people. "And I said, 'I'll run get some coffee. You guys want coffee?' And we talked awhile, so I probably didn't get home 'til 1:30 or maybe, you know, later."

"Uh-huh."

"Around that area," she said. "And when I got there his car was gone. But I thought nothing of it because maybe he did get peeved or maybe he did decide to go out for a while or maybe he did go to, you know, wherever."

"So," asked Barry, "you were the last person to see him?"

"Yes." Then she added, "Well, as far as I know. Have you asked—?"

"I haven't spoken to anyone else as far as the interview," Barry interrupted her. "Your last conversation when you left, though, when you hung up the phone, was it anything to alarm you or make you think something was wrong? Or were you comfortable with the conversation?"

"He was himself," she said. "You know, he always is real depressed this time of year. He gets real down and gets real, uh, but he was down. He was depressed. He was himself. You know, I know that him, that's him."

"Nothing unusual?"

"No."

"Is he under any doctor's care or taking any medicine at this time?"

"He takes heart medication," she said. "I think it's for, uh, blood pressure."

"Since he's been gone now, have you made contact with all the close family members, friends?"

"I . . . He doesn't have any close family at all," she said. "You know, he doesn't stay in contact with anybody. There's one uncle he hears from maybe twice a year."

Barry nodded.

"And I didn't want to call him 'cause they just told us about a week ago that he's lost a lot of weight and he's really sick, and they are having him in the hospital in St. Louis," she said. "So, I, I don't want to add to, to Lester right now. 'Cause they think he he's, got, you know, cancer."

She gave a little more information on Uncle Lester,

saying he'd been undergoing tests, that he'd had trouble with his eyes.

"So I didn't want to contact them until there's something to tell them," she said. "Maybe there's nothing, you know. As far as friends, the only people that—Ron never had friends that came to the house. We've been married over seven years. He's never had one person that ever come to the house for a visit, or call. But I called a business contact that he had."

Barry didn't ask the name of the business contact. He asked, "Any discussion that now, with hindsight, looking back, that might be indicative of him acting this way or might have caused him to take off and not tell where he's going?"

"Well, you know, because of the severity of this now . . ." Margaret became tongue-tied. "I'm not just be talking, and I'm not just try to say, uh, this is what happened or this is . . ."

Then she got her thoughts straight.

"You know, I want to verify it, so you can verify it," she said. "You know, but he's been really angry lately and a lot of times he doesn't tell me everything, you know. More than depressive. What's been coming through has been anger at everybody. Everybody. Like the bookkeeper at the office.

"He had called his CPA and said, 'I want to replace her. Get me a replacement.' So the CPA had said, you know, I'll send somebody over, he said. You know, he's tired of some of her things. He was furious."

Margaret said that bookkeeper Sharon Melton wasn't the only person at whom Ron was mad.

"And he'd talked to, uh, his electrician that he was going to fire him," she said, referring to Ron Danner.

"He was going to fire Jill in the office," Margaret said of Ron's secretary Jill Julian. "And I said, 'Please don't fire her until after Christmas.' And he'd told everybody. He complained about his friends, you know, the ones that are the business contacts. I've never seen him so angry at everything and everybody all at one time."

After telling Barry about the office turmoil, Margaret said she wanted to talk about a subject "real hard for me to get into, because I know you guys are not going to understand."

"I understand so far what you are saying," the detective said. "Did you ever see a mood swing in him?"

She ignored his question.

"Well, what I was gonna say [is] that I don't know how you guys are going to take it," she said. "Ron believed in evil spirit possession."

If this shocked Barry, he didn't let it out.

His response was: "Uh-huh."

"And he'd gone to a doctor for years that did de-possessions."

"Uh-huh."

"Up in St. George," she said, apparently referring to the Utah town along the Nevada border. "And so he kept saying he was possessed by evil spirits, and he was possessed by Peggy's spirit."

Margaret explained that Peggy was "a wife that he had that killed herself in the house." This was around Christmastime, she told Barry. She said she asked her husband if he wanted to go see this doctor in Utah.

"I thought maybe because of all of his agitation and his mood he just needed to get away for a couple of days," she said. "He just needed to go by himself. And that's why at first I wasn't that upset, because, I know that demon de-possession is something that he practices."

"Can you say it a little louder? The demon what?"

"De-possession."

"De-possession? And that's something you said he practices."

"Uh-huh."

Barry didn't follow up on the demon de-possession line of inquiry. He shifted gears and asked, "Has he ever taken unexplained absences in the past?"

"No," she said.

"No?" he replied. "Has he been on any excessive pressures from his work load or even home life? Has there been anything? Looking back on it—"

She interrupted him. "Unusual?"

"Yeah," Barry said. "Possibly add a lot of pressure or stress to him?"

"I'm gonna have to say not that I'm aware of," said Margaret. "You might need to ask at the office if there's an unusual financial problem."

"Nothing out of the ordinary?"

"Uh-uh."

Barry stopped beating around the bush. "The next part is . . ." he began delicately, "I've got to cover some bases—and certainly no accusations. But we need to go over the relationship, marriagely [sic], between you and Ron."

"In my opinion?"

"Yes," he said. "Has there been any problems or any sign that might indicate that he wanted to leave or might be leaving?"

"Ron was a real off-and-on person," she said. "He was either all good or all bad. All black or all white, you know."

"Uh-huh."

"So our whole relationship has been: It's either very good or very bad. And when it gets very bad and he thinks he's pushed you as far as you're gonna take it, then he always does everything he can to pull you back and make it good again, you know?"

She said that Ron was known for doing "about-faces."

"There have been times I think I'm just not gonna be here," she said. "I can't stay. Or maybe he felt the same way but didn't tell me, you know? And then when I'd say, 'I don't understand why things are like this,' he'd say, 'OK, this is upsetting her,' and he'd go the other direction.

"And then lately things have been very, very good."

For instance, she noted that Ron had asked her if she

wanted to open the antique shop. She said he told her: "I'll fix it the way you want. I'll let you pick [it] out."

"He was really out of character doing those things," she said. "And he tried so hard. He was over here all the time, you know: 'Let's do it this way. Let's do that. Let's have this.' And I was even surprised myself at how far he was going out of his way to be really, really nice. And really, really giving and really accommodating."

Barry said, "Uh-huh."

"He wanted me to be here. He wanted me to succeed," she said. "He wanted to go to Thanksgiving with my mom, you know? It was like at holiday time, he gets, uh, segregated. You know, he feels like he doesn't belong. He doesn't have a home. He doesn't have a parent. He doesn't [have] stability or something."

"Uh-huh."

"So he, I think he's, um, more likely to be rejecting at this time of year, but he was going out of his way not to be. So, I guess I was getting double signals."

Barry asked: "Would it be totally out of character [for him] to be having an affair?"

She said he had. "He told me that he was going to stop seeing her in September," she said, then her words became a jumble. "He just, he's just that kind of . . . of . . . He just needs a lot of . . . That sounds stupid, doesn't it? Ego. Ego."

She rambled some more. "Women get to a point where uh . . . he's . . . just, . . . say, that's been going on since time began."

Margaret said she knew who the woman was—and that she had tried to contact her the day before.

"I had called [her] work just to see if she was there, you know? You know, 'cause, call and if she answer the phone, hang up. We'll know if she's, you know? And I had the phone number."

"And did you make that call?"

Margaret nodded yes.

"Was she there?"

"She was there."

"Do you know her name?"

"I just hate to bring her into it."

"Understand," Barry said, "that we are not gonna bring anyone into it that doesn't need to be brought into. But right now, with the time frame that we are looking at, the seriousness—"

"OK," she said. "Then, I know."

"We'll do what we can to locate him. And we'll keep it as low-key as we can. OK?"

"I know this doesn't sound like something that men would probably understand, but it's embarrassing."

"Uh-huh."

"And like—never mind. It doesn't matter," she said. "It's, uh, uh, Sue, and the last name is Lyles."

Barry asked her to spell the name, which she did. He spelled the last name back to her to double-check.

"OK," he told her. "We're off the personal now. Now, on business."

"Thank you," Margaret said.

"Obviously, he's established," said Barry. "Has a lot of contacts. Are there any people out there that might wish him ill? Does he have enemies? Or people that don't like him?"

"He has people that don't like him," said Margaret, "but I don't know if I'd be the one to talk to about that."

But Margaret did talk about it—at length.

"He takes people's houses and rehabs them. And there are usually houses that people have lost," she said. "So I know he's had threats before about, uh, people would come over about, you know, losing their possession and losing their houses and things like that. So that's one of the reasons he's always armed."

"OK."

"He does a lot of work in North Las Vegas," she said, referring to the section near downtown. "And so he's had confrontations and problems over that."

And, she said, "He's a gun dealer, and so I know he,

he deals sometimes in a lot of cash. . . . I think there was some element of danger. There's an element of danger there. It's one of the reasons he's so security-conscious, you know? He's got so many systems in his—you know, guns in his possession and so on."

She stressed this was all speculation. "As far as anything on a definite level, or personal level, or one-on-one, I don't know."

"You don't know of any personal vendettas?"

"Well, not other than . . . No."

Barry was about done. He told Margaret, "We've covered quite a few of the bases," and said that he needed to confer with his partner, Frank Janise, who had no questions.

Barry asked, "Can you think of anything you might want to add before I close out the statement?"

"I just think there's always a lot of dissension in his life," she said. "He had the wife that committed suicide."

"Uh-huh."

"Supposedly," she said, "I mean this is all I know. What he told me was that she had embezzled some money from the office."

After this, Margaret said, her husband had "tried to keep everybody separated and segregated" in the office.

"He's always trying to not have one person know what the other person does about his life or his business," she said. "It kind of plays like one persona against another, or one office against another.

"He's a very, very private man," she continued, saying that he was social "on the surface."

"Uh-huh."

"He's a very good businessman in that way, but he's very closed," she said. "Nobody knows the whole picture. Nobody knows the whole run. That's the part that worries me. Maybe there's something we don't know. Maybe there is somebody he was gonna meet. Maybe there is something that was going on with the business or personal deal [that] we don't have any idea about. That's the part that I feel like there's more. There's more that we don't know now."

"We'll do our best," Barry assured her.

With that, the interview was over. The detective left for later the process of reviewing the tape and digesting all that Margaret had said, about Ron's emotional turmoil, the spirit de-possession, the troubles at work and the marital problems, including a possible girlfriend.

But before that Barry had something else he wanted of Margaret. He asked her if they could have her consent to search the house. They told her they would look for any obvious clues that could give them leads.

Again, she said she wanted to talk to her attorney. Again, they tried to talk her out of that. They told her they were simply trying to help her. Margaret consented without talking to a lawyer.

The detectives drove around the block and Margaret let them through the front gate into the circular driveway in front of the Rudin residence. Inside the house, they did what they would later call a "cursory check," poking around for any obvious signs of violence. Margaret showed them the living room and then led them into the master bedroom, which was neatly kept. It had a low, sloping ceiling, a big bed that didn't look like it had been slept in recently, two nightstands on either side, a television stand, sliding glass closet doors on one side of the room, a shuttered window on the other. Hanging over the bed was a large photo of Margaret, a glamour-style portrait in soft focus, her head against a pink background. She was resting her chin on her hand.

Janise got on his hands and knees on the right side of the bed and looked underneath, finding nothing. He walked around to the other side and opened the closets. Again, nothing.

Just off the bedroom was another room, about the size of a walk-in closet, that contained a veritable arsenal. It was Ron's inventory of firearms for his gun business. There were hundreds, perhaps thousands, of weapons of every shape and description, from pistols to rifles. Barry looked at the room in awe. "I guess a lot of guys would like to have it," he would recall.

The detectives looked inside the other bedroom, where Margaret seemed to have set up some of her things, then went outside, checking a shed and the rest of the property.

In the end, the quick search offered them no information of any use. To see if Ron had hopped town, they could check financial records for any uses of an ATM card or a credit card. They would have to canvass the neighborhood asking businesspeople if they had seen or heard from Ron. Interviewing Sue Lyles was a high priority.

As for Margaret, Detective Barry saw her as just a wife taking a wait-and-see attitude. She was concerned, the detective felt, but still had reason to believe that her husband might come walking home any minute. "There was a noted amount of urgency," Barry recalled, "but not extreme urgency."

But Barry's partner Janise didn't leave with quite the same comfort level. He noted that at least once Margaret spoke of her husband in the past tense: "Ron was a real off-and-on person," she had said. And, "He was either all good or all bad." It could have been an innocent slip of the tongue—or something more revealing. Janise wasn't sure. He just didn't like it.

"She didn't seem to have a concern that I would have if it was one of my loved ones that had been missing for a period of time," recalled Janise. "She didn't seem to be overly emotional one way or another. She seemed to be basically fairly calm, didn't voice concerns that a person would normally voice if it was somebody that would be missing for . . . this period of time."

Later that day, Janise did in fact contact Sue Lyles by phone. He reached her at her office at the Internal Revenue Service. She described herself as Ron's very good friend, but Janise didn't believe her. He asked her pointblank if she knew where Ron was, urging her to be frank because the search was costing taxpayers money.

She said she didn't know. He asked her if she knew whether Ron had any travel plans, and she said she didn't know. She told the detective that if Ron were going out of town, he would have told her. That's what he'd always done before.

Sue would later say her emotions were running wild. It was only a few days earlier that she and Ron had met in the Pecos Way condominium to sort out the crisis of the letter. They had agreed to meet that following Monday, but she wasn't too concerned when he didn't call. They would often have trouble getting in touch because they were so careful with the phones. Maybe Ron just wasn't in a position to talk. Maybe he was busy. But now the police were saying it was something else. "I was extremely upset," she recalled later. "He was missing. Something was wrong. I knew something was drastically wrong."

The same day police were interviewing Margaret, another meeting was taking place across town in the law offices of Patricia Brown. Harold Boscutti and Sharon Melton arrived separately at about 8:30 a.m. and went upstairs to Brown's conference room.

The first order of business was to clear up a misunderstanding: there were two trustees for Ron's trust, but Sharon Melton was not one of them. It was another woman with the same first name, though different spelling: Sharron Cooper, an escrow officer who had done work with Ron. At some point Ron had switched trustees without telling his bookkeeper. Since she wasn't a trustee, Sharon Melton offered to leave the meeting, but Patricia Brown let her stay. They took care of the cash situation. Sharon Melton handed over the money from Ron's desk and got a receipt from the lawyer.

Brown made it clear that Harold still was a trustee. He sort of knew that. He had recalled Ron asking him to do it years earlier. Harold signed some papers and never gave it much thought. Now, he was going to have to think about it a lot. They spent the rest of the meeting trying to come up with a strategy to keep Ron Rudin Realty afloat for the time being. They would use some of the money from the desk to pay bills, use cash desposits from Cold Creek mortgages to pay others. Only the most important matters would be handled: payroll, taxes, loan payments.

Meantime, at the Rudin residence, Margaret got on the phone with her sister Dona, who was again asking about Ron's disappearance. Margaret still didn't want to talk about that. She had something else on her mind, some documents she wanted to show Dona that had come from Ron's office. How Margaret got them, she didn't say.

Dona went to Margaret's house, where she saw Margaret and their sister Barbara going through some papers on the glass kitchen table. There was a large stack. And then there were papers in a binder.

"Look what I found," Margaret said.

It was a copy of Ron's will and trust.

12

"PROBABLY DEAD"

Las Vegas Boulevard, the north–south street on which the major casinos are located, is better known as The Strip. But a one-square-mile area just behind the rear service entrances to the hotel-casinos may be a more appropriate location for that name. Here the lure isn't fast cash but flesh. Along Industrial Road and Highland and Western avenues, amid the plumbing supply houses and auto repair places, is the city's concentration of strip clubs, both alcohol-serving topless joints and the no-booze all-nude clubs: Wild J's Gentlemen's Club, the Can Can Room, Déjà Vu Showgirls, Spearmint Rhino, Tally Ho, Cheetah's and Little Darlings.

The Crazy Horse Too Saloon is the Caesars Palace of strip clubs, if only because it shares the hotel-casino's Roman motif. Located at the intersection of Sahara Avenue and Industrial Avenue, about a block away from family-fun casino Circus Circus, the Crazy Horse beckons the visitor with Roman columns and statues of buxom women draped in cloth.

In December of 1994, the night man at the Crazy Horse Too Saloon was Joseph Blasko. Like many in this city where people live their second or third acts, Blasko had a past. He had once been a respected homicide detective until the FBI found out in the late 1970s that he was on the payroll of notorious Vegas mob enforcer Anthony "Tony the Ant" Spilotro. While still on the force, Blasko had worked for Spilotro's "Hole in the Wall" gang of thieves before he got busted by the feds and spent time in prison.

He emerged from his life of crime as the night man at the Crazy Horse. Late the evening of December 23, 1994, Blasko walked out into the alley between the club and a warehouse. It was cold and rainy, the relentless storm system known as El Niño having arrived in the desert after wreaking havoc in California. Employees sometimes parked in the alley; this is where Blasko kept his car. There, in a space he often used, was a car he didn't recognize. It was a black Cadillac, backed into one of the spaces. It didn't seem to have belonged to any of the few customers at the club, this night two days before Christmas. It looked like it had been there some time; it was coated in dirt, turned mostly muddy by the rain. The license plate read RRR-1.

That Friday morning's paper had carried a small item about the disappearance of "longtime Las Vegas businessman" Ron Rudin. The story, with a picture of a smiling Ron in a cowboy hat with a wine glass in front of him, ran above a caption that said Ron had been reported missing the previous Tuesday by his wife, who last saw him on Sunday. The story was given bigger play on the TV news. All the reports gave Ron's age, height, weight, description, and noted that he usually wore a white gold bracelet with "RON" written in diamonds. Also missing, the news reports said, was Ron's 1993 black Cadillac Brougham, license plates RRR-1.

Blasko may have left the police department under a cloud, but he still had connections downtown—one very close connection, in particular. His son, Michael John Blasko, was a patrol officer. A little after 11 p.m. Joseph Blasko called his son at home. By coincidence, Michael Blasko was watching the local news, which had led the night's telecast with a story about the disappearance of the millionaire. As Blasko remembered the TV report, police had put out an urgent request to the public for any information on the whereabouts of Rudin or his black Cadillac. Joseph Blasko was calling to do his civic duty.

After talking to his father, Officer Blasko called a colleague on the force, David Radcliffe, who was on duty that night. Radcliffe took the call on his cellular phone while driving in his patrol car, the windshield wipers slapping away the rain. Radcliffe knew all about the Rudin case; it was a hot topic at the shift briefings. He knew there was an ATL out on Rudin and the car. He drove to 2476 Industrial in a part of town that Radcliffe had worked for about 16 years, and in the alley saw the black Cadillac caked in mud. He called the dispatcher and asked that detectives be notified.

Just after midnight, in the early morning minutes of Christmas Eve day 1994, senior crime scene analyst Monte Wade Spoor was called to the alley behind the Crazy Horse Too Saloon to collect any evidence from the Cadillac in the hopes of finding some clue as to Ron's whereabouts. With the bad weather, Spoor wanted to get the car indoors. He sealed the doors with bright orange Criminalistic Bureau stickers. A tow truck brought the Cadillac to the police impound lot on Charleston. With the help of the locksmith, he popped open the trunk. There were real estate maps, road hazard flares and four boxes of shotgun shells.

It was clear that one or more people had been inside the Cadillac. The floorboard carpeting was covered in dirt, both in the front and back seats. Using a trace evidence vacuum, Spoor sucked up the dirt and debris for future examination. He also noted what looked like one footprint on the front passenger seat floor mat. It was a poor-quality print, and Spoor didn't think it would yield anything of evidentiary value.

Also in the front seat area, he found two sets of keys. One was on the floorboard below the driver's seat and was hooked up to a remote alarm device. Another key ring dangled from the tilt knob on the steering wheel. The glove compartment had the usual glove compartment things, and a little box in the front-seat divider contained business cards, handkerchiefs and napkins.

In the back seat, he found clothing, neatly folded: a tan jacket (size 46), a blue long-sleeved Van Heusen dress shirt (size 34/35) and a pair of black Haggar pants (no size tag). The right front pocket of the jacket held yet another set of keys.

He did do some limited dusting for fingerprints inside, using black powder, and found one latent print on a seat belt buckle. Spoor was told to hold off on a more extensive fingerprint search, one that required the spraying of super glue, because it would damage the inside of this expensive car. Police wanted to wait just a little while longer for Rudin to show up, so that if he did materialize he wouldn't hit them with a repair bill.

Spoor completed his processing of the car. There would be no blockbuster clues this night, no body, no smoking gun, just a dirty car that had obviously been ridden in by a person or persons with dirty feet.

Spoor sealed up the car, photographed the outside one more time, and awaited further instructions from his supervisor.

Detectives, meanwhile, worked the phones to try to find out why Ron's car would be left behind a strip club. Two women in Ron's life, his ex-wife Caralynne Rudin and his friend Sue Lyles both said it was out of character for Ron to visit such a place. He was too classy for that. And too tired. "He had a routine. He didn't go out a lot at night," Sue would recall. "He'd go home, take his medication and go to bed early." When police told her that Ron's car had been found, she feared the worst. "I felt at that time that there was something wrong, that he was probably dead."

In the days after Ron's disappearance, real estate man—and newly appointed trustee—Harold Boscutti had a lot on his mind. He was weighing whether he really wanted to be a trustee. It would require putting much of his own real estate business on hold while he worked full-time keeping up with his trustee duties. Even getting help from Sharron Cooper wouldn't be enough. He was making a good enough living. He didn't want or need the aggravation at this point in his career. And there was plenty of aggravation. The bills were pouring in to the real estate office, and not just for the usual business of buying and selling properties. One of the bills was for a $35,000 glass door for Margaret's antique business.

Margaret was on Harold's mind. Since she had called him earlier in the week with her helpless little girl voice, he wondered what she was up to.

He wouldn't have to wait long to find out. It was on either Christmas Eve or Christmas Day—Boscutti couldn't remember which. Harold knew by now that the Cadillac had been found behind the Crazy Horse Too. He had received a call from Margaret. She wanted to show him something.

They met on Christmas at her antique shop around 1 or 2 p.m. This would not be a discussion about what could have happened to Ron and how they were going to find him. Margaret wanted to talk money. She said that somebody wanted to buy Lee Canyon. Harold knew that Ron had spoken about a possible deal involving Lee Canyon just before he disappeared. But that's all Harold knew. He didn't know where this offer had come from or how Margaret had gotten it, but assumed, "Somehow she was involved with this."

Then she made her move.

"She said it would be so nice if she could be a trustee as well," he said. "She said that would make things so much easier."

Harold didn't answer. He needed time to think.

13

IF I DIE...

Christmas for the family was held, as it usually was, at Ron and Margaret's house, even though Ron was missing. But Margaret had offered to host, and the family went along. The gathering included Margaret's son, Michael Mason, his wife Shellie, and their four children; her sister Dona and Dona's son Doug Spice; Margaret's other sister, Barbara LePome, her son Scott Stavrou and his fiancée Lisa. Scott brought a couple of friends. And Margaret had a friend, Jeanne Nakashima.

Traditionally, Margaret would go all out at Christmas—lots of decorations and presents. But this year the arrangements were made at the last minute, and it showed. She did have a Christmas tree. Under it were what looked like presents but were actually fakes—books wrapped to look like presents. She was using them at the antique store for a holiday display. As a real present, Margaret gave some of the relatives personal checks. Dona recalled that Margaret got the grandchildren's presents at a drugstore on Christmas Eve.

As far as Dona could remember, nobody talked about Ron. They kept the conversations superficial. But the entire time Dona felt uncomfortable. Things just weren't right. For instance, at one point Margaret went off somewhere, and Dona looked for her. Dona walked down the hall and noticed that one of the bedroom doors was closed. Margaret's son and his wife were standing by the door, and Dona asked if Margaret was in the bedroom.

"No," said Michael, "She's not there, and she doesn't want anyone else in there either."

Then there came the point in the early evening when Margaret wanted to leave the house to run an errand—and bring her sisters with her. Margaret told them that she had overheard Ron's employees saying that the locks were going to be changed at the real estate office the next day. She wanted to get inside before that happened. The three of them—Margaret, Dona and Barbara—made the short walk from the house to the office.

Margaret tried some keys. Ron had normally kept his office keys in a safe deposit box, but earlier in the year he had gone out of town and failed to lock them up. Margaret made copies. These keys, though, weren't working. Margaret asked Dona to try. She couldn't get them to open the door either.

Margaret then called out a locksmith, Liberty Lock and Key, which for $168 picked the exterior lock to the main offices, then drilled out the high-security lock system to Ron's private office. The locksmith did the work after Margaret showed him identification.

Inside Ron's office, Margaret told her sisters she was looking for clues to his disappearance. She also wanted some documents, including the appraisal of Lee Canyon, which she believed was worth more than $3 million. She did find some papers, including trust deeds, letters, cards from Ron's family members. But she found something else even better: a copy of a police report about the confrontation at the 1978 funeral for Peggy Rudin, the report that had been submitted by Ron's police friend Jack Ruggles. This was the report that stated Ron had been threatened by one of Peggy's relatives.

"That was the best thing we found yet!" Margaret said. She told her sisters the report could be very valuable to her. At Margaret's instruction, Dona went into the copy room and made copies of the report.

Margaret was having second thoughts about leaving the bugs she had bought from the Spy Factory in the office. She told her sisters she should probably remove them. She unplugged the device from under the bookkeeper's desk and wiped it off. But she changed her mind and plugged it back into the outlet. She also decided to keep the one in Ron's office. Margaret told her sisters that she had become accustomed to overhearing conversations in the office and didn't want to be denied that.

The sisters returned to Margaret's house, where Barbara and Dona spent Christmas night.

The next day, Monday, December, 26, Margaret arranged for another meeting with Harold Boscutti. This one took place at about 1 p.m. in the parking lot behind the mini-mall, where she gave him a maroon binder containing an appraisal for the Lee Canyon property. There may also have been a copy of Ron's trust, but Harold couldn't remember. Margaret was suggesting the names of people who could help take care of things. Boscutti recalled that Margaret was all business, cold and perhaps insincere.

Feeling uneasy, he wasn't ready to make any decisions, about Lee Canyon, about appointing Margaret as a trustee, about bringing more people into the mix. Ron was still missing, not dead. Harold felt that some professional help would need to be called in.

Soon it was going to get more complicated.

Pat Brown had a holiday surprise.

On Tuesday, December 27, the two trustees assembled in Brown's law office. It was time to go over the trust in more detail. According to the trust, Ron was worth between $5 million and $11 million, though little of that was in cash. His wealth was tied up in Nevada real estate, including his mini-mall, some investment properties, his home and most important, his acreage in Lee Canyon.

Ron had stated that if he should die, his estate would be carved up this way: Harold was allotted 15 percent, Ollie Grinfelds and his wife Lilly would get 15 percent and 10 percent would go to Sharron Cooper.

The rest, 60 percent—as much as $7 million—would go to his fifth wife Margaret.

No money was to go to any of Ron's previous wives. His family members, including his cousins and surviving aunts and uncles, got nothing. There were no charities mentioned, no churches, just the three business associates and Margaret.

But the money wasn't the only thing Ron had discussed in his trust. He had attached a directive:

To my Fiduciaries:

I request that in the event my death is caused by violent means (for example, gunshot, knife or a violent automobile accident), extraordinary steps be taken in investigating the true cause of the death.

Should said death be caused, directly or indirectly, by a beneficiary of my estate, said beneficiary shall be totally excluded from my estate and/or any trusts I may have in existance. [sic].

Dated this 27 day of April, 1991.

It was signed in Ron's big, looping handwriting, with the oversized "Rs" in his name.

Harold and Sharron were stunned. For years, Ron had publicly laughed off warnings that Margaret was dangerous. But as he signed this directive more than four years earlier, he was deadly serious. At the time, Brown explained, Ron was worried deeply about Margaret's behavior, telling the attorney that she could be loving one minute and vicious the next. Margaret had gotten into some kind of a scuffle with one of Ron's employees, so he barred her from the office. He began to worry about his own safety. In one draft of the directive Ron didn't use the word "beneficiary," but specifically mentioned Margaret.

But, Brown stressed, Ron had held hope that the directive would never have to be seen. It had been kept in a safe all these years. If Ron were to have died of natural causes or an unsuspicious accident, it would have been destroyed and nobody would ever have known about it. That's why the directive was drafted as it was, as a directive, and not as a formal amendment to the trust. Each time Brown had asked Ron if he wanted to make it a permanent part of the trust, he'd said no. He kept thinking that things would work out between him and Margaret.

And now Ron was missing, perhaps even dead. If he had in fact died violently, the trustees—Harold and Sharron—would have more to worry about than paying bills and liquidating assets.

They would have to solve a murder. And Ron would have already identified the Number One suspect from the grave: Margaret.

14

RON IN THE PAST TENSE

Detective Frank Janise of the missing persons division spent the days after Christmas roaming the shopping centers and stores near Ron Rudin's office, asking people if they had seen the tall realtor or had any idea where he was. Nobody did. He also visited the Crazy Horse Too and spoke with the owner, Rick Rizzolo, who told him that he had never seen Ron in the club and that none of the dancers had remembered the man. But Rizzolo posted Ron's picture on bulletin boards and in the dressing rooms.

On December 29, Janise paid another visit to Margaret at Antique Merchants. He wanted to get the names and phone numbers of her relatives—brothers, sisters, anybody who could possibly shed some light on the situation. Janise, who had had a bad feeling about Margaret from the beginning, had to go to her because she wasn't staying in touch with police.

"During the portion of the investigation that Pat Barry and I did, we received no calls that I know of, documented or otherwise, that showed that she showed any interest in him being missing," said Janise.

He spoke to Margaret for about 10 or 15 minutes. They huddled in the corner, out of earshot of Margaret's sister, Dona, who was working that day. After Janise got the names of the relatives, he decided to talk to Margaret once again about the last night she had seen her husband. Margaret told him that she'd called Ron at about 9:30 p.m. that Sunday, but couldn't get ahold of him. She repeated her account of going to the tax preparer's office at about 1 a.m. She said that after that she went to the 7-Eleven, which she hadn't mentioned before, and then went home. She got to her house, she said, at about 1:30 a.m. Ron wasn't there, she said, and neither was his car. She said she called his cell phone repeatedly, but nobody picked up.

It was mostly rehash. Janise turned his attention to the list of relatives. One of them, sister Dona, was there in the store. He walked over to the desk where she was sitting. He took a seat. Her name was written on his small yellow pad. The detective took down her address and phone number, then asked her if she had any ideas about Ron's disappearance. She said she had none. She didn't tell the detective about Margaret searching Ron's office or about her suspicions that Margaret wasn't overly concerned. She told him nothing about the listening devices in the office.

Then, out of the blue, Margaret interrupted them for a moment.

"By the way," Margaret told the detective, "Ron always wears black pants, and Ron always wears cowboy boots."

It was slightly odd that she would make a point to tell the detective this; Ron's dark wardrobe was common knowledge by now.

Margaret walked away, and the detective wrapped up his interview with Dona. He got up from the desk and walked out of the store, telling the women that he was headed for Ron's real estate office.

Margaret sprang into action. With Dona in tow, she left the store and walked over to the house. "She wanted to go to the house because that's where the listening devices were, the monitoring equipment," Dona recalled. "She wanted to go hear what the detective was saying to the bookkeeper or to whomever else might be in the office."

When they got there, Margaret settled in to monitor the detective's work. She put the little plug from the receiver into her ear and listened. Dona didn't know what Margaret could hear. After a few minutes, Margaret stopped listening and told Dona she had to make some phone calls. She gave the ear plug to her sister, who picked up on the surveillance work. By now the detective had apparently left the office.

"I heard the bookkeeper's voice. I could hear the phone ring," Dona said. "I could hear her end of the conversation. One of Ron's employees went into the office. I could hear his voice."

Dona recalled nothing of significance going on when she was listening.

Margaret then told Dona why she had interrupted the interview with Detective Janise just to make the statement about Ron's black clothing. "I realized I had been talking about Ron in the past tense," Margaret told Dona. "So that was why I made a point to refer to Ron to the detective in the present tense."

"I hope that doesn't mean you know something," said Dona.

Margaret replied with eerie slowness, a pause between each word.

"I . . . don't . . . give . . . a . . . shit."

15

SOMETHING ABOUT MARGARET

"Oh, sure, I knew about him." It was the 1970s, when Las Vegas was a much smaller town and Phil Ramos was a young patrolman for Metro. "It's kind of funny," Ramos said. "I remembered him because he used to sponsor a softball team, and our police department team used to play his softball team all the time. We were always the top two teams. It was always the police department against Ron Rudin Realty for the championship. He didn't play, but I remember seeing him. He wasn't flamboyant, but he was recognizable. He was low-key, but everybody knew him."

By January 1995, Ramos—now a homicide detective—would be reintroduced to Ron Rudin on most unpleasant terms. Missing persons detectives had already been on the case for three weeks, interviewing dozens of people and taking statements from Margaret. The gist of the investigation was that since Ron hadn't turned up by now to retrieve his car—since he hadn't cashed a check, used an ATM machine, bought something with a credit card, made a phone call or contacted anybody in his immediate circle of friends, family and business associates—then he probably had fallen victim to foul play. That meant it was now a case for homicide.

Ramos and partner James Vaccaro, who went by Jimmy, were both relatively new to homicide when they were assigned what was then the biggest case of their careers, on January 10, 1995, having worked homicide for just about a year. They made for an interesting pair, the stuff of countless cop shows. Ramos is the low-key one, amiable, calm under the most trying of circumstances. Vaccaro had the more prickly personality, quicker to take offense, less patient with people trying to screw around with him. In questioning suspects or hostile witnesses, Ramos would play good cop, Vaccaro bad cop.

Ramos and Vaccaro say they began their investigation from step one, reading the reports, talking to the missing persons detectives and "just kind of absorbing everything that they had," said Ramos. "Then we picked up the ball and ran with it."

The homicide detectives had plenty of other leads to follow up on. Ron's disappearance and the discovery of the Cadillac had been widely publicized in the local Las Vegas news media and the tips were rolling in, some of them supposed sightings of Ron. The trustees of Ron's estate had taken out newspaper ads offering a $25,000 cash reward for "information leading to Ron's discovery and/or successful prosecution of any persons responsible for his disappearance." The detectives started prioritizing their work.

The first two weeks of January brought relentless rains to Nevada, as El Niño hit the desert in earnest. One wet day the detectives drove to the Crazy Horse Too, which seemed like one of the better places to start, since Ron's car had been found there, muddy in the late-December drizzle. A local attorney had gotten a tip that a dancer with the stage name Sahara had given a lap dance to Ron and may have been the last person to see him. "We followed up on that and got a list of all the dancers that were working at the Crazy Horse Too during that time period, and none of the dancers had a matching stage name," Ramos recalled. "There was one that was close, but it was spelled and pronounced differently. We contacted her, but that was a big zero." The photo of Ron that owner Rick Rizzolo had posted produced no leads. Rizzolo said he knew who the regulars were, anyway, and that Ron Rudin wasn't one of them. The club had some security cameras, including ones watching the patrons inside, but at the time the Crazy Horse didn't have a security camera in the back alley where the car was left.

Ron hadn't been a Crazy Horse customer, or so the owner said, so what was his car doing there? His acquaintances insisted that Ron was not the type of guy to go to a club. He was too tired, too anti-social after business hours. The detectives figured somebody else had left the car there. It was dirty; Ron never would have allowed that. It was backed into the spot; Ron's habit was to pull in forward. But why was it left there? And by whom?

A more delicate question was whether there was any significance to the fact that Ron's car was found by a man with a mob past. It was also not unheard of in the history of Las Vegas that men who carried lots of cash and guns would up and disappear without a trace. The whispers that had dogged Ron since Peggy Rudin's death had started to reach the ears of police investigators.

In the end, Ramos said, they were only whispers.

"We never found anything that backed that up," he said. "Especially at the time when Ron was coming into his prominence, the town was relatively small and we knew all the mobsters and their associates. I don't know that the mob would ever get involved in real estate unless it was large scale and there was the potential for them to make a huge amount of money."

The mob, in other words, wasn't interested in the business of rehabbing single-family homes or developing resort land on Mount Charleston, not in the 1970s when organized crime still had influence in Vegas, and certainly not in 1994, when the city was run by buttoned-down Wall Street types. As for Blasko, police never thought he had anything to do with Ron's disappearance.

So the detectives moved on to other leads. Along with the Crazy Horse owner, the detectives re-interviewed a number of witnesses and found that, while organized crime may not have been a factor, some other unsavory element could have been. Ron was certainly a character, with the potential for danger always lurking around him. Escrow officer Sharron Cooper flat-out told the detives that Ron was "paranoid." But of what? The detectives couldn't narrow it down to a single suspect or business entity. There were very strong hints of shady business dealings—the fake names on some of Ron's properties, for one—but the most that that added up to was that Ron may have been trying to rip off the IRS. And while the IRS was capable of many things, the detectives didn't think it would commit murder.

The leads poured in. In early January, three people believed they'd seen Ron Rudin around the time of his disappearance at the Oasis Motel, at the wrong end of Las Vegas Boulevard, between The Strip and Fremont Street. According to the witnesses, who included a maintenance man at the motel, a man resembling Ron was seen being removed from a room by men who looked like cops. The man was then placed in a car, which drove away.

But when Ramos interviewed the witnesses, he found them to be less than credible. Their stories kept changing. The description they gave of the man who was supposedly Ron didn't match; one witness had the man as half Ron's age. Ramos called around and found out that Metro hadn't hauled anybody out of the motel around December 18. He contacted the FBI and the DEA to see if their agents had been there; they had not. The license plate number on the car was from Arizona, but it didn't check out. Ramos impounded the motel log and guest signature cards to see if Ron's name or phone number would show up—a long shot, since people don't always give their true information at the Oasis anyway. Nothing came of this. Ramos put the lead on the back burner.

Then there was Margaret, the sweet-looking wife with the soft voice. Ramos insisted that he and Vaccaro didn't focus on her at first. Experience and crime statistics showed that although men would often be considered prime suspects in a wife or girlfriend's slaying, wives and girlfriends just didn't tend to kill their spouses or boyfriends. In 1995, just 3 percent of the male murder victims nationally were killed by wives or girlfriends, according to the FBI; 26 percent of female murder victims were killed by husbands or boyfriends. Given the fact that Ron was older—age 64 when he disappeared—and Margaret was in her fifties, and the fact that they were both white, the possibility statistically became even more remote.

Margaret already had been interviewed at some length by Detective Barry of missing persons. But as the homicide detectives reviewed a transcript of the interview, they spotted some missed opportunities. "In retrospect, we would have hoped they would have gone into a little more detail, not so much focusing on her feelings, but focused on more specific details of what happened the night he disappeared," said Ramos.

In her statement she said the last time she saw Ron was at about 6:30 p.m. at the house, when they discussed whether he would see a movie; then she talked to him by phone between 8:30 and 9:30 p.m., at which time he was described as being short with her and telling her he loved her.

She had said that at some point in between, she went to her friend Jack's house to fix her computer, a visit that checked out. She also said she went to the grocery store, but didn't say where, before making that final call to Ron. The next time her whereabouts could be confirmed was about 1 a.m. when she went to Carol Kawazoe's tax business, leaving a gap of as much as five hours. Then, she said, she got home at about 1:30 a.m. to find Ron and his Cadillac gone. The last person besides Margaret to recall having spoken to Ron was Margaret's friend Dottie Flint.

That meant Ron had taken off, was kidnapped or killed in the 12 hours between the 8:10 p.m. call from Dottie and the following Monday morning when he didn't show up for work. Aside from the half-hour visit to Carol Kawazoe, Margaret, it appeared from the investigation so far, had no alibi for those 12 critical hours.

"Also, the detectives were uneasy about her apparent reluctance to contact police at the beginning," said Ramos. "That's a huge red flag. Everybody in the world who knew him knew there was something wrong when he didn't show up for work—except his wife. His wife should have been right there with everybody else. Then, as time went on, it became more of a concern that she didn't become more concerned."

Meantime, Margaret's behavior continued to raise concerns. Margaret was under enormous financial stress. The trustees of Ron's estate, saying that they were acting under the recommendation of attorneys, had refused to release any of Ron's money for Margaret. She had no access to his bank accounts, and, since she had no money of her own—having always relied upon Ron for an allowance—she didn't have enough cash to get by on. She began selling her jewelry and furniture to make ends meet. Margaret called Patricia Brown to complain and suggested that a bank be named as trustee.

Money wasn't Margaret's only problem. In early January, she seemed to be going through attorneys. Pat Brown said that she got calls or letters from at least three different lawyers claiming to represent Margaret. Brown finally called Margaret to try to clear things up, and Margaret acknowledged that her life was quite chaotic. Margaret put in a plea for Brown to help find Ron.

Dona Cantrell seemed to get one indication after another that her sister knew a lot more about Ron's disappearance than she was letting on. Still, Dona remained loyal to Margaret, doing whatever she asked, no matter how unsettling the errand. One day in the first week of January, Dona was working in the antique shop. Margaret wasn't there, but she had left a note on a legal pad asking Dona to go through the roll-top desk in the store and look for some legal and personal papers. Dona didn't get around to it. Margaret at some point called to remind her, and Dona went through the desk, finding several papers that, she would say later, "I thought at that particular point looked bad for her with the situation as it existed."

One piece of note paper, four inches by six inches, had notations written in Margaret's hand. She had itemized Ron's assets: 20 entries on the front side that totaled $9 million. On the back of the paper it had notations about life insurance policies, trust payments, Social Security and farm payments. There, she had written "$11.2 million."

There was also a file labeled "dream house," several lawsuits that Margaret had filed against various corporations. There was an audio tape, labeled "Ron Texas 9/93."

And there was a certificate dated November 1993 with Margaret's name on it.

It was for a gun safety course.

Then there was another strange visit to tax preparer Carol Kawazoe. It happened on January 14, a Saturday, at about 6:50 p.m.—right before a 7 p.m. meeting. Carol had just put her coat on and was walking out the door of her business into a cold and cloudy night when Margaret came in.

Margaret seemed more nervous than the first time she had come into the office as she started spilling details about her personal life, giving Carol—whom she had met only once, at 1 a.m. the night Ron disappeared—all kinds of information for which she hadn't asked.

"Ron had girlfriends, and Ron was doing this, Ron was doing that. Ron was involved with this. Ron was involved with that," Carol recalled. "She was trying to make me believe a lot of different things about Ron, what he was involved in. It was like planting something in my head that had nothing to do with . . . why she would come to visit me." In short, Carol said, "She gave me an impression that he was not alive."

Margaret spoke of hiring an attorney and a private investigator. "She felt his life was in jeopardy . . . because he was carrying excessive amounts of guns suddenly," she said. "He used to always carry a gun, but suddenly he was carrying guns in his boots. He had shotguns in his bed." She told Carol that Ron may have had a girlfriend at the Crazy Horse. "She was all over the place with conversation," Kawazoe said. "She even went as far as talking about how the people that killed him were the people he was involved with in laundering money," Carole recalled, though she thought Margaret had said that the launderers were in Mexico, which didn't make much sense to her.

All the while, "I don't know why she wanted to tell these things."

Margaret then told Carol that she had hired an attorney from Reno and a private investigator, but they weren't doing what she wanted. Margaret knew that Carol had done work for attorneys and asked her for a reference.

"I was under the impression that she had a problem," said Carol, who recommended hiring "one of the highest-paid attorneys, criminal attorneys, in one of the biggest cities you could find in the Midwest or the East Coast."

But Carol Kawazoe wasn't going to get involved. "She did want me to give her a reference, but I did not."

But the most unusual thing that Margaret was said to have done was on the following Thursday, January 19, when she walked into Ron's office. Sharon Melton and Ron Danner were working there, keeping the office running as best they could, "like Ron was going to come in any time," Sharon recalled.

According to Sharon's account of the incident, Margaret walked past them to another desk, grabbed a chair and pulled it over to where Melton and Danner were sitting, telling them: "I really shouldn't be talking to you. My lawyers have advised me not to, but I am."

Margaret then proceeded to tell them all the bad things that she claimed Ron had ever said about them. She said that Ron was planning to fire Sharon, but that Margaret had urged him not to until at least after Christmas. Sharon found this ridiculous, and she told Margaret so.

"You and Ron were fighting," Margaret said.

Sharon was taken aback. "No, Margaret, what we were fighting about was you."

Then Sharon confronted Margaret. "Margaret," she asked her, "what do you think happened to Ron?"

Margaret hesitated, then said, "Oh, they found him."

"What do you mean, they found him?" Sharon asked, aghast. All that had been in the news was that police had found his car.

"Oh, yes, they found him. And they're doing tests on him," Margaret said.

Sharon thought Margaret was nuts. "I don't think so, Margaret."

And then Margaret stood up and walked away, telling them, "I have to go. I shouldn't be talking to you."

While Margaret's behavior was garnering attention, trustee-Harold Boscutti was wavering on whether he should even be a trustee. At one point, he withdrew, feeling the pressure of the workload and being uncomfortable about the possibility that he would face personal liability if he didn't carry out the financial duties properly. Ron's real estate business turned out to be quite a piece of work. There were Lee Canyon properties in the names of at least three people who either didn't exist or who didn't know they had their names on land. More than a dozen entities were involved in Ron Rudin Realty and Construction, from banks to title companies, and there were a number of pending lawsuits, loans and escrows. All this had to be sorted out, some of it in court.

Complicating matters was the fact that Ron was not officially dead. He was just missing and theoretically could return at any moment and resume his business. The trustees considered the declaration of a guardian for Rudin—so they could operate under the legal assumption that he was dead—but that procedure would take three months. Boscutti was ready to walk away from the whole thing.

"But then," he said, "everything changed."

16
NEXT OF KIN

The spectacular growth of Las Vegas in the 1990s came with a price. Readers of the *Review-Journal* rang in the new year of 1995 with this story on January 1: "Clark County homicide rate climbs 30 percent." The article explained, "With more people unfortunately come more homicides, police say; what is different are their growing randomness." There were three homicides in the last week of December 1994 alone, pushing the total number of murders in Clark County to 155. That was a stunning 30 percent increase over the previous year, when the county recorded 119 killings.

"This is a banner year for us," a police official told the paper. "I'd say it's because of the growth. We're getting up to 6,000 new people per month, so just like their cities, our homicides are up. Our murders aren't any different than they have been in the past—we're just getting more murders."

And so, on the morning of Monday, January 23, 1995, it was hardly news that somebody had found the remains of a human body near Lake Mohave. Bodies of Las Vegas residents had been dumped in the desert as long as Las Vegas has existed. The story played in the "In Brief" column behind an item about three teenagers arrested after a bar robbery and a story about a Houston man winning $3.5 million at a slot machine.

Under the heading, POLICE FIND REMAINS NEAR LAKE MOHAVE, the story reported the discovery of a human skull and human remains near Nelson's Landing at Lake Mohave and that the remains seemed to be those of a man. Foul play was suspected.

The afternoon paper, the *Las Vegas Sun*, contained a little more information about the discovery—saying that police were going through their missing persons files to help with identification.

But even as residents read their afternoon paper, police already knew whose remains were found in the desert.

In life, Ron Rudin was over six feet tall and weighed 220 pounds. In death, he was nothing more than a pound of charred bone fragments and what was officially described as "a relatively intact skull." What little that remained of prominent businessman Ronald J. Rudin now lay on the work table of Dr. Robert Jordan, deputy medical examiner for the Clark County Coroner's Office.

It would not be difficult to positively identify what for a brief time was labeled John Doe No. 95-287. The jeweled bracelet immediately pointed authorities toward Rudin as the likely victim. The well-preserved teeth in the skull would confirm it. James Becvar, the chief investigator for the Clark County Coroner's Office, had remembered that the name of Ron's dentist was contained in the missing persons report. Becvar went to the offices of Dr. Ronald R. Taylor, whom Rudin had visited about two years earlier, on August 10, 1992. Taylor had recently taken over the practice from Ron's previous dentist and on that date updated his records by X-raying Ron's teeth. Those X-rays were brought to the coroner's office and compared against X-rays of the teeth in the skull from Nelson's Landing. It was a positive match.

It was up to Dr. Jordan to determine the cause of death—and find possible clues to the identity of the killer.

With so little left of Ron, it was not much of an autopsy. Jordan inspected the skull, which was in good shape "considering the condition of the other bone fragments," he recalled. Why the head had survived the fire virtually untouched by flames, while the rest of the body was reduced to charred bone fragments, remained unclear, though the possible scenarios were grisly.

"My feeling, and my opinion," Jordan would later say, "is that carnivores probably chewed the cervical vertebra apart and the skull rolled away from where the main body of the remains was found. Coyotes have a particular delight in separating the skulls from bodies and rolling them across the desert. I've seen it a number of times."

Bolstering his theory were signs of "gnawing" on the soft tissue in the upper back, and no evidence of "sharp trauma" that could have been caused by a knife or an ax. "It looked like it had been chomped on by carnivores," he'd say. "It didn't look like it had been detached by a sharp instrument or some kind of an ax or a chain saw."

It was still possible that somebody had chopped off Ron's head, but that person would have had to have done it high on the body, between the first vertebra and the base of the skull. "It would take a pretty good knowledge of anatomy," Jordan said.

This theory would conflict with that of the detectives, who believed Ron's head was chopped off so that his body could fit inside the trunk, which was then hauled out to Nelson's Landing and set afire. During the fire, Ramos
and Vaccaro believed, the head either rolled away or, more gruesomely, was purposely left there by the killer or killers.

And Jordan himself professed to be perplexed by the arrangement of the remains. "In a death scene where you have the body parts separated, you have to try to figure out how that happened," he would say. "In this case, somebody could have separated the head from the body post-mortem [after death] purposely, or the fire separated the skull from the neck."

But the fire-separation theory also was problematic because the head had survived the blaze virtually untouched by flames. There was just a little burn area on the head. In fact, Jordan was generally surprised at how well preserved the skull was. Usually, having spent that much time in the elements, the ligaments connecting the jaw to the rest of the skull would have rotted away. But the jaw was still attached in this one.

So while the manner of decapitation was unclear, the fact that the skull was so well preserved made it easier to determine the probable cause of death. "In my opinion, Ron Rudin died as a result of multiple gunshot wounds to the head," Jordan concluded.

The coroner found three bullet entrance wounds in a triangular pattern on the back of the skull, just behind the ear. The bullets had exited. Inside the skull, he found three small-caliber projectiles. Another bullet had entered the front of the skull—the forehead area—and went all the way through the head, exiting out the back. A chip to the mandible, or jawbone, suggested a fifth gunshot wound. The coroner found two more fragmentary pieces of one or more bullets. A ballistics expert who later examined the three bullets and two fragments would confirm that three full-sized projectiles were .22-caliber bullets from a rim-fire cartridge. The bullets were lead-coated and copper-colored. They were extremely common and could have come from any derringer, revolver, semi-automatic or rifle.

After examining the skull, there was little left for Dr. Jordan to do, or so he reasoned. He never took a DNA sample from the skull. He didn't notice any brain tissue that could be used for a sample, and even if he had, he wouldn't have collected it anyway. In those days, DNA testing wasn't as prevalent as it is today. Jordan figured that the dental X-rays were more than sufficient for identification.

With identification made, it was time for Ramos and Vaccaro to do what can be the hardest part of their job. Over the years, Phil Ramos had made hundreds of death notifications. They were never easy, but he had found a pattern. "They know it's coming," he said. "They're expecting it, and they're scared. They're on the verge of tears. They know what we're going to say and they're just waiting for us to say it."

The morning paper had only contained the small story

about the remains being found in the desert, with no mention that they belonged to Ron. That information wouldn't be released until after the official notification. The notification would be done in person. Ramos called Margaret a little before 9 a.m. on Monday, January 23, to make sure she would be home.

"Margaret," he told her, "we need to talk to you."

"I'm kind of busy," she said. "Can't this wait?"

Ramos found her reaction strange.

"No," Ramos told her. "This is important."

"OK," she said. She would be there.

Ramos and Vaccaro got into Ramos' police-issued 1994 Gold Chevrolet Caprice and drove from their downtown homicide offices west on Charleston about four miles to the Rudin residence. Ramos called her again, from his cellular phone, asking her to open the security gate. She did, and Ramos pulled the Caprice into the driveway. They got out and knocked on the front door. Margaret answered.

She had a puzzled look on her face.

"What's going on?" she asked.

"Well," said Ramos, "we need to sit down and talk."

"Something has happened?"

"Yeah, it has."

They went into the living room. Margaret sat on a love seat, Ramos took a seat on the sofa. Vaccaro remained standing, discreetly looking around at the house.

Ramos explained to her that human remains had been found near Lake Mohave, and that they had been positively identified through dental records as those of her husband Ron.

Ramos paused for a moment to study her reaction. If she got too distraught, the detectives would leave. If not, they would try to use the opportunity to ask her some questions.

"Oh, my goodness," she said with little inflection her voice.

Hardly the emotional meltdown that usually comes at

this point. Then she did something puzzling. She started rubbing her right eye, very hard. Ramos couldn't figure it out, but he kept talking.

"Now that we've learned that these remains were Ron's, we need to sit down with you and go over exactly what happened the last time you saw him so we can start putting together what ultimately led to his death," said Ramos, hoping to fill in some of the holes from the missing persons interview.

"OK. That's fine," she said, still rubbing the eye.

Ramos was starting to think she might hurt herself, she was rubbing her eye so much. Then it dawned on him. She was trying to make herself cry.

This was a first for him.

He continued with the questioning. "I realize that you're upset. Can we go ahead and just get started on talking about what happened?" he said.

Margaret grabbed some papers and said, "That will be fine, but can my nephew come and sit with me?"

"Sure. There's no problem with that."

"He's in the guest house."

Ramos asked her what the nephew's name was. She told him Scott. She got up and called one of her sisters on the phone. Then she asked if Ramos would go get Scott Stavrou, the son of Margaret's sister, Barbara LePome. Ramos went over to the guest house next to the main house and knocked on the door. A tall, skinny man in his twenties answered the door. The man identified himself as Scott. Ramos explained to him that he was a police detective and that Margaret had asked if Scott would sit with her while they interviewed her.

"What's going on?" Scott asked.

Ramos told him to wait. He'd find out soon enough.

The two went back into the house and sat down with Margaret in the living room. The detectives explained to Stavrou that Ron's remains had been found and the detectives had come to officially notify Margaret. He started to ask Margaret about the events of the day before Ron's disappearance. She had stopped doing the eye-rubbing thing by now, and there was somewhat more emotion in her voice. Ramos thought she was speaking a little more dramatically. But she never asked any questions about how Ron was killed.

They spoke for only two or three minutes about the last time she saw Ron when Margaret suddenly excused herself again to get a cup of coffee.

When she came back, she said, "You know, this is really hard for me right now. Can we finish this tomorrow?"

"Sure," Ramos said, "that's no problem at all. We understand completely."

She told the detectives that she really wanted to help them in any way that she could and that she would answer all of the questions they had.

At that point, her sister Barbara LePome—Scott's mother—arrived. She had knocked on the door and come in. She didn't say anything to the detectives. As Ramos and Vaccaro walked out, they saw the two sisters start going through papers on the kitchen counter.

Afterwards, the detectives ran over the interview in their minds. "Jimmy and I walked out of there thinking that we've got to talk to her some more," recalled Ramos. "It wasn't: She did it. It was: Hmm, she didn't react the way she should have. There was just something wrong with her reaction."

Something else stuck out in Vaccaro's mind. While Ramos was talking to Margaret, Vaccaro had looked around the house. He could see down the hall, and got a glimpse of what he took to be a guest bedroom. Something had caught his eye. He couldn't take his mind off of it, though it would seem to have had little evidentiary importance at the time.

Hanging on the wall, above the bed, was a soft-focus, glamour-style photograph of a woman, her chin resting on her hand, big earrings dangling, her eyes peering straight ahead. It was Margaret.

The next day, Tuesday, the city was blanketed with news of the murdered millionaire, the story a brief no more. The *Review-Journal* played it on the front page, with a small picture of Ron, unsmiling, his tie loosened, and the headline, REALTOR'S REMAINS IDENTIFIED.

The story reported that the bones belonged to "prominent Las Vegas realtor and developer" Ronald Rudin, and gave the basic facts behind the discovery, nothing that the remains were found by fishermen early that Saturday morning in a ravine abut 150 yards from the shores of Lake Mohave.

The story also revealed that a bracelet with the name "RON" written in diamonds was found at the site.

"It's real early in our investigation," Las Vegas police Sgt. Bill Keeton told the RJ. "From December 18 till now it's been strictly a missing person investigation. We'd really like to talk to somebody about his lifestyle, about the last few days of his life that might lead us to the killer or killers," Keeton said.

The story was again carried by the afternoon paper, the *Las Vegas Sun*, under the headline METRO POLICE SEEK REALTOR'S ASSAILANT with the same picture of Ron, and by the local television and radio stations. The publicity generated scores of phone calls from people with tips about the case. Detectives Ramos and Vaccaro took most of the calls themselves and followed up on the leads that seemed promising.

Margaret's behavior during the death notification, combined with what the detectives saw as her tardy and reluctant reporting of Ron's disappearance, made her, if not a suspect, something very close to that. But all they had were their gut feelings. They had no hard evidence that Margaret was involved in Ron's disappearance or murder. They didn't even have a murder weapon. What they needed was an eyewitness or some compelling evidence.

The call came on January 25, the day after the papers first announced Ron's murder. The news that day consisted of

Rick Rizzolo of the Crazy Horse Too saying that he never saw Ron Rudin there. Ramos answered the phone from his desk at the downtown homicide office. The caller was a woman. She thought detectives ought to talk to her son.

17

THE HEEBIE-JEEBIES

Augustine Lovato was a slender, dark-haired man of 22 who lived with his divorced mother and brother in a small apartment on Charleston Boulevard, not far from Ron Rudin Realty. Hurting financially after his mother's divorce, the family for a time had no furniture in the living room, and the phone had been temporarily disconnected. His mother Terry worked as a change-maker at the Rio Suites Hotel and Casino. Augustine never knew his father, and despite his Spanish surname, he didn't speak the language.

Pressured by his mother to get a job, Augustine had signed up with a temporary employment agency called Labor Express, which did get him some work—and a whole lot more. After his mother heard about Augustine's strange and frightening experiences, she urged him to call the police. But Augustine had a police record—he had been arrested once in Arizona for aggravated assault for going after a man with a baseball bat in a fight over Augustine's pregnant girlfriend. He wanted nothing more to do with cops. So his mother called Metro homicide, and within an hour, Ramos, partner Vaccaro and a supervisor, Sgt. Bill Keeton, were on the road, driving down Charleston in a heavy rain. Parts of the city were flooded. Las Vegas had received more rain in the first 25 days of 1995 than in all of the previous year.

After they got to Augustine Lovato's little apartment, the investigators, the mother, her new boyfriend and Augustine all took their seats in the living room, now with a sofa and a couple of chairs. Terry didn't say anything. She gave her son the occasional encouraging look. A few times she got up to serve coffee. Ramos did most of the questioning. The interview was tape-recorded.

Augustine would repeat the story several times in the

coming years. He would add details and change a couple
of small matters, but the basic story would remain the
same.

On December 20, 1994—two days after Ron had failed
to show up for work, though at the time Augustine knew
nothing about Ron Rudin or his mysterious disappearance—Labor Express had gotten a call from Margaret
seeking a day laborer to move some antiques from her
shop and from her guest house to a storage unit across
the street. For $13 an hour, Labor Express gave her the
services of Augustine Lovato.

A little before 10 a.m., Marvin Eikenberry, who sub-
letted space in Margaret's shop, met Augustine and his
cousin Steve at Labor Express. Steve was going to come
along to help with the job. Marvin drove them to a walled
house on Alpine Way behind the antique store, where they
were met by a woman who introduced herself as Margaret
Rudin.

Margaret told them that before they started on the work
at the store, she had another chore for them. She had
gotten a late start on her Christmas preparations and asked
them to get some decorations from the guest house and
place them on her tree. As they decorated the tree, Margaret started telling them about her husband, Ron, and
how he was missing. She said she didn't know why he
was gone, but guessed he was on a hunting trip. She told
them she was upset, but Lovato recalled, "She didn't really seem upset. She didn't look like she was crying or
anything."

At another point, Lovato overheard Margaret talking
on the phone, telling somebody the same thing: that her
husband was missing and might be off hunting. She said
she wished he had called her. She seemed a little more
shaken this time, though far from hysterical, just "kind of
upset about it," said Lovato—but he admitted he had a
hard time reading her demeanor. She spoke so softly that

he sometimes just assumed she was upset, but he could have been wrong.

At some point Margaret left. Augustine didn't know where she went, but this would have been around the time that Margaret went to the police station with Ron Danner to file the missing persons report. After she returned to the house, Augustine and his cousin moved a piano from the hallway into a guest house next door. They went to Margaret's store and loaded some boxes of antiques into Marvin's car. Marvin drove them all to a nearby Public Storage facility, where Augustine and his cousin unloaded them.

They ended work at 5:30 p.m. Margaret asked if they could return the next day. Steve couldn't make it, but Augustine said he could.

Augustine arrived at the house that Wednesday morning, December 21, 1994. He didn't see the husband there, just Margaret. He finished the work left over from the night before, moving the rest of the boxes from the antique store to the storage facility. Then he went into one of the bedrooms, where Margaret had some cleaning that needed to be done. It seemed to him to be a guest bedroom or second bedroom. Margaret had him pick up books and papers she had scattered about. She told him she had just finished a cookbook or travel guide, Augustine couldn't remember which. She asked him to put the papers and books in neat stacks under the bed.

From there he went to the laundry room for more cleaning. Only this time it wasn't clutter. It was a stain.

Dirt from foot traffic had soiled a large section of the carpet in front of a closet that held the washer and dryer. But in the middle of the carpet was a different kind of stain: one big spot, about two and-a-half feet around. It was the color of brown dirt, but it looked different from the traffic area stains. Augustine thought something had been dumped there. Around the big spot were a few little ones, the size of half-dollars.

It appeared to him that somebody had already tried to

get the spots out without success. A rag sat there and the carpet was moist from scrubbing.

Augustine got on his hands and knees. It took him a half-hour to clean away the spots.

As he worked, Margaret was on the phone constantly, telling people her husband was still gone and that she didn't know where he could be.

After cleaning up the spots in the laundry room, Augustine tried to cut a deal with Margaret. He reminded her that she was paying Labor Express $13 an hour for his services. "I told her I'd do it for half that if she would call me at my house," he recalled. "She said that she'd get ahold of me and I'd work straight through her and not through Labor Express for about $6 an hour."

But Margaret didn't call him right away. In fact, a couple of weeks went by without any word from her. Each time Augustine drove down Charleston he'd slow down and try to get a look in her antique shop to see if she was there. He'd look for her pale-green Lincoln in the parking lot. He didn't stop, thinking that maybe she'd call. Finally, Augustine took the initiative. He was out driving with his mother and sister one day in early January when he stopped in the mall. He walked into Antique Merchants, where he saw Margaret.

She appeared upset, her eyes bloodshot.

"Have you heard anything on your husband?" he asked.

"No," she said, "they still haven't found him."

He asked her if she needed any work done. She said yes, and she'd give him a call, which she did the next day, telling him to come in on January 12.

It was a cold, gray Thursday morning. Rain was in the forecast. Augustine drove to Margaret's house in his mother's car. When he arrived, Margaret told him that she wanted to turn the master bedroom into an office—the master bedroom where Ron had slept since the early 1960s. At the time, his body had still not been found, though his Cadillac had been located at the strip club.

Augustine claims not to have known about this at the time.

Margaret wanted the bed taken out of the room and the carpeting stripped. She didn't say anything about her husband, where he might be or why she wanted to convert their bedroom into an office. Augustine didn't ask. He guessed the husband was still missing, but he didn't get into it.

The bed was large, one of those adjustable models, like a hospital bed, allowing the feet or head to move up. It had a big heavy headboard. The sheets and bedspread had been stripped off. It had plastic lying on top of it. Augustine started with the mattress. He pulled it off. Margaret was on the phone at the time.

"What do you want me to do with this?" he asked.

"Put it out on the patio," she said.

He hauled the mattress and the box spring out to the covered patio. He went back into the bedroom and took apart the heavy frame. It was too heavy for him to lift, so he got a dolly. He started to take it out to the patio. But it was raining by now. He feared it would rust. He asked Margaret where she wanted it. She said in the "ammunition room."

When he walked into the place where Ron had stored his weapons, Augustine was dazzled by the hundreds of weapons neatly stored in cases. Augustine had a great interest in guns; he used to go to the gun shop in Ron's mini-mall with his little brother. He stacked the frame in Ron's gun room, then returned to the bedroom. He moved the rest of the furniture out of the bedroom: two night stands and a little cabinet for the VCR, which was wired to a wall-mounted television.

Margaret told him she also wanted him to tear out the carpeting, a piece about 9 feet by 12 feet, which she intended to replace with an Oriental rug. Margaret then left the house. She told Augustine she had to meet with her lawyer to discuss matters dealing with her husband's disappearance. But before she left, she gave Augustine a stern instruction. "The cops think that I might have something to do with this," she told him. "If they ask you, if they come up to you and ask you, you just don't know nothing."

"You're right," he said, taken aback. "I don't know nothing anyways."

After Margaret left, Augustine looked over the carpet in the now-empty bedroom. Like the carpeting by the laundry room nearby, this section was also soiled: two large stains, on either side of where the big adjustable bed had been. Each stain was about 1½ feet wide by 2 to 3 feet long. At first it looked like dirt.

But this time, when he cut through the stained part of the carpet with a knife, the blade hit what he called "crunchy stuff that was flicking me in the face." He described it as "dried, hard, dark-brownish goop." He thought it was coffee, many, many cups of coffee that had spilled. Or Kool-Aid.

But it didn't smell like coffee or punch. It had what he described as a "really rank" odor that Augustine likened to the smell of his dogs "after they've been chewing on rabbits."

Of the two stains, one was larger—the one on the side of the bed closest to the wall. Augustine didn't know it, but that was the side of the bed that Ron Rudin slept on.

Augustine had worked for about an hour, nearly cutting out the entire 9-by-12 area, when Margaret returned. She told him she had "good news" from the lawyer. She'd just found out she was going to be getting some money she had been hoping for.

She was in a position now to buy all new carpeting for the entire room, instead of just an Oriental rug, so he could now strip the entire floor. She said she was thinking of industrial office-style carpeting.

Augustine went back to work. He found the disinfectant and returned to the bedroom, putting the cleaner on the carpeting. He rolled the carpet up and dragged it to the covered patio outside. The disinfectant was of little use. He held his nose, it smelled so bad.

Augustine returned to the bedroom to tear out the padding. The stain had seeped all the way through the carpet and the padding was moist. It was a mess. The stains had gone all the way through the carpeting and moistened the padding, which he didn't smell. "I didn't want to smell it," he said. "I was holding my nose through the whole process. I just pulled it up and got it out as quick as possible." He tossed the padding in a Dumpster behind the antique store.

He left the carpeting on the covered patio. "It was getting late and it was time for me to go home," he said.

But before he left, he made one last discovery.

He went back into the master bedroom, now bare, the furniture gone, the smelly carpeting and padding taken out. The room was dimly lit by a single lamp that he had left there.

Across the room, on the wall, was a photograph hanging over where the headboard of the bed had been. Somehow he hadn't noticed it before; perhaps it was because he was so busy.

It was a picture of Margaret. The portrait was framed, without glass. It was a glamour shot, soft-focus, of Margaret resting her chin on her hand.

"It was about 6 o'clock. It was dark," he said. "It was about the last thing in the bedroom. And it was a long day, and I don't know, it kind of—it was an eerie picture. It was an eerie feeling at the time because it looked like she was staring at me."

Augustine couldn't help but look a little more closely. Dust had settled on the top of the frame. "I was going to take it off the wall," he said. "I grabbed it and when I did I was looking closely at it, and it had splatters of something on it."

The splatters were reddish-brown, about the size of raindrops. "And they went up the picture," he said. "Up towards the right."

He put the picture back on the wall. His thoughts drifted to the stains in the house, to Margaret's admonition that he didn't know anything, to Ronald Rudin, a man Augustine had never met, but whose absence hung heavily in the house.

He said he "kind of froze" for a moment.

The drops looked like blood.

"It hit me like [all at] once. It didn't seem right," he said. "Him still being missing and me turning their master bedroom into an office and then those splatters on the picture—like, I got the heebie-jeebies."

He finished the last of his work and went home.

Two days went by. The memory of the portrait of Margaret still weighed heavily on Augustine Lovato, but not heavily enough for him to stay away from the Rudin household.

He had made arrangements with Margaret to return on Saturday, January 14, and, despite the experience from two days before, he did just that. When he got back to the house, the new carpeting had already been installed in the former master bedroom, now on its way toward becoming an office.

The bedroom wasn't the only part of the house Margaret was clearing out. Ron's gun room was next. Margaret had already started on the room. "There was stuff all over the floor," Augustine said. "And she basically wanted me to put all of the stuff that was laying on the floor in boxes. There was knives, hunting knives and hunting clothes and shoes all over the place, and she just wanted it straightened up." There were also some women's clothes in there, "like when they ran out of room in their closet everything went in there."

Margaret told Augustine that he didn't have to store everything away. If he saw something he liked, he could have it—anything but the guns. "So I took some slippers for my little brother," he said. "They were brand new, never been worn, and some tennis shoes." She told him that Ron had never worn the shoes because they were too small, at size 8. Everything else went into boxes. "She didn't know what she was going to do with this stuff," he said.

At the time, Ron had been missing for about four weeks. His body still had not been found.

Cleaning the gun room took Augustine nearly all day. As he worked, he couldn't take his mind off that picture he had seen the last time he was there. At one point, when Margaret was busy in the kitchen, Augustine quietly looked for the portrait. "I was curious where it went," he said.

It was no longer in the former master bedroom. He found it in what had been described to him as the guest bedroom, hanging over the bed in that room as it had in the other room. He stood on the bed and looked at it closely. It had changed slightly. "There was no dust on the top," he said. "It was all clean."

Something else was missing. "There were no more splatters on it."

"I just looked real quick," he said. "And I got off real quick, and went out of there."

He completed his work for Margaret that day and went home.

Six days later, despite his misgivings, Augustine Lovato was back at work for her. It was Friday, January 20, 1995—the last day he would work for her before talking to police.

Margaret wanted to get rid of the box spring and mattress that had been in the master bedroom, the one that was sitting on the stained carpet that Augustine had ripped up. She also wanted to dump a portable wardrobe that had been in the gun room, and a sofa and love seat stored in the loft over the guest house. She said that she had long wanted to get rid of the sofa and love seat, but that Ron didn't want her to. "She hated them. 'They're ugly,' " Augustine recalled Margaret telling him. "Ron wouldn't let her give them away. This was a prime opportunity to get rid of them."

Ron had now been missing for more than a month. His remains would be found that night at Nelson's Landing.

Margaret had rented a U-Haul, and told Augustine to put the furniture in there. She wanted it dropped off at Opportunity Village, a charitable organization nearby. When he finished loading the truck, Margaret told Augustine she had to go to her lawyer's office. She asked him to set up two banquet-style tables in the former master bedroom. He did as she asked. By now, the room was starting to look like an office. There were also a sofa and some antiques, and papers lying around.

While she was gone, he went into the bathroom, and got another surprise. In the bathtub there was what he called "like a blob." He heard "gurgling noises."

"It was . . . a brownish blob that was coming out from the drain," he said.

He didn't know what it was. It didn't appear to be sludge backed in the drain. This stuff was bubbling. It was dark, brownish-red. He turned on the water to try to wash it down, but the goop didn't go anywhere.

Augustine returned to his other work. When Margaret got back, the two of them drove off with the furniture toward Opportunity Village, making a stop at Augustine's apartment. "We had no furniture in our apartment at the time, so she actually gave me the couch and the love seat," he said. "It was old and green, but it was still something to sit on, so I didn't mind."

After dropping off the furniture at his apartment, they got back in the truck. They got into a little disagreement over the location of the Opportunity Village. Augustine thought it was on Charleston, Margaret insisted it was on Oakey. They drove down Charleston. Then Margaret said the Opportunity Village was behind the Red Rooster Antique Mall near the freeway. They pulled into the parking lot, but there wasn't any Opportunity Village. Margaret told Augustine to go ahead and put the mattress and box spring in the Dumpster, which he did. He also dumped an old portable closet into the bin.

They returned to Margaret's house, where Margaret got into her Lincoln. She then followed him to the U-Haul rental office on Decatur. They dropped off the U-Haul, and Margaret drove him back to her house.

There she gave him a package to mail. It was a small cardboard box that she wanted sent to her mother. She gave him five dollars for postage.

Augustine left Margaret's house. He tucked the box behind the seat of his mother's car and drove home.

Two days later, as Augustine was driving his mother and brother to the store, his brother kicked something under the seat.

"Oh, man, I was supposed to mail that," Augustine said.

Augustine shook the box. It seemed to weigh about two pounds. Something inside clunked around. He couldn't tell what it was. He showed the box to his mother.

Over the weeks he had been telling her about the strange goings-on at Margaret Rudin's house: husband missing, wife turning their bedroom into an office, the splattered, eerie portrait.

"Oh, my God," his mother said. "You are not mailing this."

By this time, the news was filled with stories about the remains of missing millionaire Ron Rudin being found in the desert by Lake Mohave. Augustine's mother called police.

Augustine finished his story. For the detectives, it seemed almost too good to be true. Possible blood in the tub, blood in the laundry room, blood in the bedroom, blood on a picture of Margaret? Was Ron murdered in his own bed, the blood spraying on a picture of the killer? But how could this be? The room had already been checked by missing persons detective Frank Janise, who actually got on his hands and knees by the bed, albeit on the other side from where Augustine said he found the stains. It was possible that Janise had simply missed it—he had said his check was quick and cursory—but it wouldn't take the world's sharpest defense attorney to suggest that one of them was wrong, or lying.

Still, Augustine had times, dates, names and information that only somebody who had been inside that house could have known. He seemed to like Margaret enough, holding no apparent grudge against her. At one point he spoke of how nice she was and how he couldn't believe she had had anything to do with her husband's murder.

But most important, he had the package, addressed to an Eloise Frost in Tennessee, Margaret's mother. If Augustine's testimony checked out, if police could actually find some of that blood he said he had cleaned up still in the house, they would have a strong case against Margaret. Would the package finalize the case? Could it contain a murder weapon?

After the interview, Ramos X-rayed the package at the courthouse security area. Unable to make out any of the objects inside, they got a search warrant and unsealed the box. The package raised more questions than it answered. It didn't contain a gun. It didn't contain anything that directly implicated Margaret in the murder. Instead, there were lotions and cosmetics, presumably for Mrs. Frost. Accompanying those was a letter from Margaret giving her mother an update on the police investigation. She told her that she had gotten a new attorney, that everything was going to be OK, that she shouldn't worry.

But there was something that would add an entirely new element to the case: an 8-by-10 glossy head shot of a handsome, dark-haired man with a George Hamilton haircut and a movie star smile. It was the kind of picture an actor would use to show casting directors.

There was also a fold-out postcard showing several tourist sites in Israel. On the back was a note to Margaret, apparently from a man, saying how much he missed her and how much he wanted to see her again. "It was kind of romantic in nature," Ramos recalled.

The letter was signed, "Love, Yehuda."

18

THE HOLY OIL SALESMAN

As best as Dona Cantrell could recall, her older sister Margaret had first mentioned the name Yehuda Sharon in the summer before Ron disappeared, in about August of 1994. "She would say things like how wonderful he made her feel, how intelligent that he was, how beautiful that he made her feel, how much fun he was," Dona said. "Things that were so special about him." Dona said Margaret gave the distinct impression that they had a "love relationship" and that her sister "certainly cared a great deal about him," but Dona couldn't recall seeing them together. She didn't know anything else about Yehuda: what he did for a living, or how he had entered Margaret's life.

Up until now, police had heard about Ron's extensive love life and, while Sue Lyles did not volunteer it at first, investigators were almost certain that she had been Ron's lover. With Yehuda in the picture, the case now included not one love triangle, but possibly two. After Detective Ramos opened the box that Margaret had given Augustine to mail, the question of Yehuda Sharon's role in Margaret's life became a burning one.

Based on the information from Augustine Lovato, Ramos and Vaccaro theorized that Ron Rudin was murdered in his bedroom—and possibly in his bed, based on the amount of blood in the carpeting and Margaret's alleged efforts to dispose of the mattress and box spring. The body then would have been transported to Nelson's Landing in the antique trunk, whose remains were found at the scene, and set afire. What the flames didn't finish off, the wild animals of the desert did. The theory wasn't perfect. For one, the missing persons detective had looked in the bedroom and didn't see any blood in the carpet or the bed. For another, there was the possibility that no fire could have burned hot enough to finish off an entire body. Plus, there was the question of the head not receiving the full brunt of the flames. Finally, there was the question of how Ron's body—all 220 pounds of it—could have been transported all the way out to the middle of nowhere, across steep, rocky ground. That activity would have been physically impossible for a skinny, 5-foot-7 woman in her early fifties. Could Yehuda be her accomplice?

Yehuda Sharon lived in a modest apartment near the University of Nevada, Las Vegas. He was of about medium height—not much taller than Margaret—with a lean, compact build. He had dark hair, brown eyes and a warm smile. He was self-employed in two occupations. One was writing computer software for businesses. The other was selling oils, or chrism, to churches for religious ceremonies.

Authorities would later suggest another vocation.

Yehuda had a number of what he called clients, older women like Margaret to whom he gave what he called financial advice and help with lawsuits, even though he was neither a licensed accountant nor a lawyer. In some cases, he described the women also as friends. Authorities would grill Yehuda on just what his relationships with these women were all about.

According to interviews and court proceedings, Yehuda Sharon came to the United States from Israel, where he was born on June 7, 1954, and where, as is the law, he served beginning at age 18 in the Israeli military. He says he fought in the Yom Kippur War and served in military intelligence. In about 1979 he came to the United States, settling in Las Vegas. While working in a hotel, he studied at UNLV, graduating with a degree in accounting. He would hold dual US–Israeli citizenship.

His first meeting with Margaret, he said, came shortly before a Christmas trip to Israel in 1992. He was attending happy hour at the Las Vegas Country Club, where he had guest privileges through an older woman whom he said he was advising on legal matters. He had a social link to her, as well, but he wouldn't say what it was. On two or three occasions, Yehuda, then 38, had seen Margaret, who at the time was 49. Ron was a longtime member of the club, having often taken his mother there over the years. This day, Margaret was at the club with a friend named Debbie. Yehuda had gone to get hors d'oeuvres, but they were nearly gone. He noticed that Margaret and her friend had plates overflowing with food. They invited him to join them at their table, which he did. They asked him what he did for a living, and he told them he worked in computer accounting.

He saw Margaret again several times the following February, in 1993, at the club, when she was there with Debbie. They would talk about his trip to Israel. He seemed to connect with Debbie, who, like him, was Jewish. Yehuda would contend that it was the women who pursued him. Later that spring, he said, Debbie asked him for his phone number, and in June or July of 1993, she called him, saying she was having Margaret and other friends over and asking if he would like to come. He declined, saying he was busy. Debbie called again that fall, and once again invited him over. He again said no.

Then, in late November or early December, he ran into the women at the country club, where they got to talking about Margaret's plans to go into the antique sales business. She asked Yehuda if he could set up a computer system for her. He said that he told her that he couldn't do it because he was involved in the software side of the business, not the equipment.

In March or April of 1994—around the time that she had first mentioned Yehuda to her sister—Margaret overheard Yehuda talking to the bartender at the country club, about computers. She again asked him about a computer system, and this time he told her about a friend. The three of them later met at a coffee shop called Café Roma to discuss the computer system for her store, but Yehuda didn't think she ever bought anything from him. About a month later, in May, Margaret called Yehuda to tell him she was writing a book about Las Vegas attractions and activities and their prices, and she asked him what kind of software to use to store the information.

In June, Margaret called Yehuda yet again, this time asking for help with a computer problem at a store where she was working. Yehuda drove to the store and fixed the computer, not charging her anything. He said that Margaret had told him that many of her friends had computers; he considered the free work a good way to build up a reference.

At some point in the weeks that followed, Margaret called Yehuda, asking why he hadn't been going to happy hour at the club. Yehuda told Margaret that club management had informed him nicely, but firmly, that he was no longer allowed in unless he was married to the woman he accompanied. She then went on to talk about her plans for a new venture, called Concierge Tourist Service, in which people could call asking for information about Las Vegas. The information would be stored on a computer program. Yehuda met Margaret several times at the coffee shop Jitters to discuss the project.

A couple of times, she met him at his house, once stopping by with her grandchildren. She borrowed $150 from him to take the kids to a show, giving him a thank-you kiss on the cheek. When she gave him a $150 check a couple weeks later, she told him that her grandchildren teased her because she liked Yehuda. He said that Margaret seemed very happy at the time—Ron had provided the rental space in his mini-mall for her antique store. She also helped him with his holy oil business, giving him phone books from Texas and other places after she returned from a trip to Tennessee over Thanksgiving 1994 to see her mother. Finding the numbers of churches, Yehuda would call to make business contacts.

In the two years that he had known Margaret, Yehuda would insist that their relationship was never intimate, though he sensed that Margaret wanted them to be closer than he did. "Put it this way, it remains as a business relationship as far as I'm concerned, but, you know, she was trying to push to have me go with her to parties or whatever," he would tell a grand jury. He said he did, in fact, dine with her occasionally, but never went to parties. He recalled that one night, as he was leaving the house at about 10 p.m., Margaret was outside, waiting in her Lincoln. He asked her, "What's going on?" and she replied, "I don't want to go home." She asked him where he was going. He said he told her, "None of your business. I'm going out." He left without her. "I mean, it wasn't her business to know what I'm doing, where I'm going, and she's married anyhow," he said.

Yehuda may have had good reason not to tell Margaret what his business was. On Dec. 14, 1994—just four days before Ron's disappearance—Yehuda met a Philippines-born woman named Maria Aquino at a club called The Hop on Tropicana Avenue. When she told him she was returning to the Philippines over the holidays, he asked if she could bring back some church directories to get contacts for his holy oil business. He knew that there were many Catholic churches in the Philippines and saw the country as a good business opportunity. Maria said she might be able to help him, telling him that her brother was a former priest. They exchanged phone numbers.

The next day, they went out to dinner, and they spent the night together at her apartment. He left her home the morning of Friday, December 16. He went to his sports club to shower, then later called US Rent-A-Car to see if they had any cars available. In a story that would later come under great scrutiny by authorities, he said he needed a car to drive to Arizona, where he would pick up bottles for his holy oils. He claimed he didn't want to drive either of his two cars, a gold Toyota 4Runner and a gray Nissan pickup, because they both had manual transmissions; in the cold weather the shifting would be difficult on his leg, which had a nagging knee injury. He preferred to drive an automatic. Why he thought he would do more shifting on a long-haul trip to Phoenix than while driving around town locally was never fully explained.

That Friday night, he attended a party with Maria, then spent the night again at her apartment, leaving the next morning. He cleaned up at the sports club that Saturday, ran some errands, then returned home to do some work, then returned to Maria's apartment for the third night in a row.

The next morning, Sunday, December 18—the last day Ron Rudin was seen alive—Yehuda left Maria's apartment at about 6:30 in the morning, going home to make early morning business calls to churches in a later time zone. At 8 a.m., Margaret called him. She said she was having a problem with her computer and wanted to see him. She was annoyed because the computer had broken during the grand opening of her store. In 10 minutes, she was at his apartment. He told her he couldn't fix her computer—that he only knew software, not hardware. Margaret seemed irritated that he couldn't do anything about the problem. Before she left, she reminded him to attend the grand opening. She had sent him an invitation. He never went.

At about 7 p.m., Margaret called him. "She wanted to know, very demanding, why I didn't come to the opening of the shop," he told a grand jury. "I got the invitation. And then she asked me to come, and it just happened, you know, that I was busy, you know, and I didn't understand why she was pushing for it." About two hours later, he walked a block-and-a-half to the US Rent-A-Car outlet at the corner of Tropicana and Paradise Road, where he rented a four-door Chevrolet Cavalier with automatic transmission for his trip to Phoenix to buy 4-ounce–sized bottles for the holy oil. He drove the car home, parked it, and at about 10 p.m., Maria called. She was getting ready to leave a Christmas party at the MGM Grand Hotel and Casino and invited him to spend the night. He drove to her apartment about a half-hour later, and waited another 20 minutes for her to arrive. When she got back, she let him in, and he stayed the night—the night that police believe Ron Rudin was killed.

Police would later talk with Maria Aquino, and no matter how many ways they asked her, the answer kept coming out the same way. Yehuda Sharon was with her all night Sunday, December 18 through Monday, December 19, 1994. Police would find her a credible witness, an upstanding citizen with no reason to lie and every reason to tell the truth.

But Yehuda would not be in the clear. He would never make it to Arizona to pick up the bottles. That Monday morning, after he returned home from Maria's house, he said that Margaret had left several messages for him saying that Ron was missing. Finally, in the afternoon, they spoke, and she told him that Ron hadn't shown up for work. "She told me that her husband wasn't there and everybody was waiting for him," Yehuda recalled. "I mean, the employees were waiting for him because he's the only one that had the keys or something like this, and then about 1 o'clock they all disperse."

At some point that day, he said, he also called the bottle company and found out that it was out of the size he needed. That meant that he would have to go elsewhere to a company in the Los Angeles area that only sold them in huge quantities, by the pallet. The Cavalier wouldn't be big enough.

So, Yehuda claimed, he returned the compact car to US Rent-A-Car at about 9 p.m. Monday and got something bigger, a blue Chevy Astro van with automatic transmission. Before he drove off, he had somebody at the rental agency remove the back seats, so, he said, he would have room for the holy oil bottles.

Detectives would say the van also had room for something else: an antique trunk with a body inside.

19

"I'VE BEEN HERE BEFORE!"

On Wednesday, January 25, 1995, the same day that Augustine Lovato was talking to police about cleaning up the goopy stuff in the Rudins' bedroom carpet, Margaret was having a chat with a newspaper reporter. While she had little to say to detectives when they informed her of the discovery of Ron's remains, she had a mouthful for *Review-Journal* reporter Carol Huang, telling the journalist that she was baffled by Ron's murder. "He was a very private, mysterious person, and nobody knew him. I thought I knew him as good as anybody, but now with the things I'm finding out—nobody knew him," Margaret said, in an article published the next day. "It's beyond my comprehension. I can't imagine that this would have actually happened to him."

This was the beginning of several interviews Margaret would conduct for newspaper and television reporters. For the readers of the *R-J*, she painted an ominous portrait of her late husband, a man who was something of a gun nut, with a pistol stuffed in his boot, who traveled frequently to Mexico and Colombia for yearly hunting trips—and possibly other, more sinister business. "Afterwards he sent guns to people he met on these trips. That I know for a fact, but how many or how often, I don't know," she told the paper. As for his real estate business, she told Huang that this was mysterious, too. In the months before her husband's death, he became more secretive, she said. She didn't know why. He made some deal on 100 acres of Lee Canyon land at Mount Charleston that he didn't tell anyone about, not even his business associates. How she knew about this, she didn't say. She said Ron also tore out phone records usually kept by his secretary.

"There were just so many, many mysterious things that

were going on lately," Margaret told the paper. "He was extremely secretive about what he was going to do. Nobody knew anything. . . . He wasn't confiding in anyone."

Margaret repeated what she had told the missing persons detective about the night before Ron's disappearance, how Ron had told her he wanted to see a movie, then changed his mind. "He said, 'No, there's nothing on any good.' And his words were, 'You don't have to go to a movie with me. I have somebody to go to the movie with. Somebody answered my personal ad,' " she recalled him saying. "I thought he was kidding, so I said, 'I hope she's young and pretty and likes your kind of movies.' "

She said that she'd left to drop off a computer at a friend's house, and called Ron from the car on her cell phone at 7:30 p.m. "I had asked him if he was all right, and he said, 'Yes,' and 'I love you,' " she told the newspaper. "Everything seemed fine."

As for any sort of memorial service, she said there would be none. Ron had left explicit instructions that there be no services for him in Las Vegas and that he be laid to rest in the small Illinois town where his parents were buried. And, in fact, that same day, Margaret went to Davis Funeral Homes on Charleston Boulevard. Ron's remains had been released by the coroner's office to Palm Mortuary, then transported to Davis, where they were prepared for shipment to a funeral home in Dieterich, Illinois, not far from the family farm in Effingham.

Along with the newspaper interview, Margaret was making behind-the-scenes moves, hiring yet another lawyer, this one John Momot, one of Las Vegas' best-known criminal defense attorneys, who specialized in representing tough guys in big trouble. Margaret also continued to confer with her private investigator, Anthony R. Desio of Colt Protective Security, whom she had hired four days after Ron's disappearance. According to Desio's invoice for services, he had his initial consultation with Margaret on Dec. 23, 1994, then met with her three times in January before Ron's remains were found, including one meeting at a Marie Callender restaurant. Desio also logged two meetings with Momot before the discovery of the remains. On the day that Margaret was notified of her husband's death, the private investigator logged this duty: "Confidential source utilized."

Margaret's efforts, however, would do nothing to stop what was now a full-bore police investigation against her. Tipped by Augustine Lovato, detectives and crime scene technicians gathered in a cold, steady rain in a muddy area behind a building at 307 Wall Street, in a run-down section of Las Vegas frequented by homeless people. It was here that Augustine told police that he and Margaret had dumped the mattress and box spring from the master bedroom. The detectives theorized that if what Augustine found in the carpeting was blood, then Ron may have been shot in his bed, leaving blood also on the box spring and mattress, critical evidence that would tie Margaret to the killing.

Ramos, Vaccaro and the technicians searched in the rain. The wooden box spring set, caked in mud, lay on the ground near a Dumpster. The mattress wasn't with it. They searched some more but couldn't find it, deciding at last that a homeless person might have carried it off. The box spring was hauled back to the police lab for closer inspection. A technician sprayed one section with a chemical called luminol, which can detect the smallest amounts of blood, even invisible residue from stains that have been wiped away. Luminol reacts with the properties in blood and glows in the dark. The technician dimmed the lights. The area of the box spring that had been sprayed put out the tell-tale greenish glow: a positive test, though not a definitive indicator of blood. Luminol treatment is what is considered a presumptive test for blood because other non-blood substances can also set it off. The box spring would need further testing.

But with what Augustine had told police, it was a very strong indication that Ron had been killed in that bedroom in his own adjustable bed. The fact that no buttons or zippers were found in the fire pit at Nelson's Landing suggested that Ron was in his nightclothes when killed. It provided enough probable cause for a judge to grant search warrants for the Rudin house, Margaret's antique store and a storage facility. A judge also approved placing a wire tap on Margaret's home phone and cellular phone. Earlier, police had set up what is a called a phone trap on the Rudin phone, which doesn't record the actual calls but does record the outgoing numbers that are dialed.

On the afternoon of Friday, January 27, 1995, police made their move against Margaret. The operation was a big one, involving not only homicide technicians and crime scene analysts, but a crew of undercover surveillance officers who would keep tabs on her while the detectives searched her house and store.

At 4:30 p.m., surveillance officers saw Margaret Rudin emerge from the front doors of the mini-mall where she had her antique store. She got into her large light blue-green Lincoln Town Car, with license plates RRR-6, and pulled out of the parking lot onto Charleston, driving around the neighborhood before making her way back to her house on Alpine Way. She was seen cruising by the house at about 15 mph talking on her cell phone.

From her house, she made her way to a Circle K convenience store on South Valley View Boulevard, about a mile away, and pulled into the parking lot. She was seen talking on the cellular phone inside the car. She then got out and walked over to a pay phone next to the Circle K, dropping money into the phone and punching in a number.

As she did this, Detective David F. Kallas of Metro's intelligence squad, strolled to a pay phone next to Margaret and pretended to make a phone call. "I'm not going back there," she was overheard to say, then soon finished the call. Kallas couldn't tell who she was talking to.

Kallas returned to his unmarked car. He watched through his binoculars as Margaret made several more calls at the pay phone. She then walked back to her Lincoln and made yet another call on her cellular. Then she returned to the pay phone to make more calls.

This went on for more than an hour, leading police to wonder whether she already suspected her home phones were tapped. Finally, after making her last call at the pay phone, Margaret went back to her car and opened the passenger-side door, retrieving a dark plastic bag. She walked to a trash bin and tossed it in. She got back in her car and pulled out of the parking lot at 6:33 p.m., driving back toward her antique store.

Kallas went to the Dumpster to see what Margaret had thrown away after making all those calls. The trash bin was full of boxes and old pieces of meat from Larry's Meats, the butcher shop next door to the Circle K. While Margaret was making her calls, Kallas had seen employees from the butcher shop throw those things into the bin. But in the corner of the Dumpster he found what looked like the plastic bag that Margaret had put there. He pulled the bag out. It was black with the logo of the Golden Nugget casino hotel downtown. It contained something heavy, but he didn't open it.

He also saw in the Dumpster a box containing calendar pages apparently torn from a day planner, and a newspaper. He left them there.

Crime scene technician Daniel Ford was summoned to the Circle K, where he photographed the inside of the Dumpster. Kallas gave him the Golden Nugget bag. Ford removed a box full of torn pages from a calendar book. The calendar pages appeared to trace Margaret's appointments and activities of the last few days. On the January 22 page, a notation in the upper right-hand corner made reference to power of attorney, something to do with a court motion, an appointment with a Pat Brown and the words "lease ASAP" and "trust." There were also references to such things as Ron's document, John's office, Terry Y with a phone number, Cooper resignation, Davis trust and the word "movie."

That page also made reference to a Jeremy at TWA. There were also clippings from the *Las Vegas Review-Journal* listing a travel agent.

The January 23 page had notations about tickets and a bank account, and the January 26 page had the phrases "assets not to be put into trust" and "want to put into probate ASAP."

The page for that day, January 27, had another reference to power of attorney, the court motion, the name John, a $500 figure, and the word "horses."

There was no page for the following day, January 28. The pages for the 29th and 30th were both blank.

Ford then inspected the Golden Nugget bag. Inside was another bag, from a Target store, which contained two 64-ounce bottles of red-colored lamp oil, both unopened, with the seals still on them. Ford found another newspaper article, this one about hiking in the Lake Mead National Recreation Area—the same area where Ron Rudin's body was dumped, and where somebody had set a large fire.

As Margaret was making her phone calls at the Circle K, the search was underway at her home. Police arrived in the early evening and rang the bell, but nobody answered. Detective Vaccaro, who would lead the house search while Ramos would later go to the antique store, forced his way into the house. Margaret's nephew, Scott Stavrou, heard the commotion and came out of the guest house.

Stavrou at first asked if he could stay during the search. Police said he could, but he soon left anyway, either driving his own car or getting picked up by somebody else.

Once in the Rudin house, the search team did a quick walk-through to get their bearings. They then headed for the master bedroom, the key area they wanted to search, where Augustine had said he cleaned up the crunchy stuff from the carpeting. The room was small, with a sloping ceiling, and had been converted into an office. Gone was the big bed, replaced by a folding table, desk and chair, which sat on new, industrial carpet. A typewriter was on the table. There was a fireplace with a cozy sitting area in front of it. Other chairs and folding tables were lined up against one wall.

As he looked at the bedroom, one of the detectives, Dave Hatch, said: "Wow, I've been here before."

Hatch was the lead investigator in the death of Peggy Rudin, 16 years earlier. As his recollection of that case came back, he told the other detectives and the technicians that this room had already seen one bloody death, when Peggy blew the top of her head off with the .357 Magnum. This added a new wrinkle to the search. Depending on how well the room had been cleaned, police could very well expect to find blood and other biological evidence from two people: Ron Rudin and his third wife.

Still, for a room that may have been the site of two deaths by gunshots to the head, it would take some effort to find any evidence of blood. Searching the slump block wall, on the south side of the room behind where Augustine said the head of the bed had been, technician Mike Perkins finally found something: reddish-brown spots. They weren't very big, about 1/16th of an inch to an eighth of an inch in diameter, but it was more than enough to collect and to test.

Perkins then looked to the wall to the left, on what would have been the side of the bed where Ron slept. There, in the grass-cloth wallpaper, were more tiny spots.

On the other side of the bed, there was another red-brown speck on the mirrored door about nine inches from the ground. Another spot was on the track to the door.

Perkins turned his attention higher in the room. On the south wall where he had seen those first spots, he found more reddish drops on a plastic electrical outlet about a foot from the acoustical ceiling. And there were more little splatters in a circular pattern amid the popcorn-like bumps of the sprayed-on ceiling. He noticed that some of the little bumps had apparently been picked off recently, leaving white spots against the yellow-stained ceiling.

Though the spots looked like blood, Perkins needed to

conduct a test to be more sure. He tested all of the spotted areas except the switch plate with a chemical called Hemastix, which, like luminol, is a presumptive test for blood. The switch plate wasn't tested because there wasn't a big enough stain and Perkins didn't want to destroy what little was left. All of the areas that underwent the presumptive test came up positive for blood.

Perkins and his crew then collected a total of five samples of the reddish-brown spots, removing both the stains and the materials on which they were splattered. They chipped away small sections of the block wall to preserve the entire stain sample. They also took off pieces of the acoustical ceiling, removed the stained outlet plate and clipped off some of the stained grass cloth.

With the larger samples now taken, Perkins searched for blood that couldn't be seen with the naked eye. As had been done with the box spring, he conducted a luminol test on the south wall where the head of the bed had been. He sprayed the chemical and turned out the lights. A green glowing circle appeared just over the former site of the bed, a positive result. He did the same for the other two walls on either side of where the bed had been. A fainter pattern emerged on the wall covered in the grass cloth, another positive. There was no glowing on the wall with the mirrored doors.

The newly installed carpeting in the room was clean of any obvious stains. Near where the bed had been, technicians ripped up the carpet and found a stain about where the headboard of the bed would have been. This was sprayed with luminol, and the test was positive.

The search turned to the master bathroom, where Augustine had claimed to have seen the gurgling goop in the bathtub. Technicians performed a Hemastix test on the drain in the tub; it came back positive.

Another likely blood stain was found on a remote control device that had worked the big bed. The final sign of blood was found in a vacuum cleaner that was being stored in Ron's gun room. Technicians tested the bottom of the vacuum cleaner with Hemastix, and on the air intake area got a positive reaction for possible blood.

If the spots in the bedroom were in fact blood, then the search of the Rudin residence had proved to be a major advance in the investigation—and strengthened the case against Margaret, perhaps to the point that she could be arrested.

But one major issue remained. How could police know that this blood belonged to Ron? Although it was unlikely that the blood from Peggy's apparent suicide would still be in the bedroom 17 years later, investigators needed to be certain. They needed to identify the source of the blood drops to confirm whether they had come from Ron.

The problem was they didn't have a sample of Ron's blood. Tests can determine whether blood comes from a male or female, but police needed a known sample of Ron's blood against which the drops in the bedroom could be compared. Ron had been incinerated, leaving no body to provide a blood sample for DNA testing. All that was left was the skull, and while there may have been some usable tissue for DNA testing, the coroner didn't take such a sample before releasing the remains to the funeral home.

In a stroke of luck, during the search of the house, police believed they had found a sample of Ron's blood. In the top left drawer of a vanity in the bathroom, technicians found, sitting amid the combs and brushes, an off-white handkerchief with many little brownish-red spots on it, the kinds of spots caused by dabbing shaving cuts. Police would later find a witness linking Ron to that handkerchief—the housekeeper. Police felt they now had a Ron Rudin blood sample for DNA comparisons.

There was still one last item that police couldn't find. Augustine had spoken of the portrait of Margaret hanging over the bed—the portrait with little splatters on it. A search of the entire house turned up no portrait, splattered or otherwise. The best police had to settle for was finding a nail driven into the block wall, in the place where Augustine said the picture had hung. Vaccaro, who had first seen that picture a week earlier when they had come to give the death notification, was eager to find out where it had gone.

Coincidentally, as the police search team was scouring the house for the missing picture, who should drive into a parking lot next to the house but Margaret herself. She had called her private investigator, Anthony Desio, at about 5:50 p.m. to tell him that police were at her home. They arranged to meet in the parking lot next to the Winchell's donut shop, then together met with Vaccaro.

Vaccaro got word of her arrival and walked up to Margaret's Lincoln, telling her that the police had search warrants for her home and business. He asked her to unlock the antique store and disable the alarm so that police wouldn't have to smash their way in. She complied, allowing the other investigators into the store. Margaret, her PI and Vaccaro then returned to the parking lot, where the detective asked her to sign a form consenting to a search of the car. He wanted to know if the picture was inside.

She refused, saying she wanted to talk to her attorney. According to her private investigator, who later filed a report, Vaccaro told her he could confiscate the car because it technically belonged to Ron's estate and not to Margaret. She still wouldn't allow the search. Vaccaro then asked if he could just look in the trunk for the picture.

"I have no problem opening the trunk of my car," she said, and popped open the trunk. Vaccaro looked inside. There was no picture, but he did see a green hard-sided suitcase about 10 inches deep and two-and-a-half feet across. This concerned the detective.

"Are you traveling somewhere?" asked Vaccaro.

"Oh, no," she said. "There's a problem with the latch on this suitcase and I'm having it repaired."

If it had a bum latch, Vaccaro certainly couldn't tell by looking at it. It seemed to be shut just fine. But he let the matter drop, and Margaret drove away. Vaccaro said he had no legal cause to detain her.

Inside the antique store, meanwhile, Detective Ramos was rummaging through hundreds of papers in an old roll-top desk. He would be at it for about an hour, looking at every receipt, invoice and inventory sheet for any trace of an antique trunk of the sort whose parts were found at Nelson's Landing.

"Oh, boy!" he said aloud.

In his hand were two invoices for two antique trunks. From all the other work, he could account for one of the trunks. A receipt in a file cabinet showed that the trunk had been sold.

But there was no such receipt for the other trunk.

Meanwhile, surveillance officers had followed Margaret from the parking lot of the mini-mall to a restaurant, Blueberry Hill, just off Charleston, where she was seen meeting with an unidentified white man. From there she went to a Vons grocery store on East Flamingo Road, then drove down Flamingo to a cul-de-sac just a block off the boulevard, in the southeastern end of the city.

Although the surveillance officers couldn't tell what she was doing, it would be reported later by Margaret's sister Dona that Margaret was huddling with her family at the home of her sister, Barbara LePome. Barbara's son Scott Stavrou had called to tell his mother that Margaret's house was being searched by police, then drove to his mother's home for a family gathering that also included Scott's fiancée Lisa, Dona and her son Doug, and Margaret.

Dona knew her sister well, through times good and bad between them, and this night Margaret didn't quite seem herself. "She's pretty tough under fire, but it was one of the few times where I did detect nervousness," Dona would tell a grand jury. "She was hyper, a little excited."

The family spoke about the police serving the search

warrants. In addition to Scott being at the guest house when the cops arrived, Margaret told her family that she had driven by the house and seen the police there—then drove right by, until she returned to meet her private detective in the parking lot.

During the meeting, Barbara gave Margaret the papers that Dona had taken out of the antique desk, including the list of Ron's assets and the gun safety certificate. Barbara also gave Margaret the cassette tape from the desk, the one marked "Ron Texas 9/93." Margaret pulled the tape out of the cartridge.

As Margaret went through the papers, she warned Dona that police were looking for three things. "She said that they were looking for a picture, a portrait of her," Dona recalled. "They were looking for a trunk that had been used to move guns in, and they were looking for a gun that was in my possession, my personal possession. And she said for me to get rid of it, to get rid of the gun."

In 1991, Margaret had given Dona a .38-caliber pistol. As far as Dona knew, that gun had never left her possession; she kept it by her nightstand. It was unclear why Margaret thought police might want that gun, and it was never linked to Ron's death.

After this discussion, the family decided to go to a restaurant. They got into separate cars, Dona riding with Margaret. They didn't go far, just a block away to a place called the Suburban Lounge in a shopping center on the corner of Flamingo and Sandhill Road. For reasons Dona couldn't remember, the family didn't eat at the Suburban Lounge, and instead went across the street to a restaurant called Thumpers. While in the parked car at the restaurant, Margaret got a phone call from private detective Desio. Dona got out of the car to give her some privacy.

Margaret wrapped up her phone call and joined the others at Thumpers. But when they got inside they found out they couldn't eat there—Thumpers had just had a kitchen fire and wasn't serving food. As people walked back to their cars, Margaret lagged behind the rest. Dona

watched as Margaret tore up a piece of notebook paper
on which she had written something and dropped it into
the garbage can near the restaurant.

From Thumpers, the group got into their cars and drove
to the third corner of the intersection to a restaurant called
the Blue Ox. They all parked and walked inside, but
couldn't be served there because Dona's son Doug wasn't
21.

Finally, they went to the fourth corner, a 7-Eleven. "I
remember laughing at the time, talking to my sister Barbara," recalled Dona. "I remember laughing and saying
we must look ridiculous here just bouncing from corner
to corner."

The irony was that they *were* being looked at—by Detective Michael Givens of Metro's intelligence unit.

The family members went back to Barbara's house, but
Margaret didn't stick around for the rest of the evening.
She left Barbara's house—as did Givens.

By now it was after midnight, in the early morning hours
of Saturday, January 28. Givens followed Margaret to an
apartment complex on Escondido Street, near the main
campus of the University of Nevada, Las Vegas. There,
she met a man in his thirties with dark hair and dark
complexion. Surveillance detectives were given copies of
the 8-by-10 photograph of Yehuda Sharon—the photo
they had found in the package that Margaret asked Augustine to send. The hairstyle was different, but as best
detectives could tell, it was the same man.

According to the surveillance log, Margaret got there
at 12:52 a.m. and stayed for more than an hour, being
watched by Givens, who had a poor view from his unmarked car. "Inside the apartment complex all I could see
was the garage door, the top of her vehicle, and the top
of his vehicle," Givens said later. "When the garage door
would come open I could see them going to and from the
different vehicles, but I could not tell if they had anything
in their hands or not."

At 2:17 a.m., Margaret and the dark-haired man left the apartment in separate cars, Margaret in her Lincoln, the man in a Toyota 4Runner. They made their way west to The Strip, where both pulled their cars into the valet parking lane at the entrance to the Excalibur Hotel and Casino. In the valet area, Margaret got into the man's 4Runner. The valet attendant parked her car, while the 4Runner headed for the self-parking lot. Margaret and the man were then seen going into the hotel at 2:38 a.m. Givens didn't follow them inside, and he didn't know what they were doing. But they didn't check in. They only stayed there for 22 minutes, and were seen coming back out of the hotel at 3 a.m.

They got back into the 4Runner, and drove out of the hotel down Las Vegas Boulevard, going south for about 20 miles on the frontage road until they stopped in Jean, Nevada, at the Gold Strike Hotel and Gambling Hall, where they got gas and coffee. They then got on Interstate-15 heading south, toward Los Angeles. Las Vegas police followed the pair as far as the state line, which the 4Runner crossed at 3:45 a.m. Police assembled at Buffalo Bill's Resort and Casino in Primm, the town on the Nevada side of the border, then radioed for help from Los Angeles authorities.

Around Barstow, officers from the Los Angeles Police Department spotted the 4Runner and followed it for 140 miles through Victorville, into California's Inland Empire, across downtown Los Angeles and finally to a cheap motel near Los Angeles International Airport. Margaret and the man spent a few hours in the motel, then drove to the airport. Los Angeles police watched Margaret as she and the man believed to be Yehuda walked up to an American Airlines counter, where she appeared to purchase a ticket. The officers photographed the pair there. At one point Margret and the man embraced. Margaret boarded a plane and the man was followed back to the motel. Surveillance was then called off.

Ramos would later say that one of the surveillance officers knew the ticket agent and convinced the agent to look up what flight Margaret had taken. It would take several hours to find out because of a computer snafu. It initially appeared that Margaret had headed for Tel Aviv, Israel, because of the TLV code typed onto the ticket. It wasn't until later that police and the ticketing agent realized that the TLV was a typo; it should have said TVL, the abbreviation for "travel." A supervisor sorted things out. Margaret was traveling to Chicago's O'Hare Airport, via St. Louis.

Two days later, on Monday, January 30, Lowell Landrus, owner of the Wright Funeral Home in the southern Illinois farming community of Dieterich, drove the company van across southern Illinois to St. Louis, Missouri about 100 miles to the west, to pick up the remains of Ron Rudin. Davis Funeral Homes of Las Vegas had shipped the remains to St. Louis on Delta Airlines. They were contained in a metal box, slightly smaller than a coffin. Although he didn't open the box, Landrus assumed there wasn't a complete body in it. As the box was loaded into the van, Landrus could hear something rattling around inside.

Landrus had only met Ron Rudin a few times. But he did know Ron's family, the cousins and aunts and uncles who still lived in the little rural towns of southeastern Illinois. Several years earlier, Landrus had handled the funeral arrangements for Ron's mother, Stella Rudin. At that funeral, Landrus spoke to Ron and met his then-new wife, a beautiful, well-dressed, soft-spoken—even glamorous in his view—woman whom Ron had introduced as Margaret.

After Landrus returned from the St. Louis pickup of Ron Rudin's remains, he would again see Margaret Rudin, now a widow. She came into the funeral home with two other women. Landrus couldn't remember who they were, though he recalled Margaret saying that one was a friend and the other was a relative. Margaret was there to make the final arrangements for her husband. Landrus got the information from her for the death certificate and the obituaries that would be placed in the local newspapers.

In his years in the funeral business, he had been witness to a lot of tears, and as expected, Margaret cried and made expressions of grief. But Landrus wasn't buying it. "I thought she reacted really fake," he said. He showed her his line of caskets, and Margaret picked out the cheapest one in the shop, a metal casket costing about $1,000. This, in and of itself, wasn't unusual; other customers couldn't afford more expensive caskets. But Margaret, he said, wasn't interested in looking at anything else. "She went into the casket room and said, 'I'll take that one,' " he said. "Then she went over to the other woman and she was kind of crying and stuff. She said, 'Oh, this is so terrible.' She said to me, 'You know that he had been decapitated, did you?' I said, 'No, I didn't know anything about it.' "

After wrapping up the business, Margaret and the two other women left. Landrus would later send a bill for all the costs: about $3,500. One of Margaret's attorneys sent him a check. Landrus placed the box of Ron's remains in the casket. The box was so big he had to cut out some of the lining in the casket.

Margaret then made her way to the home of Ron's cousin, Karen Pitcher, in Montrose, not far from Dieterich. It was Tuesday, the day before Ron's funeral, and Margaret had called earlier, telling Karen that she was in Illinois, having flown in from Las Vegas for the funeral, and was on her way to the Wright Funeral Home to buy Ron's casket. Margaret arrived at Karen's home with a friend. Karen's sister, Marilyn Anderson was there, too. As Karen served them lunch, Margaret told them that she and her friend had met up in Chicago, then picked up Margaret's daughter, who lived in the Chicago area. They all drove down to southern Illinois and checked into a motel in Effingham; the daughter was still in the motel because she wasn't feeling well.

Then Margaret spoke about the tumultuous events following Ron's disappearance. "A lot of what she talked about was the police chasing her and suspecting her and how they hounded her. She also said how the trustees wouldn't let her in the house, how she did not have any money," recalled Karen.

Ron's cousins asked Margaret how she felt Ron was killed, and she told them she thought it was either the mob or some of the relatives of Ron's former wife, still upset about Peggy's death and blaming Ron for it.

Then Margaret started criticizing Ron.

"She was just saying terrible things about Ron that day," said Karen. "I thought it so odd the day before his funeral she was telling his cousins what a terrible person Ron was. She said that he was very paranoid, that he had actually gone to the Mayo Clinic thinking that Margaret was poisoning him, that he was terrible to his mother, which I could hardly believe."

Margaret seemed hurt, sad and upset, which seemed natural to Karen. But Karen couldn't reconcile those emotions with the awful things Margaret was saying about Ron. "Marylin and I were sitting there with our mouths open," said Karen. "I remember telling Margaret, 'You should write a book. This would make a wonderful book.'"

At the end of the lunch, Karen and Marylin each gave Margaret $50 for gas money and expenses to get back home; they were assuming she was returning to Las Vegas. Margaret never asked for any money, but her talk of being shut out by the trustees made it clear she was in dire financial straits. Margaret said that that night she and her friend and daughter would have dinner near the motel and they arranged to have Karen pick them up the next morning for Ron's funeral.

The next day, just as Karen and Marilyn were going out the door for the service, the phone rang. It was Margaret. She told them she wasn't going to the funeral and wanted Karen to explain why to everybody else. Margaret said she was being followed. She had seen two men watching her and her friend at the restaurant the night before. Karen tried to explain to her that it was all probably innocent enough, that Effingham was a small town and that a couple of nice-looking women would attract the attention of any local men who might be at the restaurant. But Margaret didn't want to stay.

"I'm afraid there will be someone at the funeral to grab me and take me back to Las Vegas," she told Karen.

Karen couldn't make sense out of this. She thought Margaret was going back to Las Vegas anyway. She tried to talk her out of missing the funeral, saying that it was a small church and that anybody who didn't belong there would be sent away.

"There's no use," Margaret said. "We're halfway back to Chicago. I'm calling from a pay phone."

The service was held in St. Paul's Lutheran Church, a small brick church surrounded by fields of corn and soybeans. It was a morning service, about 11:30 a.m., and about 30 people attended, mostly aunts, uncles and cousins of Ron's. Karen recalled there was a casket—"closed, of course"—with a floral wreath in front. She only remembers the pastor, Glenn Renken, saying some words, and everybody singing a few hymns. Ron was interred at 12:30 p.m. Otherwise, the morning was a bit of a haze.

"I was kind of in shock," said Karen. "Bizarre is what I thought this whole thing was."

While Margaret was in Illinois, surveillance detectives in Las Vegas kept watch on Yehuda. On Monday, January 30, two days after he returned from Los Angeles—and the same day Ron's remains were being picked up in St. Louis—Yehuda was seen going about his business. He went to the Jitters coffee shop, then the post office, before returning to his apartment by UNLV. At 2:20 p.m., homicide detectives Phil Ramos and Jimmy Vaccaro drove up to Yehuda's apartment house. Vaccaro called Yehuda on his cell phone to tell him they were coming. He opened his garage door and met them there, before letting them in the house through the garage. The detectives had braced themselves for this meeting, having heard so many rumors about Yehuda and thinking that this could be an accomplice to murder. Instead, they were greeted by what Ramos described as a visibly nervous—trembling even—man who was shorter than he looked in pictures.

Yehuda let them in. The detectives sat on a couch and surveyed the modest apartment. Ramos considered it a "dump," cluttered with papers and other items and just seeming generally dirty—in sharp contrast to the impeccably neat Rudin home. By plan, the detectives, in questioning Yehuda, played the good cop, bad cop routine. The amiable Ramos was good cop, the harder-nosed Vaccaro acted as the heavy. Vaccaro told Yehuda that he potentially faced big trouble, that there was a risk he could be arrested and charged with harboring a fugitive. The detective told him it was time to tell them what he knew.

Vaccaro clearly rattled Yehuda. He seemed on the verge of losing his composure, but he never quite did. It quickly became apparent to the detectives that Yehuda may have been nervous, but he was no fool. As they started the tape recorder for a formal statement, Yehuda wouldn't give them any details about his relationship with Margaret or any information about Ron's murder. He claimed not to know anything about anything. He didn't even own up to taking Margaret across the state line until the detectives told him that he had been followed.

They asked him why he didn't say anything about taking Margaret to California. He told them that he was seeing another woman and he didn't want that woman to know that he was with Margaret. The detectives kept asking him questions and Yehuda kept dodging and weaving. Finally, it became clear that he wasn't going to tell them anything. The detectives turned off the tape recorder and left.

*   *   *

Yehuda would later admit that he didn't say everything he knew because he first wanted to determine what the police were up to. He said he was worried about being arrested. "It wasn't things to hide as much as find out what they want," he said. "I mean how they going to treat me because when the detectives came over—I believe it was Detective Vaccaro—I mean he threatened to arrest me for helping her flee the scene of a crime."

In time, however, Yehuda would tell police more. In dribs and drabs, he gave them the details of his business dealings with his female clients and told them about his alibi, spending the night with Maria. He told them about renting the car for the trip to Phoenix, then exchanging it for the van the day that Ron disappeared.

But he insisted he had nothing to do with disposing of Ron's body, though his explanation for what he did with the van would strain credibility among police. Yehuda said he had driven the van to California to pick up holy oil bottles from a distributor in the Santa Fe Springs area, but turned around somewhere around Barstow—in the middle of the southern California desert—because a trucker had told him bad weather lay ahead. Yehuda said he didn't want to get caught in rain or snow. All this, he would say, explained why he put 348 miles on the van but never got to his bottle supplier. Police continued to suspect that he'd put those miles on the van by driving out to Nelson's Landing.

He did confirm that he remained close to Margaret in the weeks after Ron's disappearance, going through financial documents with her even before Ron's body was found. When he was confronted with the fact that he had been under surveillance the night of the search warrant, he also acknowledged that he did in fact drive Margaret to Los Angeles International, but he said that Margaret had actually planned on leaving town earlier, from Las Vegas, except that she'd missed her flight due to the commotion around the search.

He confirmed that they had left his place in separate

cars, but he'd had to return because he forgot his wallet. While at home, he realized that he still had one of her boxes of documents, which he loaded into his 4Runner because he didn't want it left at his apartment. They hooked up at the Excalibur, where he went into the casino with her to cash a check, accounting for the 22 minutes that had been logged by the surveillance detective. During the drive to Las Vegas, Margaret told him about the search of her house. After getting to Los Angeles International Airport, Margaret went from counter to counter looking for a flight to Illinois while Yehuda waited in the car. By now, it was about 6 a.m. Saturday, and Yehuda having driven all night, was exhausted. They went to the motel near the airport, where Yehuda got some sleep while Margaret called airlines.

At about 1 p.m., he drove her back to the airport from the motel to the TWA counter, where she got her ticket to Illinois. Two days later, after detectives Ramos and Vaccaro showed up at his apartment, he knew that he had to get in touch with Margaret and convince her to come back to Las Vegas. "I didn't exactly wish to protect her as much as protect myself," he later said, adding, "I didn't want to be arrested."

For a few days, Las Vegas police lost track of Margaret. They knew she was in Illinois, and suspected she was staying with family members; her daughter lived in northern Illinois near the Wisconsin border. They knew she hadn't attended Ron's funeral. They had called Ron's relatives, who told them about Margaret's no-show.

It was time to put some more pressure on Margaret. Homicide Sgt. Bill Keeton told reporters February 3 that Margaret had refused to talk to police since her husband's remains were found and that she had blown town without her husband's remains after the search warrants were served January 27 at their home, their storage unit and the antique store. The part about the remains wasn't entirely correct; Margaret didn't technically go with the remains, but she did make the arrangements to have them flown to Illinois.

Keeton didn't go so far as to label her a suspect, but did note: "All I can say right now is that they were married for seven years and they had their ups and downs."

Another story, on February 3, from John L. Smith, the respected columnist for the *Review-Journal*, went even further, saying, "Now the missing persons inquiry–turned–homicide investigation has begun to focus on Rudin's widow, Margaret." The well-connected Smith cited "sources." He found it odd that Margaret would hire a hard-hitting criminal defense lawyer, John Momot, before her husband's remains were even found. Sources told him that she'd missed Ron's funeral because "she took ill."

Although Margaret was temporarily out of sight, the case against her continued to progress. That same week, on February 6 or 7, Ramos got a call from a worker at Michaels craft store, on the corner of Russell and Pecos in the south end of the city near the airport. Yvette Renee Eddy, who put frames on posters and pictures, had remembered that one of her customers was Margaret Rudin.

Margaret came to the store on Tuesday, January 24.— the day after she was visited by Ramos and Vaccaro to be informed of the discovery of her husband's remains. The craft store worker recalled Margaret as "well-dressed, well-groomed" when she came into the store, telling Yvette that she had three pictures that needed work. Yvette took them and recorded Margaret's name and phone number.

Yvette could only remember what two of the three items were. One was a cheap poster, badly damaged. The other was a glamour photograph of Margaret in a gold frame—a picture that sounded exactly like the one that Vaccaro had seen in the guest room, and which Augustine Lovato had seen with splatters on it. It was the same picture that Vaccaro couldn't find during the search of the house. Yvette said she noticed that the portrait was damaged. There was a mark, a vibrant yellow in color, about two to three inches long, and about a half-inch wide, in the lower right-hand corner of the photograph.

She said that she asked Margaret: "Do you want this repaired?"

"No, I just want to have glass on it so it doesn't get further damaged," Margaret was said to have replied.

Margaret explained that the maid had damaged the picture while trying to clean it. But to Yvette it didn't look anything like a cleaning mark, no swipe marks or other signs she had seen in other damaged pictures. The mark instead looked like someone had scratched the portrait with a razor blade or knife—as if trying to scrape off the top layer from the photograph.

Margaret would never get that picture back. After talking to Yvette, Detective Ramos drove to Michaels to pick up the portrait.

Margaret's whereabouts didn't remain unknown for long. The taps on her home and cell phones ended up yielding nothing of evidentiary value for investigators, who would discover that Margaret made calls from pay phones, but it did tip them off that Margaret had returned to Las Vegas after about two weeks away. Yehuda picked her up at Los Angeles International Airport and drove her back to Vegas, where she was immediately confronted by her sister, Dona, who asked her point-blank who killed Ron.

"The mob did it," Margaret said.

Dona was incredulous.

"Tell me," she said to her older sister, "who got into your high security house, surrounded by dogs, shot and killed Ron in the bedroom, removed him, cleaned up the room so you didn't notice anything amiss, drove him 40 miles into the desert, decapitated and burned him, and brought his car back to town? Margaret, does that sound like the mob to you? Does that sound like random street crime? Does that sound like burglary?"

Margaret didn't say anything.

"It doesn't sound like it to me," Dona said. "And if it

doesn't sound like it to me, it doesn't sound like it to police."

For as long as she could, Dona tried to give Margaret the benefit of sisterly doubt. "Well, I still had absolutely no proof," she would later recall. "I only knew what I thought. I was confused by a great deal of the events. It may sound more clear-cut talking about them now, but at this particular time Ron was missing. I wasn't sure. I was really uncomfortable with what I was seeing and hearing, but I wasn't sure what happened and in what time frame."

But by February, she didn't like what was going on. It seemed that everyone else in her family was taking Margaret's side—and pressuring Dona to go along. "I was the only one in my family that was showing—that was wanting to have any real conversation about it, that was showing any curiosity, that was forming any opinions," she said. "I felt like I was in this alone. No one else seemed to have the same concerns that I did, and I just felt a little overwhelmed by it all and wasn't sure what to do and so I didn't know what to do."

Until this point, Dona had remained silent about her concerns, even as the missing persons detective was questioning her in the antique store. Margaret had already instructed Dona on what to tell police if they should come by her home, which they in fact did. Detectives Vaccaro and Ramos had shown up at her second-floor apartment and left their business cards. She didn't talk to them. But if she ever did, she was to say that Margaret and Ron were getting along better than ever, that Ron had just spent $30,000 to open Margaret's antique shop, and that Ron was no longer having an affair. Dona knew that this wasn't all true. It was time for her to decide whether to continue to go along with Margaret, or break from the family. It would be one of the hardest decisions she ever made.

They met over coffee at the Skyline Restaurant and Casino on Boulder Highway near Dona's home in the Las

Vegas suburb of Henderson. Detective Jimmy Vaccaro
didn't take a formal written statement or use a tape recorder. He was trying to be careful with this one. Dona
had the potential to be the most important witness in the
case since Augustine Lovato—and the only witness in
Margaret's inner circle. Dona had been seen working with
Margaret in the antique store and was seen with her when
the family went restaurant-hopping the night Margaret
went to Los Angeles. She very well could have been privy
to many private conversations about Ron and the circumstances of his murder.

Normally, detectives only tell witnesses the most basic
information about an investigation, so as not to plant ideas
in their minds or taint their testimony at the time of trial.
But with Dona, Ramos and Vaccaro had decided they
would divulge a little more information than usual. They
felt that they had to make a case that Dona's sister could
very well be a murderer. If Dona were sufficiently convinced, they believed, then her conscience would force
her to turn on her own sister.

So at the meeting in the coffee shop, and in subsequent
phone calls, Vaccaro told Dona some information that at
the time only police knew: about the blood in the bedroom, about the blood in the vacuum cleaner bag, about
the blood on the handkerchief that would be used for comparisons. For detectives, the tactic paid off.

On March 17, Dona gave a tape-recorded statement at
the homicide offices in the City Hall building downtown.
She told them of Margaret's complaints about Ron, how
she had once considered getting a divorce but decided to
wait because of his bad health. Margaret had told her sister that she would just wait until Ron died.

Dona told them about the tense moments when Ron
came into the antique store the weekend before he disappeared. She told them how Margaret kept saying, "I
don't want to talk about it," when asked about Ron's disappearance. She told them of going into Ron's office on
Christmas Day and retrieving the papers and the police

report about the confrontation at Peggy's funeral.

She told them what little she knew about Yehuda, that Margaret had spoken fondly of him, that he made her feel pretty. She told them about the trunk that had been in the antique store on the grand opening weekend, but then disappeared—right around the time that Ron disappeared.

She also said she thought that Margaret might have been listening in on her husband's conversations in the office, but she didn't initially tell police all she knew about the bugs that had been purchased at the Spy Factory. That would come out over the next few weeks.

Then Dona disclosed what could have been the most damaging information of all. She told the detectives about a night in late January 1995—she guessed it was Saturday, January 21—when she drove over to the house of her sister Barbara to meet her to go out to eat. At Barbara's house, Dona recognized the car that was being driven by the fiancée of her nephew Scott Stavron. Scott and his fiancée had recently moved into Margaret's guest house, but they were over at his mother Barbara's house this evening. Atop the car sat a large roll of what looked to Dona like carpeting. It was light in color. Dona couldn't tell if that was the shag or the underside. It was rolled up tightly.

The four of them went out to eat in another car. When they returned to Barbara's house, the roll of carpeting was gone.

Dona saw some carpeting again at her sister's house. She thought it was some time that week. There were strips of carpeting and padding in Barbara's garage. It was beige, the same color as the carpeting that had been in the master bedroom of Ron and Margaret's house.

There seemed to be something on it.

Dona took a look. She put a strip across the hood of Barbara's car. There were three or four small stains on the carpet, one big stain on the padding.

"I thought it was a strange color," Dona recalled. "I said at the time I don't know if it was spaghetti sauce or blood or wine. It was a reddish-brown purplish color."

It looked like somebody had been scrubbing at the stains.

"I leaned over and smelled it," Dona said. "[It] smelled really, really strong of cleaning solution."

After that day, she never saw the carpeting again. She didn't know what had happened to it.

20

COURT INACTION

The interview with Dona was a major development in the investigation. It helped link Margaret to the trunk found at Nelson's Landing, and it corroborated the testimony from Augustine Lovato about the apparent blood in the carpeting. It also offered damaging details about Margaret's seemingly suspicious activities after Ron's disappearance. By March of 1995, two months after Ron Rudin's remains were found, detectives Ramos and Vaccaro felt they had a reasonably good case against the widow Margaret Rudin. She'd had the motive and opportunity to kill her husband and appeared to have engaged in a cover-up, hiring a man to clean up the scene of the crime, then dodging police. Her statements and activities seemed to the detectives to be those of a woman suffering no grief over her husband's death; on the contrary, all she seemed to care about was finishing the plan: getting at his multimillion-dollar fortune.

But the case had some holes. It was highly circumstantial. Nobody had seen Margaret commit the crime. Nobody had heard her admit to committing the crime. The only physical evidence—the apparent blood spots in the bedroom—was still undergoing DNA testing. There was no murder weapon. What's more, key people in the case—Scott Stavrou and his mother, Barbara LePome—weren't talking to authorities. Yehuda Sharon was giving some information, but none of it under oath and none of it incriminating, for him or Margaret.

It wouldn't take much of a criminal defense attorney to raise doubts about that case in court. So in March of 1995, Margaret Rudin wasn't arrested and wasn't hauled into court to face charges in the murder of her husband. The detectives and the officials in the DA's office reasoned that there was no hurry, that time was on their side. The DNA tests would be coming back, and police were certain—correctly as it turned out—that much of the blood in the bedroom would be genetically consistent with the blood on the handkerchief. In the meantime, authorities thought that maybe they could squeeze Yehuda or Scott, maybe put some more pressure on Margaret. Maybe the wire tap would turn up something.

In early March, the district attorney's office expanded the investigation by presenting a case before a grand jury. Prosecutors would later acknowledge that they didn't intend to get an indictment, but wanted to use the subpoena powers of the grand jury to compel testimony from witnesses who wouldn't talk to police, namely Stavrou, his mother Barbara and Yehuda. The grand jury probe would also put more pressure on Margaret; maybe she would make a mistake.

Grand jury proceedings are supposed to be secret, but this one was as discreet as the Circus Circus marquee after dark. Even before it began, a story appeared in the *Review-Journal* on March 2, in which "two law enforcement sources" divulged that Margaret herself would be called to testify in a "pending Clark County grand jury probe." After the earlier press leaks, this story effectively announced to the city that Margaret was under the official spotlight. It noted that she had already been fingerprinted—to exclude her as a suspect if necessary—and that a small amount of blood was found in the master bedroom of her home. By now, Margaret had hired yet another attorney, noted criminal defense lawyer Dominic Gentile, after parting ways with John Momot. Gentile told the paper he didn't know anything about a grand jury probe but did know that police were trying to railroad his client. "We are more than willing to cooperate with their investigation but we are not going to be giving any statements," he told the press. "It seems to me she would be foolish to talk to the police when they have already made up their minds that she has done something."

While the grand jury probe proceeded, Margaret was also fighting the trustees of Ron's estate for money. Harold Boscutti and Sharron Cooper, saying they were acting under lawyers' advice, wouldn't give Margaret anything. They had taken away her Lincoln, which was actually leased in the trust's name, and had kicked her out of the house on Alpine. She was living in motels and staying with friends. Scraping for money, she sold off antiques and jewelry to pay for lawyers, her private investigator and her basic necessities. For a time, she would work at the front desk of a lodge on Mount Charleston.

The day after Gentile spoke to reporters about the grand jury probe, Margaret filed papers asking that trustees Cooper and Boscutti be removed because of their alleged knowledge of fraudulent real estate deals by Ron. Claming that the trustees—who also stood to inherit a share of Ron's estate—had conspired to take away Margaret's community property, the papers called for placing the estate in the hands of an impartial third party to sort things out.

At the same time, the grand jury began hearing testimony once a week. Police would also release to the media details of the removal of bedroom carpeting stained with what resembled blood. They told reporters that they had talked to the worker who actually removed the carpeting. But it wasn't just the authorities waging a PR campaign. Local TV and newspaper reporters began receiving an anonymous, four-page letter suggesting that Margaret was innocent. Police looked at the letter and speculated that Margaret herself had written it.

Behind the closed doors of the grand jury room, prosecutors were hitting roadblocks. Yehuda refused to testify, citing his Fifth Amendment rights against self-incrimination, even though he had already given information to police and would also speak to lawyers in the civil case. According to sources in the secret session, Scott Stavrou and Barbara LePome testified, but they didn't reveal much. The most that came out of them was Barbara confirming some of the events that Dona had spoken of, including the meeting at Barbara's house the night of the search warrant, but she said little more.

Prosecutors didn't panic. Their decision to wait did pay one more dividend: They had just obtained other pieces of evidence against Margaret that could subject her to more than just murder charges.

Sharon Melton is the one who found them. By March of 1995 she was no longer Ron's bookkeeper, *per se.* She was working for the trustees, Boscutti and Cooper, who were also now working full-time for the Ronald Rudin Trust, sorting out Ron's finances and fending off the challenge from Margaret. The trustees were paying themselves $75 an hour out of the trust. Sharon continued to work her usual three days a week in Ron's offices. By now, the locks had been changed. The only people with keys to the office were her and the two trustees.

In March 1995, the offices were painted. The painters, she had noticed, had left a little electrical-looking thing on one of the filing cabinets in her office. It appeared to be one of those adaptors that allow you to expand one outlet into three. "Actually, I didn't pay any attention to it," she would recall. "I kept moving it from one filing cabinet to another. It was in my way. It just looked like an extension, if you wanted to put more plugs into a wall."

Then one day she spoke to Harold Boscutti, who had been informed by police that Margaret may have been bugging the office. A private detective working for the trust showed Sharon a picture of what a bug would look like. "I know where that is," she told the PI. "I can show you."

The private detective, retired Metro police investigator Charles A. Leveque, was directed by Sharon to a filing cabinet. Inside, there was a cardboard box that contained a rectangular plastic object with electrical plugs.

"Don't touch it," he told Sharon.

It was too late. "I've been moving this thing for

weeks," she said. "My fingerprints are all over it."

Leveque carefully placed it into an envelope. He took it to his office and tested it. It was not only an electrical adaptor. It was an electronic listening device that could send a signal to a receiver. Police used very similar devices.

He turned it over to Detective Vaccaro.

After finding this first bug, Sharon Melton went through the office again looking for more. A few days later, in early April, she found the second one in a box of other items that had been removed from Ron's office.

By mid-May 1995, five months after Ron's disappearance, the grand jury investigation of Margaret had been put on hold while the district attorney's office awaited the outcome of DNA testing. But the propaganda war continued, with authorities now exerting pressure on Yehuda. Chief Deputy District Attorney Charles Thompson told reporters that he believed charges would be brought against one or more people. He didn't say who these other people were, explaining that he was bound by law not to discuss grand jury proceedings. "I can tell you there will be charges brought. One person committed the murder, but more than one person was involved in the disposal of the victim's body," said Thompson. But "police sources" told the *Review-Journal* that Margaret and her friend—as the paper called Yehuda—were the "target of the probe from the beginning."

Behind the scenes, prosecutors were frustrated because they couldn't get Yehuda to testify before the grand jury. They thought they knew why he was taking the Fifth. Although his alibi was solid for the night of the murder, police believed that Yehuda had helped Margaret dispose of the body, hauling the antique trunk out to Nelson's Landing in the Astro van that he had rented. The mileage on the van was more than sufficient to drive out to Nelson's Landing, dump the trunk, and come back to Las Vegas. Police believed that Yehuda was lying about the business with the holy oil bottles and the thwarted trip to Southern California, and not lying very well. The question was how to get Yehuda to tell what authorities believed was the truth. No other tactics had worked so far, not the threats and cajoling, not the statements to the media about him being a target.

So the DA's office came up with a plan. On October 26, 1995, Yehuda was dragged before Judge Don Chairez for a special proceeding that prosecutors hoped would result in Yehuda turning on Margaret.

"Your Honor," prosecutor Dan Bowman told the judge, "for the last few months the Clark County Grand Jury has been conducting hearings . . . into the cause and manner of death of Ron Rudin. Mr. Sharon, who is present here today, has appeared before the Clark County Grand Jury in the past, and in the past he has refused to testify, taking his Fifth Amendment privilege."

Bowman explained that Yehuda had been subpoenaed to appear that morning before the grand jury, and that Charles Thompson of the DA's office drafted an order of immunity for Yehuda, protecting him from being prosecuted as a result of anything he said. But he still refused to testify. Bowman said he wanted to ask Yehuda a few questions "and see if he has changed his mind and will testify."

If not, Bowman said he would ask the judge "to order him to testify."

The judge asked Sharon: "Mr. Sharon, first off, do you understand English?"

"I do," said Yehuda.

"How long have you lived in this country?"

"Fifteen years."

The judge read him the proposed Order of Immunity:

"It is hereby ordered that Yehuda Garach Sharon, is granted immunity in any future investigation relative to any testimony given before the Clark County Grand Jury or future trial in any court of record and is re-

Ron and Margaret Rudin in happier times. COURTESY DORIS COWMAN

Ron Rudin at
his high school
graduation in 1948.
COURTESY DORIS
COWMAN

Ron (*left*) during
the Korean War.
COURTESY DORIS
COWMAN

Ron and his beloved mother, Stella, in 1976.
COURTESY DORIS COWMAN

Ron and Peggy Rudin. Peggy committed suicide in the same room where Ron would be killed years later.
COURTESY DORIS COWMAN

The Las Vegas strip mall at 5110 West Charleston where Ron operated his real estate business. The sign still bears his company's logo.
MICHAEL FLEEMAN

The bunker-like home where Las Vegas real estate baron Ron Rudin lived—and died. MICHAEL FLEEMAN

Ron's car turned up in a parking lot behind the Crazy Horse Too Gentlemen's Club shortly after his disappearance.
MICHAEL FLEEMAN

The rugged landscape surrounding Nelson's Landing—where fishermen found Ron's charred remains.
MICHAEL FLEEMAN

Pyramid Island, in Lake Meade, where a scuba diver made a startling discovery: the gun that killed Ron Rudin.
MICHAEL FLEEMAN

Almost three years after skipping Las Vegas, Margaret Rudin turned up in Revere, Massachusetts, where she lived on the second floor of this apartment building. JEFF SCHEID, *LAS VEGAS REVIEW-JOURNAL*

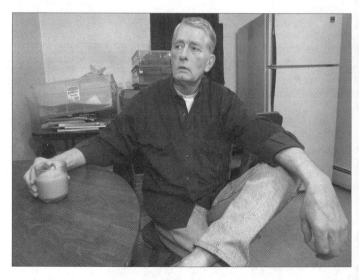

Joseph Lundergan, the disabled former firefighter with whom Margaret was sharing an apartment at the time of her arrest.
JEFF SCHEID, *LAS VEGAS REVIEW-JOURNAL*

Clark County Courthouse in Las Vegas, Nevada— where Margaret Rudin would finally face justice.
MICHAEL FLEEMAN

Prosecutor Chris Owens preparing for the trial.
JEFF SCHEID, *LAS VEGAS REVIEW-JOURNAL*

Phil Ramos, one of the two lead detectives on the Ron Rudin murder case, during Margaret's trial.
JEFF SCHEID, *LAS VEGAS REVIEW-JOURNAL*

Margaret Rudin's defense team. *Left to right:* Michael Amador, Margaret, John Momot, Thomas Pitaro.
JEFF SCHEID, *LAS VEGAS REVIEW-JOURNAL*

During the trial, the defense presented a recreation of the bedroom where Ron Rudin died. Here, defense attorney Tom Pitaro hangs the infamous glamour shot of Margaret Rudin while she and Private Investigator Michael Wysocki look on.
JEFF SCHEID, *LAS VEGAS REVIEW-JOURNAL*

Defeated defense attorney Michael Amador with a female acquaintance moments after Margaret was found guilty of murdering her husband, Ron Rudin.
JEFF SCHEID, *LAS VEGAS REVIEW-JOURNAL*

leased for all future liability to be prosecuted or punished on account of any testimony or other evidence the said witness may be required to produce in regards to the circumstances surrounding the investigation pending before the Clark County Grand Jury."

Bowman told the judge about the civil proceeding in which Margaret was attempting to get money from the trust, and that "Mr. Sharon has testified without taking the Fifth Amendment" in a deposition in that civil trial.

Bowman then spelled out what authorities thought Yehuda's role was in the Rudin case.

"In short, Your Honor, we know Mr. Sharon did not kill Ron Rudin," said Bowman. "We also believe very strongly that he knows a great deal about the disposal of the body and probably participated in that disposal. We need to ask him those questions."

Bowman said that as long as Yehuda "testifies truthfully, he will not be prosecuted for anything he testifies to," but if he lied, "I can tell him right now on the record I intend to charge him with perjury."

Yehuda didn't like the deal. He said he worried that even if he had immunity from criminal prosecution, anything he said could haunt him in the upcoming civil trial. He said he believed that prosecutors were in cahoots with the civil attorneys for the Rudin trust.

"They go ahead and give question to the civil lawyer. They asked me criminal questions from the civil lawsuit, so it's basically all tied together, the way I see it," he said.

The judge asked if Yehuda was a party to the civil lawsuit.

"No, he is not a target of these proceedings. He is not a part of any civil proceeding that I'm aware," said Thompson.

"I disagree with it," said Yehuda. "In the newspaper April first, they put my name as the suspect in the murder. No matter how much they say in the newspaper it was

by—I forget the name—published twice that I'm a suspect in the murder."

"Your Honor," Bowman said, "the order of immunity
takes care of that."

"That's what this does," the judge told Yehuda. "It
makes sure you're not a suspect. Even if they are making
an agreement, they did not prosecute you with anything
related to the murder."

"Meanwhile, the civil courts will sue me," said Yehuda. "I'll lose my job, lose my house."

Bowman ran out of patience. "Your Honor, at this
point if it appears that he understands that Order of Immunity, I would ask that this court order him to answer
questions before the Clark County Grand Jury regarding
Ron Rudin's death today."

The judge told Yehuda that "the long and the short of
it" was that the Fifth Amendment applied to the right
against self-incrimination. "Since the state has offered you
this order of immunity, you no longer have a legal right
to be claiming the Fifth Amendment," he said.

"I have no choice," the judge said, "but to order you
to testify in front of the grand jury and not allow you to
claim the Fifth Amendment right against self-
incrimination."

With that, prosecutors had hoped that they had essentially forced Yehuda to testify by imposing immunity
upon him. It was a tricky move.

And it backfired.

Yehuda went before the grand jury and told the panel
essentially what he had been telling police and the civil
lawyers: that he had had nothing to do with the murder,
that he knew nothing about Margaret having any role in
the murder, that he hadn't transported any bodies anywhere. The van was rented for the purposes of his holy
oil business. And that was it. Prosecutors gave Yehuda a
get-out-of-jail-free card and got nothing in return. The detectives, who had tried to talk prosecutors out of the deal,

were frustrated. They thought they still could have built a case against Yehuda.

In the final analysis, the District Attorney's Office violated the Golden Rules of dealing with possible accomplices: never give immunity unless you know what you're getting in return. The deal, struck just a block away from the Fremont Street casinos, was a sucker bet, and everybody but the DA's office seemed to know it. With Yehuda now useless and untouchable, authorities looked to the civil case between Margaret and the trustees for a break. If she or Yehuda testified, maybe they would say something that could be used against them at a criminal trial.

21

MARGARET FIGHTS BACK

By late 1995, nearly a year after Ron's remains were found, Margaret was fighting for millions of his dollars. The fact that she was the top suspect in her husband's murder—and the target of a grand jury probe—didn't slow her down. Not even her ongoing problems with attorneys could stop her. Margaret was going through lawyers the way she had gone through husbands. At times she either didn't have a lawyer or not enough lawyers for the complicated job at hand, single-handedly taking on the trustees and their high-powered legal team, led by attorney Mark Solomon, a well-connected Las Vegas civil lawyer. With the newly immune Yehuda helping her, she would collect and read through thousands of pages of documents dealing with Ron's Byzantine business dealings. She even questioned witnesses in deposition, making for the odd spectacle of Margaret both asking questions and defending herself at the same time.

In December of 1995, Margaret, without the aid of a lawyer, questioned Ron's financial attorney, Pat Brown, in a pre-trial deposition. As Margaret listened, Brown spoke about a memorandum Brown had written about how Ron described Margaret as suffering a "dual personality" disorder that made her a "lovely wife" one moment, then a "vicious and violent individual" the next.

"OK, Pat, let's go backwards," Margaret then said. "This is the first time I have seen this, and, of course, it's going to be upsetting for a little bit." Margaret became overwhelmed by emotion. "So you guys are going to have to bear with me."

"Do you want to wait a minute and take some time?" asked trust attorney Earl Monsey, working with Solomon.

"Do you want to take a break?" asked Solomon.

"No," Margaret said. "I'll be OK now. I'm sorry. Maybe you shouldn't try to represent yourself."

She then began with a rambling question.

"The time—because we have the papers—I know they were November 1993 that you talked with him about that," she said. "And at the same time that he was saying he'd been to a physician in Utah—this was a psychic healer. And at the same time that he said to you that he believed he was being poisoned by me, he also increased the share of my percentage of the estate at that same time, because you made a new amendment at that time stating my share went from 40 percent to 60 percent?"

"Yes," said Brown.

"At the very same time," Margaret continued—making, in an awkward way, a very good point: If Ron was so concerned about Margaret wanting to kill him, why did he increase her share of his inheritance from 40 to 60 percent?—"it seems a little contradictory that he would do both at the same time. Can I go into more of why he said to you, or what he said to you—I guess I can't say why—he believed he was being poisoned?"

"It was just a comment that he had made, and it was, he was going for another physician in Arizona, as I recall. In fact he was leaving the day that he stopped in to execute the documents."

"Going to Arizona?"

"That's my understanding."

"Did he say it was the Mayo Clinic?"

"I don't recall that."

"OK, he did state to you that we were in counseling at that time?"

"He indicated that he thought the counseling was working, as I believe—is what I believe this—I can recall of the conversation."

Margaret fumbled around looking for a document, finally giving up. She asked about Ron decreasing trustee Sharron Cooper's share of the trust, then asked about Ron's demeanor when he met with Brown in March 1991.

"And did he seem distraught at the time or like, like he was drinking?"

"I don't, I don't believe it was a drinking type of discussion," Brown said. "I know that it was a concerned conversation. But I wouldn't say an illogical discussion."

"Well, it was illogical," Margaret replied, "because we have never been under counseling, and I have never been diagnosed with having any kind of personality disorder. And that's one of the things that I wanted to go into with you is we've never had counseling. Did he say with who? Where? How long?"

"He didn't."

"And he said that at one point she can be a lovely wife, but her schizophrenic personality turns into a vicious and violent individual. Did he say what vicious acts I was supposed to have ever done?"

"He did indicate, and I believe I have it in that memorandum, about a gunshot. That, about two months prior to that, that he, that you had attempted to take his life with a gun. It was in that second paragraph."

Margaret noted that she had been in a serious car accident around that time, implying that she couldn't have fired a gun. Margaret also pressed Brown on the limited information that she had, that Ron was known to ramble on and on and would have told her a lot more about the gun incident and other matters.

"I have been in the office when you have had some conversations with him where you told him all about taking Tai-Chi and your exercises, and him talking all about exercises that he does and health foods that he does and vitamins that he takes," Margaret said. "So you know I have overheard some of the conversations that he's had with you. And that's why I know he elaborates a great deal when he is emotional."

At this point, Solomon finally objected on the grounds that Margaret was arguing with the witness.

"You're right," Margaret said. "I apologize."

And on it went, with Margaret interrogating Brown,

questions that were more statements than questions, facing objections, but always pressing on.

A few days later, Margaret questioned her sister, Dona. By now, Dona was back in Illinois, wanting to have nothing to do with Las Vegas or the mess involving Margaret. Dona had made her statement to police, and did show up for the grand jury proceedings, but was not called as a witness. The deposition was conducted over the phone, with Margaret and the trust attorneys in Las Vegas, and Dona and her attorney in Illinois. Dona refused to answer all but the most innocuous of questions from both sides, citing her Fifth Amendment rights against self-incrimination. This made Margaret furious, although Dona insisted that it was actually in Margaret's best interest if Dona kept what she knew to herself.

Either way, the deposition again featured Margaret acting as her own attorney. She fired off questions to her sister: "Didn't I tell you . . . that the trustees refused to give me money to live on?", "Didn't I tell you that my daughter, my friend and I were being stalked and followed by someone?", "Didn't I tell you that the police seized my house and threw me out while I was attending Ron Rudin's funeral?"

To each question, Dona would refuse to answer on Fifth Amendment grounds.

Still, none of these pre-trial obstacles kept Margaret from seeking what she felt was rightfully hers: 60 percent of Ron's estate. By the time the trial was scheduled to begin in January, she had yet another new lawyer, this one Charles Kelly, a former federal prosecutor and high-profile Las Vegas criminal attorney, whose full-page ad in the Yellow Pages says, "Do not plead guilty until you talk to me."

As lawyers filed into the courtroom for the non-jury trial before District Judge Jack Lehman, police and prosecutors would be watching very closely for more leads and evidence that could be used against Margaret. Authorities fully expected that Margaret would take the witness stand and testify in her own defense, setting herself up for troubles later on. Margaret's new lawyer worried about that very thing. Kelly asked the judge to postpone the trial until the criminal probe was completed. Lehman decided not to. "Obviously, this investigation could go on for a long time," the judge said.

The trial began on January 16, 1996. To keep Margaret from obtaining her 60 percent share of Ron's estate, the trustees had to prove that she'd killed him. Ron had spelled out in his directive that if any of his heirs were shown to have caused his violent death, then they were to get nothing. The trustees would have a theoretically easier time of it than prosecutors because the burden of proof was lighter in a civil trial than a criminal one. With only money at stake, the trustees would have proven their case by a preponderance of evidence—the "more likely than not" burden—rather than the proof beyond a reasonable doubt standard in criminal court.

Mark Solomon's opening statement for the trustees resembled that of an opening statement by a prosecutor in a murder trial: "Margaret was the only person who had the motive, the means and the opportunity to cause Ron's death."

News accounts at the time said that Margaret showed no emotion while Solomon laid out the evidence against her, starting with the details of a marriage that "to say the least was rocky from the start to the end." Solomon said it was so bad that a year after the 1987 wedding, Margaret had fired a gun at Ron a reference to the incident Margaret had documented in her diary, when she confronted Ron over his sex chat on the phone with another woman. Solomon contended that the couple's marriage was on the verge of collapsing in December 1994 and that after Ron had gone to sleep on the night of December 18 Margaret fired four or five bullets into his head.

"He didn't trust Margaret," the attorney said. "In the last few months of his life, Ron believed that Margaret was trying to kill him . . . poison him." Solomon said he would prove that the murder was the result of a plot between Margaret and a man she was said to be having an affair with, Yehuda Sharon. Solomon said that Yehuda rented a van to haul the body—apparently decapitated to fit into an antique trunk—to the remote site where it was dumped. He also told how the carpeting and bed were removed and discarded in the days after Ron disappeared.

When it was time for Margaret's side to speak, Kelly countered the prosecution-like statements of the trustee attorney with a criminal defense–like opening statement. Kelly portrayed the trustees' evidence against Margaret as a weak circumstantial case "built upon innuendo and misinformation."

"I can see why the grand jury hasn't indicted this woman, because there isn't any evidence," he said. Looking at what he said was the feeble collection of evidence, he asked, "Is that all there is for a murder case?"

Kelly acknowledged that money could have been a motive for murder, but not just for Margaret. He noted that the trustees "stand to take what Margaret loses" and that they were "building a case . . . to deprive Ron Rudin of what he wanted—that Margaret Rudin have 60 percent of what he owned."

Kelly said that Ron "knew he had enemies," and was so concerned he wore a bullet-proof vest, tinted his car windows and put reinforced glass in his office. Margaret, by contrast, was a concerned wife who checked her voice mail over 300 times between Ron's disappearance and the day his body was found, always hoping he would he would call. If the marriage had been as bad as the trustees said, then Ron would have ended it. Instead, he changed the trust three times to increase Margaret's share of the inheritance.

As for the physical evidence, Kelly said the blood found in the bedroom didn't necessarily mean Ron was murdered there, even if it was determined to be Ron's blood. Ron, the lawyer said, frequently suffered nosebleeds in the dry desert air, and it wouldn't be unusual to find drops in Ron's home of 30 years.

Finally, Kelly made the promise that prosecutors were hoping to hear. He said that Margaret had nothing to hide and that she would testify under oath.

The trial was scheduled to last about two weeks. One of the earliest witnesses was also one of the most important. Sue Lyles described Ron as a "gentleman," saying he was a "caring, sensitive man. I valued his friendship." She told the judge about the anonymous letters to her children and how an upset Ron concluded that the letter had come from Margaret. "He said that he had forgiven Margaret over and over again and that you can only forgive so many times," she said. Sue explained that Margaret believed that Ron and Sue were having an affair and apparently sent the letters to break them up. The judge wouldn't let Margaret's lawyers ask Sue about the details of her relationship with Ron. In a newspaper account, Sue was described as Ron's "friend and former employee."

But behind the scenes, Sue's secret would be out. After she testified, she told her husband about her affair with Ron. "I knew it was going to be in the newspaper because everything is in the newspaper," she said. "And I showed him the letter."

The next year, they would be divorced.

The civil trial moved swiftly. Vaccaro testified that even though Margaret had not been arrested or charged, the evidence showed she had the "availability, motive and the ability" to murder her husband. He considered her to be the "prime suspect." "Everything comes back to Margaret Rudin," he said. "I still believe she was responsible for his death." Vaccaro described the interview with Augustine Lovato about the apparent blood in the bedroom. He testified about the glamour picture that once had spots on it; by the time it was picked up from Michaels, it was clean. He spoke of the search of the house that turned up the blood spots on the walls and ceiling—blood that a

DNA expert would testify had the same genetic makeup of the blood found on one of Ron's handkerchiefs.

Vaccaro did acknowledge that another violent death occurred in that same room. He gave some of the details of Peggy Rudin's suicide. He also testified about Peggy's relative threatening Ron at Peggy's funeral. Vaccaro acknowledged that police never attempted to find that relative.

Vaccaro's partner Ramos gave more of the details of the investigation, telling the judge about Yehuda renting a van the day after the murder was believed to have been committed, then returning it with 348 miles on it. Yehuda's name had surfaced several times during the trial, and at one point Margaret's attorney revealed that Yehuda had been granted immunity from prosecution—and it still didn't bolster the criminal case against Margaret. "In October of '95 they give him the ultimate truth serum, and what did it reveal? Nothing," Kelly said.

In fact, the civil trial judge was about to see for himself the results of the immunity agreement, when the trial took a dramatic turn. After Vaccaro's testimony that Monday, attorneys from both sides entered into settlement negotiations. The talks went into the early morning hours of Tuesday, the day that Yehuda was scheduled to testify. Then, at 4:30 p.m. that day, an agreement was reached.

On January 23, 1996, one year and two days after Ron's remains were found, the civil case was over.

Publicly, neither side would discuss the details of the plan. "It is what the trustees agreed to do," said Solomon, even though he insisted he was winning the case. "I really can't say more than that." But Margaret's attorney had more to say. "We are extremely pleased with the results," Kelly said. "We feel it is fair to all parties, and we hope that now, once and for all, Margaret Rudin can finally have her life back and that we can all go forward."

Privately, the deal they struck called for the trust to keep the bulk of Ron's estate, including the house on Alpine Place and, more important, the 200 acres of Lee

Canyon property that was worth as much as $8 million. When the land was finally sold, the trustees got hefty sums, about $1 million each. Margaret was given $600,000, far less than the $5 million to $8 million she thought she deserved, but certainly a large sum, considering that authorities believed she got it by killing her husband.

The abrupt agreement caught prosecutors and the detectives in the case by surprise, and it was a major blow to their strategy to squeeze Margaret over time. They had been working closely with the trust attorneys and investigators and couldn't believe that the trust was going to let Margaret off the hook before she or Yehuda were put on the stand. Authorities had to go after Margaret now without the help of the trust. Ron's friends and co-workers were astonished that the trustees weren't upholding his wishes that they use extraordinary means to solve his murder. "I felt they betrayed him," Sharon Melton would say. "They didn't do what he asked them to do."

Officials tried to put the best public face on things. The day after the settlement was announced, a "source close to the investigation" was quoted in the *Review-Journal* as saying that Margaret wasn't in the clear yet. A new grand jury could be investigating the murder as early as that March, the source said.

That timetable proved to be overly optimistic. A grand jury would in fact begin hearing evidence, though it would happen much later. And by the time the panel did start considering charges against Margaret, the case would be bolstered by the discovery of a key piece of evidence. But would it be too little too late?

22

LAKE MEAD

Just to the south of the main marina of Lake Mead, 25 miles southeast of Las Vegas, is a parking area and beach designated for scuba divers. The desert offers at least a dozen scuba diving schools and stores. Among those teaching diving in 1996 was Peter Price, a muscular, sometime security guard with a black belt in karate. The proprietor of Lake Mead Diving and Instruction, Price had been teaching diving since 1993, but had been exploring Lake Mead since 1980, making more than 600 dives. A favorite spot was the area just off of little Pyramid Island, about a mile offshore but reachable by car over a causeway. In the summer, when algae blooms cloud the rest of the lake, the waters remain relatively clear off the island.

At about 6 p.m. on a warm Sunday night in July of 1996, Peter Price parked his Grand Torino at a spot where the causeway meets the island. He was there with a friend and student, Bill Schaeffer. They unloaded their scuba gear, including the tanks they had rented in nearby Boulder City, and suited up for a half-hour dive around the island. They got into the water and began snorkeling at first, working their way around the southern end of the island toward the eastern edge, where three water pipes ran from the island down the underwater slope, 120 feet to the lake bottom.

By the time they got to the eastern side of the island, Price and Schaeffer had started using their scuba tanks. In the shallow waters off the island, home to striped bass and snapping turtles, the water visibility was about 20 feet, very good for the summer. The two divers followed the island slope to a spot about 15 feet offshore and down about 15 feet, then paused for a safety stop, allowing their bodies to adjust to the use of compressed air.

It was there, resting on the rocky bottom, that Price saw the object. It was wrapped in plastic and held together by rubber bands. He picked it up. It was L-shaped and contained something heavy and solid. Divers generally remove any foreign objects from the lake, particularly plastic, because it can harm the fish if they eat it. Price had a good idea of what was in this bag.

The divers swam back around the island, then got out of the water and walked to Price's car, where he unwrapped the package, removing the rotting and brittle rubber bands. The package turned out to be a series of supermarket-type plastic bags, more than a dozen of them, held with dozens of rubber bands. When Price got to the contents of the package, he discovered that his suspicions were correct.

Price knew a few things about handguns. He had worked as an armed security guard in casinos and was trained to handle firearms. He recognized this one as a Ruger .22-caliber. It was corroded. Some of the blue finish was peeling off. Its mechanisms seemed to be rusted in place. Still, it was remarkably well preserved for a weapon that had been sitting 15 feet under the surface of Lake Mead.

Price figured there were a number of reasons somebody might want to toss a gun into the lake, and most of them spelled trouble. On his cellular telephone, he called for a park ranger, and a dispatcher alerted National Park Ranger James Warren Sanborn, who drove his government-issued Chevy Suburban to the parking area on Pyramid Island. It was about 7 p.m., still light in the long summer day. He had never met Price before but recognized his name. Price had a government business permit to teach diving in the lake, and the ranger assumed that's where he'd heard of him.

Price handed the ranger the bundle of plastic bags with the heavy object inside. The ranger pulled away the bags and saw the gun. Using a rag from the Suburban,

Sanborn picked up the weapon. It had a long barrel, about 11 inches—longer than what one would expect on a handgun. Although it was corroded, it was in good enough condition for Sanborn to see its serial number : 13-53941. The ranger photographed the gun, then wrapped it up in the rag and brought it to the ranger station's evidence locker for drying.

A day or two later, he gave the gun to Malcolm Demunbrun, a criminal investigator for the National Park Service who had worked at Lake Mead for nearly 20 years. It was still wrapped in the rag and hadn't yet completely dried. Demunbrun ran the serial number through the NCIC and didn't get a hit on it as being stolen. Still thinking it may have been used in a crime, most likely one in Las Vegas, he called an old friend, Sgt. Bill Keeton of the Metro homicide unit.

The gun that had been found on July 21 made its way to Torrey Johnson, a criminalist with the Metro Police Department who specialized in both scientific evidence analysis and ballistics. He easily identified the weapon as a Ruger .22-caliber semi-automatic pistol, also known as the standard Ruger. This one was the Bicentennial model, issued in 1976.

It was a common gun, except for one thing. The barrel was longer because it had a silencer. It was a two-chambered silencer, with one chamber surrounding the barrel, and the other an extension that catches the gases that come out of the muzzle. By looking at the markings on the silencer—the initials AWC—Johnson knew the silencer came from Automatic Weapons Corp., which was affiliated with S&S Arms in Albuquerque, New Mexico. Silencers may be staples of television shows, but they're actually uncommon in the real world of crime. They have to be registered with the federal government, and, more important, they cut down on the range and accuracy of the weapon.

He cleaned up the gun. It was in good enough shape

that he could fire test rounds, which he did near the end of July 1996, keeping the bullets in case he ever needed to compare them against bullets used in a crime. He packed away the gun and didn't think about it for months.

23

"ASK ANYTHING"

Ron Rudin's cousin Doris Cowan couldn't remember the exact date; it was probably some time in 1996. But the details were vivid in her memory. Margaret Rudin was in Illinois, visiting her daughter in the Chicago area. "She was up there, I was up there, and she called wanting to get together and wanted to talk, because things were happening that were pointing the finger at her, and she wanted to talk. I said, 'Fine,' " recalled Cowan.

Margaret wanted to meet at a Holiday Inn near Gurnee, Illinois, not far from her daughter's home. Cowan and her parents, both in their nineties, drove to the hotel and hung around the lobby for an hour and a half waiting for Margaret, but she never showed up. They went back to Doris' parents' home in Arlington Heights, another Chicago suburb, and got a call from Margaret, who claimed she had also been waiting in the lobby and didn't see them. Somehow there was a mix-up.

So Margaret asked if she could meet them at their house. Doris agreed and gave her directions. After getting lost a couple of times, Margaret finally arrived, driving a beat-up old car that she said she had borrowed. She came inside and sat on the couch. She never cracked a smile.

"Ask me anything," she said, looking at Doris and her parents. "I'll tell you anything you want to know."

Doris had heard the news out of Las Vegas. She didn't want to believe what she was hearing, but she couldn't ignore it. She asked Margaret about the blood in the bedroom. "How did it get all over the ceiling?"

"Oh, Ron had nosebleeds and he would fling his head, and that's how the blood got on the ceiling, flinging his head," Margaret replied, according to Doris.

Doris then asked why Margaret took the furniture out

of Ron's bedroom before his body was even found. She told them in great detail about her plans to open a coffee shop in the house, that she knew a couple of women who were great cooks and she thought she could make it work.

Doris, who had visited the fortress-like house—behind a brick wall and off the main boulevard—asked Margaret about the wisdom of opening a coffee shop there.

"Oh, it's a wonderful location," Margaret told them. "I think it's just wonderful."

After Margaret left, Doris could only shake her head.

24

ANOTHER GRAND JURY

In 1995, the first time Clark County prosecutors went to the 16 members of the grand jury in the case against Margaret, authorities had no serious intentions of getting an indictment. They were trying to get people to talk. But by January 1997, two years after Ron's remains were found, persecutors were nearly ready to seek charges against Margaret. They had been under pressure to take action. Calls were coming in to the DA's office from Ron's angry family and friends, still seething over the fiascos that were the civil trial and the Yehuda Sharon immunity decision.

Two veteran prosecutors, Gary Guymon and Chris Owens, were assigned to the case. Privately frustrated themselves by the Yehuda immunity deal, of which they were not a part, the prosecutors went about steadily building up the case against Margaret, lining up witnesses, organizing the findings of the various tests on blood and trace evidence, compiling documents, phone records, maps, charts and photographs. News was leaked to the newspaper that the grand jury would be ready within a month to present a case against Margaret, again.

On February 27, 1997, the two deputy district attorneys started calling the first of some 60 witnesses to the once-a-week sessions—usually held on Thursdays—for a proceeding that would last two months. The witnesses represented every important person connected with the case, from detectives Ramos and Vaccaro to the various technicians. They included the women in Ron's life: ex-wife Caralynne, bookkeeper Sharon Melton, lover Sue Lyles, and Margaret's sister Dona Cantrell, who had decided to no longer take the Fifth as she had in the civil trial deposition. Prosecutors didn't bother to call Barbara LePome or Scott Stavrou. And they couldn't call Ron

Danner; he had died of cancer about a year after Ron's disappearance.

For the most part, the witnesses testified as expected, describing Margaret's demeanor before and after Ron's murder and presenting the physical evidence against her, including the blood in the bedroom. Scientists testified that blood found on the walls, the box spring and the switch plate all came from a male, and had the same genetic makeup as the male blood found on the handkerchief. Some samples had fewer genetic markers than others, making the odds of a match less certain. But none of the samples from the room were inconsistent with the handkerchief blood. Technicians found no blood on the glamour portrait.

All that was to be expected, and repeated what police had known for months, in some cases years, though there would be some surprises.

Augustine Lovato, for one, came in and told his story about cleaning up the stained carpeting and seeing the eerie picture of Margaret with the splatters on it. But he had something more to say. On the last day he worked for Margaret, after they'd dumped the mattress and the box spring and then returned the U-Haul, he said that he got into her Lincoln to be driven back to her house.

"On the passenger seat there was a newspaper and then under the newspaper was a handle of a gun sticking out," he told the grand jurors. "I stuck it under the newspaper and sat down."

He believed this was a real gun; no toy. "I could see the back end of the trigger. It was a revolver," he said. "It was a pretty small gun so I think it was a smaller caliber."

Augustine told the grand jurors he didn't know what to say to her, so he didn't say anything about it.

An even bigger surprise for prosecutors came in what normally would have been dry ballistics testimony. Torrey Johnson, the criminalist, had inspected the bullets that came out of Ron's skull and told grand jurors that they were common .22-caliber bullets. Then, as he went back to his lab after testifying, something nagged at him. There was something about those bullets that needed a second look.

"The marks on them were somewhat unusual, a little more coarse than you'd normally expect," he would tell the grand jury. Normally, bullets that have traveled through a gun barrel pick up fine markings on the surface. "It sort of triggered something in my mind of a weapon that had come into the laboratory previously which I had worked on, restored and test-fired," Johnson said.

So "on an off-chance," he pulled those files. "As I began to compare them, I found more than just a casual coincidence of marks," he said.

The bullets found in Ron Rudin's skull had the same markings as the test-fired bullets from the Ruger found in Lake Mead. These markings were a combination of the fine marks from the barrel plus gross markings from the silencer that overwhelmed and obliterated the other markings. He concluded that three of the bullets found in Ron Rudin's skull had been fired by this gun. The fourth he couldn't be sure either way.

Without even knowing it, police had the murder weapon from the Rudin case in their own evidence storage area. But that wasn't all Johnson found. Through the serial number investigators traced the gun back to one that Ron Rudin had once owned. It was the same gun that had turned up missing in the year after he married Margaret. Ron was murdered with his own gun.

Although they had no evidence that Margaret had taken the gun, she certainly had unique access to it in Ron's heavily secured gun room.

In all, the prosecution had laid out the guts of their case: Margaret, out of greed or jealousy or probably both, shot her philandering husband Ron at least four times in the head, stuffed his body into an antique trunk from her shop and dumped the trunk and body at Nelson's Landing, where it was set on fire. Prosecutors could link Margaret to the killing through the blood in the bedroom, her suspicious activities after Ron's disappearance and through evidence that she'd once owned a trunk.

But there were still some holes to fill. For one, Sharon Melton had told the grand jury she heard gunshots the morning Ron didn't show up for work. Since Ron was killed with a gun with a silencer, it would have been impossible for Sharon to have actually heard the lethal shots. It was still possible that Margaret, or somebody else, was shooting away that morning with another gun. A more logical explanation, Detective Ramos would argue, could be found next door to the mini-mall, in a car repair shop. There, mechanics used impact wrenches that let out loud bangs, sounding very much like gunshots. Prosecutors would have to convince a jury that Sharon was simply mistaken.

A larger issue was the question of how Margaret could have committed the crime by herself. She must have had at least one accomplice to dispose of the body. Clark County prosecutors had not given up on the idea that Yehuda Sharon was their man. He still had immunity. He still could turn on Margaret. Authorities had received word that Margaret had severed her financial relationship with Yehuda. Maybe now he would be ready to say what prosecutors believed the van was really used for.

The stage was set for testimony that could blow the case wide open—or leave prosecutors looking like fools again.

Before the grand jury, Yehuda Sharon was given the standard oath, to testify to the truth, the whole truth and nothing but the truth, and said, "I do."

That was about as easy as it would get for prosecutor Gary Guymon, as he went about trying to pry information once again from Yehuda on March 27, 1997.

"Can we just clear something? Am I under immunity? Am I not under immunity?" Yehuda had more questions, it seemed, than the prosecutor. "I just need to have that because if not I go ahead and take the Fifth."

Guymon tried to assure Yehuda that the immunity he was given in 1995 was still in effect. Yehuda could not be prosecuted for anything he said, as long as he told the truth.

"Will we have the truth from you in these proceedings then?"

"To the best of my knowledge, yeah."

With that, Yehuda began his testimony, telling the grand jurors that his occupation "basically is on computers," that he has dual citizenship in the United States and Israel, that he served in the Israeli Army but was prevented by "military law" from disclosing whether he served in Army intelligence, although he would discuss his military history in a media interview.

He said that Margaret came into his life when they struck up a conversation during happy hour at the Las Vegas Country Club at the end of 1992. He told the jury about his business of installing computer systems in churches and how she had helped him with that. He downplayed any suggestion that he had had a romantic relationship with Margaret. When asked whether he signed "I love you" to the postcard to Margaret from Israel, he denied it. "I don't remember signing 'I love you,' he said. "I remember signing 'love.' " He added, "Besides, I sent others."

The prosecutor tried several times to paint Yehuda as a gigolo, but he rejected the characterization. Asked if he was courting one particular female client, he said, "Put it this way: When you say 'courting a woman,' I just have European attitude, and for me a woman can be a friend just like a man, and yes, I did sleep with her, yes." But, he said of this other woman, "We weren't lovers. What determines what lovers are and what lovers not? If we have an intimate relationship, if I would see her, she wasn't married. I wasn't married. And I don't know what the occasion would bring."

In any event, whatever it was they had between them, it ended in October 1994.

Guymon then led Yehuda through his actions in the critical days surrounding Ron's disappearance. Yehuda told jurors that he had met with Margaret at 8 a.m. on December 18, 1994, that she came to his house to see if he could fix a computer, but he couldn't, being unfamiliar with the model. Then, that night, Margaret called him to complain about failing to show up at the grand opening of the antique store. He told her he was busy.

Busy, with another woman, Maria—with the brother who used to be a priest in the Philippines. The night of the eighteenth, he said, he rented the Chevy to pick up his holy oil bottles—the Chevy he needed because it had the automatic transmission.

"You said you had a bad leg?" Guymon asked.

"Right leg."

"When did you sustain that injury?"

"Eighty-six, eighty-five. No. Seventy. What am I talking? Eighty."

"When?"

"I don't remember. Seventy-two, seventy-three, seventy-four. Somewhere. I really don't remember when."

"What would injuring your right leg have to do with not being able to operate a clutch with your left leg on a manual transmission?"

"I have pins in there. I had an operation."

"You have pins in your right leg?"

"Yes."

"Do the pins in your right leg enable you not to move your left leg?"

"Just when it's cold," Yehuda said. "You have a clutch on the left, and you have the—you know, you have the right, and you have the gas. You know, when you have an automatic you can switch legs. You can have a rest to leg when it gets cold. Yes, it hurts. I mean, I feel it."

Either way, he said, he didn't need the Cavalier because he called the Phoenix company and it was out of bottles.

The prosecutor continued to try to shake Yehuda's story.

"Do you know the name of the company that you called in Phoenix?"

"No, I don't," he said. "It's one company, but they have—they use different names all along from Illinois to California."

"If you didn't know the name of the company, how is it that you knew who to call?"

"Because I was there a year earlier, and I had the receipt. I bought from them."

"Do you still have the receipt from this company in Phoenix?"

"I believe I did."

"And I take it that phone records would assure us that you, in fact, called this company?"

Yehuda, who at this point could still be charged with perjury, responded, "I don't remember where I called. I don't remember where I called."

"Did you call from your home?"

"Might be. I don't remember."

"You've indicated that you didn't have a cellular phone in '94; is that correct?"

"Yeah, but I go ahead and use other phones. You know, depends on what I did."

"What other phone would you have called this company from on the nineteenth?"

"I have no idea. Depends on what I did on the nineteenth."

And on it went, with Yehuda concluding he "probably" called from a pay phone.

In any event, Yehuda didn't go to Phoenix in the Cavalier, then didn't go to Los Angeles in the van that he had gotten in exchange for the Cavalier.

He did, however, put 348 miles on it before returning it at the end of the week. Yehuda explained his itinerary. He said that although he rented the van on December 19, he didn't leave town that day—or the next day, the twentieth, or the twenty-first. He said that he put off the trip—though still kept the van—while he worked out some affairs with Maria.

"I wanted to be with Maria as well that I had—I didn't know if I was going to be working or get the list of the church from the Philippines because to my recollection she was going to go away for the holidays."

Guymon suggested that Yehuda was just using this woman.

"Maria was another woman that you could have financial gain from as a result of your acquaintance?"

"I wouldn't say financial gain."

"Well, if you got the directory of the churches from the Philippines, it was going to allow you to do business?"

"You're right," Yehuda said. "And as a matter of fact, talking about all this, I got the first order this year."

The prosecutor returned to the issue of the van, and Yehuda couldn't recall now if he'd left for California on December 21 or 22. He settled on the early morning hours of December 22, about 2 to 4 a.m. Yehuda said he drove as far as Barstow or Victorville—he claimed not to remember which—to a gas station somewhere in the California desert, but had to turn back because of the weather.

"I talk to a guy, to, I believe, a truck driver, and he said that it was raining so I decided to avoid it."

Only the prosecutor said it wasn't raining.

"Have you since been shown weather consensus reports that indicates that there was no precipitation in Victorville, Barstow, Claremont, California, or the Los Angeles area on December 22, 1994?"

"Nope."

He said that he turned around and drove back to Las Vegas. That afternoon, Margaret asked if she could borrow the van. He said he didn't remember what she needed it for. She returned it to him the next day, Friday.

Guymon would soon wrap up his questioning about the van, but then the foreman of the grand jury had some questions of her own. Grand jurors in Nevada are allowed to question witnesses just as prosecutors do.

"On the nineteenth of December, 1994, did you drive that van that you rented down to Nelson's Landing?"

"No."

"Did you place a humpback trunk in the back of the van?"

"No."

"And take the trunk to Nelson's Landing?"

"No."

"Did you have anything to do with the removal of Ronald Rudin's body from his residence?"

"Nope."

"And take it to Nelson's Landing?"

"No."

The foreman asked whether Yehuda, if he stood to gain financially from Margaret Rudin in "an endeavor she asked you," would he do it?

"Put it this way," he said. "In the crime of it, the answer is no. My life was just getting too good, too nice, you know?"

But he was advising her on financial matters linked to Ron's estate. Eventually, he started charging her $125 an hour to go over documents linked to Ron's business and trust to determine what money she may have been entitled to. He was doing this even before the remains were found. By the end of his association with her, he would be paid $42,000—though he claimed he was entitled to $300,000.

His duties, however, weren't limited to financial advising. He also played chauffeur. On Thursday, January 26, 1995, the day before police searched the house and found the blood, he confirmed that he drove Margaret to McCarran International Airport in Las Vegas to buy a plane ticket to go to Illinois the following day for Ron's funeral.

That next day, Margaret came over to his apartment to give him three boxes of financial documents. The boxes contained real estate transaction records, tax records and a copy of Ron's trust. He saw her later that night, the

evening of the search. She had called him earlier. "She
can't make the airplane to go to the funeral and [asked]
if I would take her to LA," he said.

Margaret was being squeezed by the trustees, she told
him. They had shut off her electricity. They had canceled
her car insurance. They had shut down her health insurance, she told him.

She arrived at his apartment at about 10 p.m. At the
time, Yehuda apparently didn't know she was being followed by police and that they were being watched. Yehuda showered and got ready for the four-hour–plus drive
to Los Angeles. They loaded his car. Among the things
was a suitcase containing tapes. "I asked her, 'What are
the tapes?' " said Yehuda. "And she told me that she was
listening to her husband's conversations."

Yehuda was eager to get going.

"My concern was I wanted to get her stuff out of my
house," he said. "I had very much interest with her to get
her out of here and get her stuff out of my house."

They went to the Excalibur to cash a check, then made
their way to the airport, and the motel. "We got to a room.
And I had to go to sleep," he said. "And she was talking
on the phone or whatever or arranging her stuff, and she
woke me up as the time to the flight came."

Asked if Margaret had expressed interest in being intimate with him during that long day, he answered, "One
might say, yeah."

"I mean, you know, we in the same room," he said. "I
was tired. I had to go to bed. She was in my house [ear-
lier]. I took a shower, so there was—you see the bodies."

After dropping her off at the airport, he returned to the
motel for a nap, then went back to Las Vegas, where he
was met two days later by Ramos and Vaccaro. These
were tense days, he said. That's why, he claims, he was
willing to drive Margaret all the way to Los Angeles on
a cold winter night in his stick-shift car, even with his
sore leg.

"At the time I was just under commotion," Yehuda

said. "I didn't know what was going to be. I want to get the things out of my house, just get clear and just disassociate with her."

Guymon asked if Yehuda gave the detectives the "runaround" and "didn't give them the truth."

"The whole truth?" Yehuda asked.

"Yes."

"I give them some of the truth until I find out what they—how they going to treat me."

"When you find out what they know, the truth sort of changes because they know the truth, and then you have to give them the truth that they know about; isn't that true?"

"Uh-huh."

"You gave them the truth as they knew it."

"I gave them the truth as they knew it, as I knew it."

Margaret called him from Illinois and he urged her to return to Las Vegas.

"I had very much a interest for her to come back so I'm not going to be arrested," he said. "And so I said, 'Margaret, come and I'll help you.'"

He also claimed that he persuaded her to get the lawyer, Dominic Gentile. She agreed to return. He picked her up at Los Angeles International Airport in mid-February 1995. At first she stayed in motels because the trustees had blocked her from going into the house on Alpine Way. By now, her Lincoln had also been taken from her. Yehuda was about to leave for Israel. Needing a house sitter, he allowed Margaret to stay in his apartment for about a month, from late April to late May 1995. After he returned from Israel, "I had hard time getting her to leave."

Through 1995, when the grand jury was investigating the case and Margaret was preparing for the civil trial, Yehuda saw her two to three times a week. "There was a lawyer, there wasn't a lawyer, there was a lawyer, there wasn't a lawyer," he said. "Things were moving."

He said her lawyers "didn't exactly communicate with

me," but Margaret did. "She was going to the lawyer. She come to me. They have this. They have this," he said. "You know, everything was going back and forth until the trial, and then after the trial I think she went to Illinois and things dissipated."

But there was no dissipation in prosecutors' interest in Yehuda, who returned to the grand jury room a week later. The main subject was money—and what he was willing to do for it.

Prosecutor Guymon reviewed Yehuda's credentials as a financial adviser to Margaret and "a couple of other women."

"You're not a lawyer, are you?" he asked.

"I'm not."

"You're not a licensed estate planner?"

"I'm not."

"And yet you felt that you deserved to be paid several hundred thousand dollars at one point for your financial advice?"

"Put it this way: people can hire my services," Yehuda said. "That's my fee. They don't want it, they can go somewhere else. I don't hold them with a gun, and I don't hold them. I have other things to occupy my time with."

"Did you feel your services were worth that kind of money?"

"For what I was put through?"

"Yes."

"Yes, I do."

Yehuda said that in the civil case between Margaret and the trustees he was "basically holding the whole case in my hands," and he took credit for the outcome, saying, "There was a settlement because of me."

Guymon asked if Yehuda had recommended that Margaret take the settlement.

"Put it this way: They offered her lower settlement."

"Let's not put it that way," Guymon snapped back.

"Let's put it the way that the question requires that I'm asking you."

He finally said that during settlement talks Margaret did call him from her lawyer's office and told him the first offer.

"I said, 'If I were you, I would walk out of the lawyer's office if you don't get half a million,' " he said. "That's how it was."

She paid him for that advice, though not the amount they agreed upon.

"Is this a way that you supplement your income—by advising people on financial matters?"

"No," Yehuda said. "I do everything that I can do to make a—you know, to make money."

"It's primarily women that you advise?"

"No, it's primarily whoever wants it. It just happens to be women."

He spoke of helping another woman with an insurance problem.

"I had an accountant relationship with her, sure."

"And none of the money that you receive in this regard is for sexual favors or relationships?"

"Nope."

"None of it?"

"None of it," he said. "Put it this way: Not that I'm aware of. If you suggest that I'm that good that I should get paid, well, thanks for the compliment."

Yehuda's efforts to make money off the Rudin case didn't end with his partnership with Margaret. He showed that he was, if anything, flexible.

In mid-January 1997 he went to the offices of Rudin trust attorney Earl Monsey, without an appointment, and said that he needed to speak with him.

Monsey met Yehuda. Yehuda asked the lawyer, "How much is it worth to you guys for me to crack the Rudin case?"

He explained that he had an "intuition" that, if proven correct, could have solved the case. For a fee, he would follow up on this idea. The actual price of Yehuda's services never was discussed with Monsey—but it was later, with prosecutors.

Monsey referred Yehuda to authorities. Yehuda then made the same offer to them, this time giving a dollar amount. First he offered to crack the case for $1 million, then he lowered his offer to $500,000.

"You're saying you got a hunch?" Guymon asked in the grand jury proceeding.

"That's basically it. If it's correct. If it's not, it's not."

"This is based upon some knowledge that you have, something that you have seen, something that you've heard?"

"Probably, yes."

"And something that you haven't shared in your testimony previously, isn't it?"

"Because I wasn't aware in the testimony previously, and then nobody asked a question about it previously."

"And now your position is that you don't want to give this information out or cooperate unless you get a half million dollars; is that what you're saying?"

"Put it this way: The trustees went and took $10 million. They tried to steal from the IRS $3.5 million by escaping the estate tax, and I shouldn't go ahead and get compensated?"

"I'm going to give you an opportunity here, Mr. Sharon, to share with this grand jury any information that you have hidden from the grand jury in the past."

This information, he said, involved Sharron Cooper "moving quickly in to go ahead and take possession of the assets" and not helping Margaret with the funeral expenses. He said that Ron tried to get rid of Cooper a year before his death.

Unimpressed, Guymon asked, "Is there anything else that you have concealed during this investigation that you know about that you'd like to share at this time?"

"Ask me specifically. I mean, I don't know exactly what, you know, you're shooting at. So if you ask me specifically or give me example of what, you know, something, then it will be—I'll know what to say."

Guymon asked: "Are you hiding anything at this point?"

"I'm not hiding anything at this point."

He asked if Yehuda had shared everything he knew with investigators.

"I don't know. I have so much knowledge."

The prosecutor said that if Yehuda had nothing to hide, "What is it that you were willing to sell us some two weeks ago for a million dollars?"

"What I was willing to sell you, whatever you want to buy, and I didn't want to sell to you because I didn't exactly went to you. I went to Earl Monsey."

Asked point-blank what information he was willing to sell Monsey, Yehuda said: "I didn't have any information. I had a hunch. Information and a hunch is a whole different story."

Guymon left it at that.

But the grand jurors wouldn't let it go.

"Are you saying that for a hunch you wanted a million dollars?" asked one.

"I said that if I could crack the case—"

"With a hunch?"

"With a hunch, and go forward with it—"

"I mean, is anybody that stupid to pay a million dollars for a hunch?"

"I didn't ask for a million dollars. I said: We're going to put it in an escrow account. We put it in an escrow account. I get two attorneys that I trust that will oversee it. It's the same thing when you go ahead and you buy a house. You go ahead and you open an escrow account."

"On a hunch?"

"If it's going to go through. If I can help, if I can deliver, fine, I get paid. If I don't, the money's there."

Another juror was more blunt.

"So what I'm seeing is you're an opportunist, and any

chance you have to make money you pretty much will do that? Correct?"

"Absolutely. I making a living."

"There's no limit really to what you would do for money?"

"Except the liberty," Yehuda said. "I don't like to lose my liberty."

"What's that mean?"

"I don't like to be involved in criminal activity."

What's more, Margaret's lawyers got paid, her accountant got paid, "But when it comes to me, I shouldn't get paid? That's what you're saying?"

"But you—OK," the juror said.

"Maybe you volunteer all your life."

The juror asked why Yehuda wouldn't just provide whatever he was offering for free.

"Because the law doesn't support me freely," he said. "I'm like everybody else. Everybody else have businesses, have expenses, have things to pay . . . The District Attorney is going to come to me and say, 'You, Yehuda, or Mr. Sharon, you're going to get paid nothing, but other people that the trustees owe, they can get money. We're not going to protect them.' Well, I don't go for it. I'm sorry to tell you, if I work for something, I expect to get paid."

"You answered my question."

"Thank you."

"You're quite welcome."

Still fuming at Yehuda, another grand juror asked him why he'd waited so long to offer his services.

"In the beginning," Yehuda explained, "I didn't know what was going on. I really didn't. I was caught off by surprise. I was basically trying to, you know, protect my butt. I didn't know what was going on. Had no idea."

Several more jurors and the foreman continued to pummel Yehuda with questions about this "hunch," none getting anything close to an answer they wanted. A couple asked him again if he participated in the murder, and again he denied it. He was asked if he knew who did it; he said he didn't. The tone grew increasingly testy, until a juror asked, "You're telling us that you had nothing to do with this murder?"

"That's correct."

"You're also telling me that if you had information that would find the perpetrator or the murderer, you would give it to them if they paid you? If they wouldn't pay you, you'd let a guilty man walk free?"

Yehuda went on a tangent.

"Very nice detectives, good detectives," he said.

"Don't talk about the detectives," the juror said. "I want an answer from you."

"If I have the knowledge?"

"Yes."

"If I go ahead and accuse you, I have a hunch that you're involved—"

"I don't want to hear hunches. I'm trying to say, if you had information, you wouldn't give it unless they paid you for it?"

"No necessarily."

"What the hell are you saying to me? You're just going around in a big circle."

"OK," Yehuda said. "If that's what you think, that I'm going in a big circle, that's OK. If that's the impression, I'm sorry you got that impression."

And on it went for several more minutes before the prosecutor mercifully brought the questioning to a close. Guymon asked Yehuda to return the following week with receipts from the companies from which he'd bought the bottles.

Yehuda did return, but not with the receipts.

It would never be known for sure what Yehuda was up to. But prosecutors had a theory. It occurred to them that the gun that had been fished out of Lake Mead was very well wrapped, as if somebody had wanted to keep it in good condition until such a time as it could be found. Did Yehuda know that the gun was in Lake Mead? Was that what he was selling? If so, it would have been too late anyway. The gun had already been found. But Yehuda wouldn't have known that at the time he offered to crack the case for $1 million.

A week later, Yehuda was called back to the grand jury for a third and final time. This time, prosecutor Chris Owens did the questioning.

Owens then showed Yehuda Grand Jury Exhibit 89B, a handgun. By now, it had been identified by police as the murder weapon.

"You ever seen that before?"

"No."

"Have you ever handled that gun before?"

"Nope."

"You don't know anything about it?"

"I don't know anything about it."

"Do you know anything about that handgun being thrown into Lake Mead?"

"Nope."

The prosecutor then switched to the subject of the bottle company that Yehuda was headed for in Southern California.

He still didn't have the receipt that gave the name and address.

25

WANTED: GRANDMOTHER

The prosecution never got what it wanted from Yehuda. But on April 18, 1997, after hearing eight weeks of testimony, the grand jury indicted Margaret on three charges: murder with the use of a deadly weapon, accessory to murder with use of a deadly weapon and unauthorized surreptitious intrusion of privacy by listening device. The accessory charge was exclusive of the murder charge: a person can't be an accessory to a murder they also commit.

In announcing the indictment, Deputy District Attorney Gary Guymon also revealed that the murder weapon, a .22-caliber Ruger with silencer, had been located in Lake Mead. Because the grand jury proceedings were secret, this had not been released to the public. Guymon said that the gun was traced back to Ron Rudin, and that Margaret had unique access to it. He said it was unlikely this was a weapon Ron was carrying at the time of his killing because it was too bulky with the silencer.

"It would be a lot like walking around with a rifle," he told the press. "The silencer makes a gun very difficult to conceal. The evidence is he walked around with a concealed weapon."

The discovery of the gun, Guymon said, proved to be a critical development. He said prosecutors didn't ask for an indictment from the first grand jury in 1995 because the weapon had not been found.

A no-bail warrant was issued for Margaret's arrest. Officials from the DA's office told the press they weren't exactly sure where she was, but that they believed she was in the Las Vegas area.

They believed wrong.

* * *

Detective Phil Ramos placed a phone call to attorney Charles Kelly.

"Charles, I have Margaret's indictment here, would you like to surrender her or how do you want to work that out?"

"I no longer represent her," Kelly said, according to Ramos.

Shocked, the detective said, "Well do you know who does? I mean, this is the first we've heard of this, we'd like to work out some kind of arrangement to turn her in."

Kelly repeated, "I no longer represent her. Thank you very much."

Police searched around town. They went to the home of a woman they thought was friends with Margaret and had given her a place to stay. She wasn't there. They tried her sister Barbara. No Margaret. Ramos contacted Yehuda, who said, "I haven't heard from her and I don't know where she is."

The detective was beside himself. First the Yehuda immunity debacle, then the settlement in the civil trial, now this.

As of April 24, 1997, Margaret Rudin was a fugitive from justice.

"Of course in 20–20 hindsight we probably should have had a surveillance on her," Ramos said later. "We were thinking: We're almost there, we're almost there, and when the gun showed up, boom, it put us over the top, and let's get in with the grand jury. Everybody was so focused on getting that good case presented neat and tight, we never considered she would take off."

Behind the scenes it was surprisingly calm. No fingers were pointed, no blame placed. Police insisted that they simply hadn't had the manpower to keep 24-hour surveillance on Margaret around the time of the indictment. And even if they had, it didn't seem necessary. While it may appear like a common reaction, people facing criminal charges, even murder charges, don't tend to run away, if only because their attorneys tell them not to: it can be construed as showing consciousness of guilt.

Margaret had shown no lack of courage so far, not in the days after Ron's disappearance, not during the civil trial when she often had to provide her own legal counsel. Why panic now—and in the process give the prosecutors another piece of ammunition against her?

It was left to Guymon to give the public the news. The office that had granted immunity to Yehuda Sharon, only to get aggravation in return, had now just let a 53-year-old grandmother slip through their fingers. "The police have vigorously pursued her whereabouts and to date they have no idea," Guymon said at the time. "She is nowhere in town to our knowledge."

To find Margaret Rudin, police set out to do many of the same things they had done to find her husband back in late 1994 and early 1995. They put out the Attempt To Locate bulletins and entered her information into the NCIC computer. They kept on the lookout at airports and bus stations. They called friends, family, anybody Margaret may have known. They put together an old-fashioned wanted poster, with "Krafve" misspelled.

WANTED

FOR MURDER

* * * * * * * * **MARGARET RUDIN** * * * * * * * * * * *

W.F.A/D.O.B: 5:31-43 5' 7" 130 LBS. BLND HAIR

A.K.A. MARGARET MASON/ A.K.A. MARGARET KRAFBE

WANTED FOR: MURDER WITH A DEADLY WEAPON, ACCESSORY TO MURDER, AND UNAUTHORIZED, SURREPTITIOUS INTRUSION OF PRIVACY BY LISTENING DEVICE.

The poster listed the Secret Witness hotline number and Metro homicide's number. And right in the middle of the poster was one of the least–sinister-looking fugitives from murder charges in law enforcement history. It was the glamour picture of Margaret, smiling demurely in soft focus.

Then police went to the airwaves. The television show *America's Most Wanted* had at the time led to the capture of nearly 500 suspects since it went on the air in 1988. In early June 1997, about six weeks after Margaret fled, the program aired the first of several shows about the case. The results were immediate. Phone calls flooded the Las Vegas Metropolitan Police Department with tips. Detectives Ramos and Vaccaro sorted through them looking for those that were most promising.

Police announced that they had begun getting leads that Margaret was in the Chicago area where her daughter lived. After a story about the case aired on a local station, dozens of calls came into Metro, but none panned out.

By October 1997, six months after Margaret had fled—and no sign of her anywhere despite more broadcasts of the story on *America's Most Wanted*—people close to Ron were starting to get edgy. Sharon Melton was angry, both with the trustees for settling the civil case, and with the pace of the criminal investigation, wondering why police hadn't made an arrest. "They had everything they needed years ago," she told the *Review-Journal*.

District Attorney Stewart Bell, Margaret's old divorce lawyer who had gone on to be elected head of the prosecutor's office, acknowledged that his office may have had enough evidence for an indictment years earlier, but not a conviction. "We weren't confident we could prove beyond a reasonable doubt that she pulled the trigger," he said. "We were concerned that she could fabricate a story that could not be disproved by the then-existing evidence." He also defended giving immunity to Yehuda. "We needed to try to get information from one of those insiders, and so we chose the one that seemed least likely to be involved," he said.

Attorney Charles Kelly, who had told Ramos he didn't represent Margaret when she had fled, was still speaking out in her defense. While Margaret was on the lam, he blasted the prosecution's case. "The vast extent of the case against Margaret is based on circumstantial evidence held together by nothing but supposition and speculation," he told the media.

"There are a number of reasons people could flee other than consciousness of guilt," he said. With her gone, he said, "It's pretty easy for everybody to just sort of gang up and make a decision before they have heard both sides of the story. And believe me, there are two sides to this story."

He added that he didn't know where Margaret was.

26

PHOENIX FIASCO

On a hot summer night in Phoenix, the police radio crack-led with one call after another. Officer Christopher Mendez, riding a cruiser alone, would have to scramble to answer all the calls on his graveyard shift. It was the weekend, which was always a busy time. And the warm weather was drawing people outside—and into trouble. So the call that came over the radio sometime after 10 p.m. Saturday, August 29, 1998, would not have the highest priority. The dispatcher said that a lady who worked at the Hotel San Carlos on North Central in downtown had recognized somebody featured on that night's episode of *America's Most Wanted*. It took about 20 minutes for Mendez to get to the hotel.

Built in 1928, the Hotel San Carlos is a local landmark with a glamourous past. With 133 rooms, three restaurants and a rooftop pool, the hotel was once a magnet for Hollywood stars. Its guests have included Humphrey Bogart, Mae West, Clark Gable and Carole Lombard, and Marilyn Monroe. These days, visitors can buy special hotel package deals in which they can sleep in the same suites where the stars slept. Officer Mendez was about to find out that another famous name could be added to the roster. Only this one wasn't a guest.

When he arrived at the Hotel San Carlos, Mendez was met by a woman behind the bell desk. Vicki Drapkin was on the verge of panic. She was pale and she chain-smoked. She explained that she worked as a hotel auditor and that one of the other employees at the hotel, a woman who staffed the gift shop, appeared to be the same woman who was being referred to as the Black Widow on *America's Most Wanted*.

Vicki had turned on the show while waiting for *The*

X-Files to come on, before leaving for work. She said that the woman she knew as Annette Boatwright bore a striking resemblance to Margaret Rudin. The faces were the same; only the hair differed. The woman she knew as Annette had dark brown hair; the wanted woman had lighter-colored hair. First Vicki called *American's Most Wanted*, but didn't get anywhere, then called the police. She told the officer that the woman had been working in the gift shop since May—about a year after Margaret had fled Las Vegas. The two of them also lived in the same YMCA building nearby on North First Avenue. She gave him the woman's room number, 314.

Mendez left the hotel for 350 North First Avenue, a half-mile away. The YMCA building, which is a cross between a hotel and a halfway house, where men and women—living on separate floors—can go to get their lives back together. Mendez was met by a second officer, Bryce Kollum, his backup that night. A woman on the ground floor of the YMCA greeted Mendez, who explained why police had arrived. The woman then went upstairs and brought back a dark-haired middle-aged lady wearing blue jeans and thick brown glasses. If she was a fugitive from a brutal murder, she certainly didn't act that way. Mendez seemed almost smitten by her, recalling, "She was actually really calm, really, really nice, very cordial, very upstanding and very well educated."

The officers asked for identification and she produced an Arizona state identification, a legal ID similar to a driver's license, giving her name as Annette Boatwright. It had her picture on it. The ID seemed to be real; it had the hologram and magnetic strip on the back.

Mendez asked her if she had been involved in any criminal activity for which she might be wanted. There was a long pause, as she leaned back a little and said finally, "No, I have nothing like that at all."

Then she peppered the officer with questions. "What exactly are you looking for? What do you need?"

Mendez was thrown off. He started thinking, if this had

been any other older woman—his own mother, say—being confronted with such questions, it would be horrible. She didn't act anything like a fugitive, just a lady who had gotten called down in the middle of the night to answer a cop's questions.

He apologized for bothering her and left.

When he got back to the cruiser, the radio was going nuts: a homicide, an aggravated assault, a burglary. His supervisor was pressuring him to respond. He had no immediate second thoughts about letting this nice lady go.

He went off to the other calls, spending about 45 minutes on them. But as midnight arrived, Mendez began to worry. Something told him he wasn't finished with the woman at the YMCA. He tried calling the TV station that aired *America's Most Wanted*, but couldn't get any help. He tried to get some assistance from his police station, but everybody there was too busy. It was midnight. The city was hopping. Nobody was in the mood.

Then he got another call from dispatch to go to the Hotel San Carlos. When he got there, he was met by the same woman, who had made the first call, Vicki Drapkin. She had more news to report.

Not long after Vicki had last spoken to the officer, the woman—Annette/Margaret—came to the hotel, which was unusual because she had to work a morning shift the next day in the gift shop. The woman was dressed casually. She was calm. She asked Vicki for some cigarettes from the gift shop. Vicki didn't have the key to the shop, so she gave the woman one of her own. The woman then went into Vicki's office and calmly smoked. She didn't say anything about talking to police just an hour earlier.

By now, Vicki was a wreck. She was trying to run the front desk while a person who may well have been a wanted murderer was in a back office puffing her cigarette. The hotel controller came by, and Vicki had him call police a second time—the call that Mendez got just after midnight.

*   *   *

Mendez arrived at the hotel a second time, along with his backup, Kollum. They were led to the office where they saw Margaret. She was dressed the same, acted the same: casual inside and out. They walked her out in front of the hotel, sat her down, and questioned her in more detail. They asked her point-blank if she knew a Margaret Rudin. She paused a long time, then answered calmly, "No, I don't know anybody by that name."

"Have you killed your husband?"

Arms crossed, she shook her head. "No, I wouldn't do that."

"Have you done anything malicious toward your husband?"

"No, I wouldn't do that."

Now, Mendez got worried. She was too calm. If somebody had asked him if he'd murdered somebody, he'd be furious. But this lady just sat there, as cool as the night was warm, saying no.

Mendez went into his cruiser, and tried to get some information from his computer, the MDT, or Mobile Data Terminal. He checked the state and national criminal databases for the name Annette Boatwright for wants and warrants, and came up with nothing from a criminal standpoint, but did get a description that matched the woman seated in front of the hotel. He also tried the name Margaret Rudin and claims—even though police had entered that name into the NCIC computer, which links to the MDT—that nothing came back.

He got out of the patrol car and walked up to the woman. He tried something else, asking her if she would go down to the police station for fingerprinting. She'd have to do it voluntarily because he had no probable cause to arrest her. This time there was no long pause before she answered.

"I don't want to go down there. No."

She said that it wasn't a good time, that maybe she could do it on another day.

Failing at that, Mendez got on the phone, calling the

television station to try to reach *America's Most Wanted* or his own police station, not getting anywhere with whoever was on the line. He also tried the Las Vegas Metro Police Department, but it was a weekend and he couldn't reach anybody in homicide. He ended up with the records department, which couldn't help. While on hold, he tried to make small talk with the woman. He kept telling her that he was really trying to avoid being rude, and that maybe this was all a big mistake that she could help him clear up. He asked her what had brought her to Arizona, and she told him that she had just come in from Guadalajara, Mexico. He asked her if she spoke Spanish, but he couldn't remember what she said. All the while, she was relaxed, friendly, laughing.

They were at this for more than an hour. Finally, Mendez's supervisor got on the radio. "You guys have been there long enough. You have to come out," he said.

The radio blared with more calls. Mendez made one last attempt to get the woman to go to the police station for fingerprinting. Again, she said no, that maybe they could set something up for later. She told them to contact her any time. As they watched Margaret walk away, an uneasiness fell over Mendez. I've been talking to Margaret Rudin, he thought.

Mendez and Kollum left to deal with the mean streets of Phoenix. A burglary call commanded their most immediate attention. They caught the suspect, wrestling him to the ground, handcuffing him, then hauling him off to the jail. That's when they got the third call of Mendez's shift to deal with the woman at the YMCA.

By now, it was early morning. Vicki Drapkin had seen police question this woman and let her go. Fearful, Vicki went back to the YMCA to get her belongings. Her boss would let her stay in the hotel for the time being. But at the YMCA, she ran into the woman, walking down toward her room.

"Hi," the woman said.

"Hi," said Vicki.

"Where are you going?"

"I'm going to stay at the hotel a few days," said Vicki.

The woman said she had tried to do the same thing but couldn't.

Vicki said, "I had pre-arranged this a few days earlier to see if I could do this."

The woman said, "I'm thinking about going to stay at the Holiday Inn."

"Why would you do that?" Vicki asked. "You're due back at work at ten."

"I think it's better."

Vicki started to leave, but the woman stopped her. "Vicki," she said, "I just want you to know one thing."

"What's that?"

"I would never do anything to hurt you."

"I believe you," Vicki said. "I believe you."

Vicki then went down the elevator and back to the Hotel San Carlos.

At some point, Officer Mendez got to the YMCA for that third call, but the woman wasn't there anymore. She had left, driving off in, of all things, a limousine.

Officers Mendez and Kollum never filed a formal report on that night's events involving the calm dark-haired lady. It was too embarrassing for the department. They had Margaret Rudin in their grip—not once, but twice—and let her go. The department did follow up informally, calling Las Vegas homicide detectives to give them the bad news.

Not surprisingly, the woman, Annette/Margaret, didn't come to work at 10 a.m. the next morning at the gift shop. About a week-and-a-half later, detectives Ramos and Vaccaro met with Vicki Drapkin. They had found out about the Phoenix events within hours of Margaret's limo ride, but it was too late. The detectives were crestfallen. Prosecutor Gary Guymon told reporters: "I'm sick about it."

Now, days later, sitting with Vicki, they learned that

she and the woman she had known as Annette were acquaintances, though not close friends. She said the woman had told her that her husband had died. His relatives wanted to "cheat her out of what was rightfully hers." She said that she'd owned an antique store in Las Vegas. She even once offered $2,000 to Vicki to represent her in court in Las Vegas. One day, Vicki said, she had seen a pile of identification cards on the woman's bed. She was suspicious but didn't do anything.

Police had searched the room at the YMCA. They found makeup, photos, canned food, and a set of keys. The key tag read, "Ron Rudin Realty" on one side, "L/ Canyon" on the other.

It turned out there really was an Annette Boatwright who lived in the Phoenix area, and she did in fact look a lot like Margaret with the dark hair and glasses. She had actually met Margaret, and the two were friendly, but the real Annette Boatwright claimed to have had no idea that the fake Annette was a fugitive. But Annette did confirm one thing. Annette Boatwright—the real one—did own a place in Guadalajara, Mexico. The Rudin murder case was about to go international.

About four months after Margaret slipped through the fingers of Phoenix police, Las Vegas police got a report from Mexican authorities that Margaret was in Guadalajara, staying in a condominium complex popular with American retirees. She had apparently gone there almost immediately from Phoenix. Las Vegas police sent word to Mexico to have her arrested for deportation to the United States on murder charges. But to their astonishment, Mexican authorities wouldn't do it. "What we had to do—and this was really aggravating for us—is we had to literally translate the entire case into Spanish, send it to the Mexican Attorney General, and they would review it," recalled Ramos. "And what they told us was, 'We'll read your case and if we think you've got enough probable cause to arrest her, we'll go detain her.'

"It didn't matter that we had an indictment and that she was a fugitive in the United States. They had to give their stamp of approval to our probable cause before they would detain her."

Ramos had dealt with Mexican authorities before, and while it was always a little tricky, "they've never made us jump through those kinds of hoops." This went on for months. Las Vegas police knew where Margaret was, but the police in Mexico simply never arrested her.

Ramos thought he had a good idea why. This was a testy time for U.S.–Mexican relations, particularly between law enforcement on both sides of the border. Mexican authorities were still angry over the arrests of a dozen foreign bankers, including officials of three of Mexico's biggest banks, in what was described as one of the largest drug money–laundering cases in U.S. history. As part of a May 1998 sting called Operation Casablanca, the arrests were made at the CasaBlanca hotel–in Mesquite, Nevada. The case angered Mexican officials, who claimed that the United States had intruded on Mexican sovereignty by keeping Mexican authorities out of the operation. A defense motion in the trial that followed accused U.S. Customs agents of "outrageous misconduct" by telling Mexican authorities about the sting only after it was completed.

"You know, Mexico was a little pissed off," Ramos said. "So this case [with Margaret] is the first case that came their way, and they said, 'Well, we'll show you guys.' "

Ramos tried to flush Margaret out of the country by releasing false information to the media claiming that police believed she was hiding out in Chicago. "We would purposely publicize information that was not as accurate as we knew to make her think we were not on the right track so that we could close in on her without knowing," he said. But in the end, they lost her. Mexican authorities told Las Vegas police that she was no longer there.

* * *

For a few moments, police thought Margaret had returned to Las Vegas. A security guard at a Home Depot store near the police station called Metro homicide and said, "Hey, this Margaret Rudin lady, she's here in our store."

A Metro patrolman was sent to hold the woman, while homicide detectives were notified. Ramos jumped in his gold Caprice and got to the store in two minutes. He took one look at the attractive middle-aged woman and said, "Oh, my God."

If Ramos hadn't spent the better part of his career in homicide dealing with Margaret Rudin he might have made the same mistake. This woman, Linda Strunk, who lived in Las Vegas and Florida, looked just like her. Ramos apologized and showed her a picture of Margaret.

"Wow, I do look like her," Linda said. She even had the Southern accent, having grown up in Virginia, though her husband—a retired Nebraska newspaper publisher— was still very much alive, and seemed to get a kick out of the whole thing.

Ramos gave the woman his business card. On the back, he wrote: "This is not Margaret Rudin."

Margaret had been gone now for more than two years. Police desperately needed a break. Somebody out there would eventually have to tip off authorities.

What they didn't know was, somebody already had.

27

CHOWDA

In the summer of 1997, Roma Scott Jones, a receptionist for a chiropractor in St. George, Utah, began to worry about her friendship with Margaret Rudin. She had known Margaret since 1987 when Margaret and Ron would visit the doctor. She and Margaret would have lunch, talk on the phone. Sometimes, Roma would visit Margaret in Las Vegas. In time, Margaret would complain about Ron, calling him cheap. "I remember she told me that she sold some of her jewelry because Ron wouldn't give her enough money," Roma recalled.

In 1997, as the second grand jury was hearing evidence, Margaret went to Roma with a request. "She told me she was leaving Las Vegas," Roma said, "and she indicated she was fearful, and she wanted her mail forwarded and sent to her." Roma agreed. "I was trying to help a friend, I guess." But after four or five months, she started having second thoughts. She had heard that Margaret had been indicted, then had become a fugitive. Roma started worrying that she might be breaking the law by forwarding a fugitive's mail to her friends and family.

"I didn't want to commit a crime," she explained. "I had felt sorry for her. It didn't seem wrong when I first started doing it."

Roma wanted legal advice. Her daughter's husband happened to know a criminal lawyer in Salt Lake City, Utah. She went to him.

The lawyer called the FBI. In September of 1997, they met in the lawyer's office—Roma, her lawyer and the FBI agent. A deal was made. Roma the receptionist would become Roma, confidential FBI source. She would show them any letters or packages that Margaret sent. She would get approval from the Bureau for anything she sent to Margaret.

Over the months, she would occasionally get mail to forward, but nothing that indicated where Margaret was located. Then, in late October of 1999, Margaret sent Roma seven boxes, six of them bankers' boxes, the seventh slightly larger. She called her contact at the FBI. He told her to poke through the boxes and see if there was anything with an address for Margaret.

The boxes contained documents, books, photographs and wrapped Christmas presents for Margaret's three grandchildren.

Roma also found an address, from a place called Revere, Massachusetts.

They don't serve Boston clam chowder at the Blues Diner in Revere. They serve Boston clam chowda. That's how they pronounce it. That's how it's spelled on the menu board. That way there would be no mistake: you were in the very heart of New England.

A suburb located just 5 miles away from downtown Boston, Revere is a densely populated, working-class city of 46,000. The city has two claims to fame. It is the birthplace of Horatio Alger. And it was the site of the nation's first public beach. Opened in 1896, Revere Beach was the Coney Island of New England, with more than 250,000 bathers on the sandy shores of the Massachusetts Bay. There was also an amusement park, with a ferris wheel, a fun house and a cyclone ride. It was a place where blue-collar folks went for entertainment and escape. It was, in some ways, the Las Vegas of the turn of the century, before neglect and, finally, a blizzard wiped out much of the old Revere Beach.

When Jackie Bello, who owns the Blues Diner, was growing up in Revere, the city was dominated by Jews and Italians. These days, it's more diverse, with Moroccans, Brazilians, Cambodians. "It's nuttin' like when I was growin' up," said Bello, taking a break during his 14-

hour day at the diner. But Revere still has a small-town feel. People know each other, or at least know of each other. Nobody bothers anybody, nobody gets into each other's business.

So when the attractive, soft-spoken, middle-aged woman with the bad wigs came into the Blues Diner for a cup of coffee with the cobbler she knew down the street, Bello didn't give her much notice. "It was, 'Hi, how ya doin'?' We didn't get into anything elaborate or anything like that," he said.

But she was friendly, courteous and sweet. She didn't look like she could hurt a fly. Bello was charmed by her. "She was a stand-up woman," he said. "I never had a bad thing to say about her. She never gave reason. We have a lot of nice people around here. You know trash from trash. And she's a nice person."

In Revere, she went by the name of Leigh Simmons. Some thought she spelled it "Lee." Everyone could tell she wore wigs; they could see the blond hair underneath. "I didn't pay attention to it for the simple reason that a lot of women wear wigs for one reason or another," said Paul Winthrop, owner of First Quality Shoe Repair on Broadway, who figured that the woman he knew as Lee may have undergone chemotherapy.

She'd walked into his store around September 1999, asking him to repair the heels on her shoes. "She was a nice person, well-dressed, nicely groomed, very polite, very friendly," he recalled. "I didn't think, 'Oh, gee this is a crook on the run.' She didn't give me that impression. She started talking. She told me she was writing a book, I told her about my projects."

In addition to his shoe trade, Winthrop writes novels and children's books and had been trying to get published. They talked about the problems with getting a book agent and other authorly frustrations. He couldn't remember what she said her book was about. "Some kind of technical book," he said.

She was looking for work, and he offered to train her

in the shoemaking and repairing business. But she couldn't get used to the dust and grime in a cobbler shop. Instead, she kept him company, stopping by every few days, watching his cat Shu Shu when he went out. He gave her a note telling anybody who might ask that she was allowed to be in the store when he was gone.

She read over his manuscripts and offered him constructive suggestions. "She was very encouraging. She'd say, 'You're very talented. You have a gift.' "

In addition to being a cobbler, Winthrop was also an ordained minister, from the Universal Non-Sectarian Church, and the two would talk about the Bible. They went out for breakfast once, got coffee a few times at the Blues Diner. She didn't tell him much about her past life, and he didn't ask. She said she was sharing an apartment with somebody in town. All she said was that she had family in Austin, Texas.

"She was in here a few times when the beat cop was here," he said. "He'd come in and we'd talk and whatnot, light and friendly. I didn't see any change in her demeanor. When I stop and think about it now, she was cold-blooded about the whole thing."

Once, she brought a few boxes over to his store for him to keep until the UPS man showed up. He'd also stored an old brown suitcase for her. He had almost forgotten about it. In time, he would stack some of his stuff on it.

She lived in a second-floor walkup apartment in a two-story house at 30 Yeaman Street, not far from the post office, where she had instructed that all her mail be delivered. As modest as her home was in Las Vegas, this place was considerably worse. It was dark and spartan. She stayed in a little room off the hallway, sleeping on a mattress on the floor and keeping her few possessions, including family photos, on a dresser. A woman who had married two millionaires in a row, Margaret now lived with a retired firefighter named Joseph Lundergan, a thin chain-smoker who had met her when they were staying in a Guadalajara apartment complex popular with American retirees. In Mexico, she had gone by the name of Marie, and she told him she was wrongly accused of her husband's murder. She said a former Israeli agent of the Mossad named Yehuda was working for the trustees of her husband's estate and wanted her dead.

They started spending more time together, going out to dinner.

"Of course I was curious, and sometimes I would ask her in more detail about her past," Lundergan would later tell reporters. "As she would get into it, though, she would start crying. I figured it was too painful for her, so I just let it alone."

Lundergan finally left Guadalajara after recovering from a knee injury. He gave the woman he knew as Marie his phone number in Revere. A month later, Marie, now calling herself Leigh Brown, showed up at the front door of his apartment, where she started taking care of him. She cooked him meals, got his prescriptions. She stayed in the bedroom down the hall. They would spend their evenings reading or watching television.

Margaret became friends with her upstairs neighbor, Carol Reagor, with whom she had dinner twice a week. Reagor recalled that when she first moved into that apartment, she was shocked to see the woman huddled in the empty unit, reading a book. "I figured she was running from something, probably a boyfriend who wanted to kill her," Reagor told the *Review-Journal*. "A couple weeks after we met, she said, 'If anyone comes knocking for me, you don't even know me, you understand?' We figured she was just scared of him."

Vincent LaPorta, who ran a print shop, thought that the woman he knew as Leigh worked for a battered women's shelter, because she often had fliers made about domestic violence, or as a nurse, because she had him laminate nurse identification cards. Vincent liked the woman so much he gave her a four-leaf clover from his collection.

But once he saw another side of her. After he had left one of the nurse cards on a stand near the front entrance of the store before he was able to laminate it, "Leigh" became nervous and told him she'd laminate it herself. He got the impression she didn't want anybody seeing her picture.

She had good reason to worry.

In late October 1999, the FBI's fugitive task force in Nevada contacted the Massachusetts State Police's Violent Fugitive Apprehension Section, a 20-member unit made up of state police troopers and officers from the Department of Corrections. A possible address had been located, through a confidential source, for Margaret Rudin, by now known as the Black Widow of Las Vegas, even though by all accounts her four previous husbands were alive and well. The address was on Broadway in the heart of the business section of the city. At the same time, the Boston Police Department had also independently received a tip that Margaret was in Revere. Representatives from the state police and Boston PD met and pooled their information.

The decision was made for the state police to handle the arrest. On the afternoon of November 4, 1999, Sgt. Mark Lynch of the Massachusetts State Police met in downtown Revere with seven other officers from the state police and the department of corrections. They first went to the Broadway address provided by the FBI's source out West. It was for a small cobbler's shop called First Quality Shoe Repair. Nobody was inside. So the officers went across the street to the post office, figuring that somebody there would likely know who was handling the mail for the cobbler.

The officers showed postal workers two pictures of Margaret, one the glamour shot, another a snapshot from Las Vegas police. Although the woman in the picture had blond hair, the workers immediately recognized her as the dark-haired Leigh Brown who shared a post office box with Joe Lundergan. The postal workers knew where

Leigh Brown lived—the apartment she shared with Lundergan was less than 100 yards from the post office—but she'd told them never to deliver her mail to the house, only to the PO box.

"We decided to hit the house," Lynch said.

The next evening, the fugitive squad officers, now joined by two officers from the local Revere police department, staked out 30 Yeaman Street. It was close to freezing and the officers wore gray jackets. Shortly before 9 p.m., they saw a Domino's deliveryman drop off a pizza at the apartment. Lynch had an idea. He wanted to avoid going in with force because of the danger of gunfire. A quick check of Lundergan found that he had applied for and received a handgun permit in Revere four months earlier. Lynch also was told by Las Vegas authorities that Margaret was accused of using a handgun to kill her husband.

Officers approached the Domino's man, who had just brought a pizza to Lundergan's unit, and asked him if they could borrow his shirt, a car placard and an empty box. Wearing the Domino's uniform, one of the officers, Sgt. Joseph Pepe of the corrections department, walked up to the second-floor apartment where Lundergan lived. He was followed by several officers. Two other officers went to the back door.

Pepe, disguised as the Domino's man, knocked on Lundergan's door, which had a peep hole. Lundergan opened the door, and the cops, carrying semi-automatic handguns and big Maglite flashlights, stormed in. Lynch was the first in the door. He grabbed Lundergan and passed him back to other officers behind, who frisked him. Lynch went four steps into the tiny apartment and saw a door to the right, a bathroom. He opened it and shined his flashlight.

There, cowering in the darkness by the bathtub, was a woman in a dark wig.

"Do you know why we're here?" Lynch asked her.

"Yes," she said. "This is about Las Vegas, isn't it?"

Margaret surrendered without a fight. As she was escorted out into the cold New England night toward a police cruiser downstairs, she was read her Miranda rights. After those few words in the bathroom, she didn't say anything at first, didn't ask for a lawyer. She was booked at the Revere Police Department, then transferred to the state police offices—called "the barracks" because officers used to sleep there—in Framingham, 15 miles to the southwest. She was placed in a five-by-eight holding cell with a metal cot. If she was cooperative, she would get blankets and a pillow and be allowed to use the women's bathroom rather than the toilet in the cell. That would not be a problem. She would be cooperative, eerily so.

"From the first time I saw her, she was very subdued, but wasn't very nervous," said Lt. Kevin Horton, who heads the fugitive unit. "She wasn't nervous, wasn't panicky in any way. Just very calm. It did hit me, as I looked at her, that she's acting awfully calm like this was routine for her, or she expected it. Maybe in her mind she knew this was going to happen someday. But it was too calm for me. She's got to know that she's going to go back to Las Vegas to stand trial for murder. She didn't seem like she was too worried about it."

But the people of Revere were stunned. Some still don't believe she could have killed her husband. The arrest was big news in the little seaside city, and the Boston area news media invaded the streets. Lundergan told reporters in his cramped kitchen, "My feeling is that she's physically incapable of that kind of crime, and psychologically and emotionally, too. I believe her." Lundergan also wanted it made clear to all media people that he never slept with Margaret, that they were just friends.

At the Blues Diner, Jackie Bello thought Margaret got railroaded like another famous defendant out West. "If you look around at the circumstances, I don't believe police dug enough. Look what happened to O. J. That's what happens. With her, the husband did shady dealings, was a shady character, was dealing guns. You don't know what he was dealing with. I think she's getting a bum rap."

The cobbler, Paul Winthrop, who became increasingly angry over the TV crews in front of his store and even at his house, said, "I was flabbergasted. She just did not strike me, she did not faze me as being somebody on the run. To think that she was on the run, allegedly killed somebody, just took me simply by surprise."

In Las Vegas, detectives Ramos and Vaccaro made plans to go to Revere. District Attorney Stewart Bell said the case that had taken so long to yield an arrest was now on the fast track. He said authorities would press for a speedy extradition and that the trial could begin as early as August or September of 2000. He was once again overly optimistic.

Massachusetts state police returned to the second-floor apartment at 30 Yeaman Street to serve a search warrant, finding the tools that had helped Margaret evade authorities for more than two years. There were two wigs—dark brown and light brown—hair dye by L'Oréal and fake ID cards. One card identified her as Susan E. Simmons, a practical nurse licensed in the state of Connecticut. Another identified her as Kathleen M. Larkin, an employee of Massachusetts General Hospital. They also found a catalog, with an address sticker for Lee Lundergan, that sold mail-order police badges, ID cards and guides on creating new identities. Among the items circled in pen were the books *How to Investigate by Computer, Secrets of Surveillance: A guide to tailing subjects by vehicle, foot and airplane, The Master's Guide to New Identity* and *New Identity in America*. There was a paperback book called *How to Legally Obtain a Second Citizenship and Passport, and Why You Want To* and the non-fiction book *Perfect Murder, Perfect Town*, about the JonBenét Ramsey case. At the cobbler's shop, police also found the brown leather suitcase that Margaret had stored there. Inside was a laptop computer.

*   *   *

On the morning of November 8, 1999, three days after
her arrest, Margaret was transported in an unmarked
Crown Victoria from the barracks to court for her arraignment. Sgt. Lynch, who had apprehended her in the bathroom, was in the car with her. She asked Lynch a little
bit about what was going to happen to her. He explained
arraignment court in Massachusetts. She fell silent for a
couple of minutes. Then she shook her head. She told
Lynch that she didn't have any money left, that everything
she had gotten from the settlement with the trustees she
had spent on lawyers. She had spent $50,000 on one law-
yer as a contingency in the event that she was indicted,
but even that money didn't go to good use. She said the
lawyer was supposed to advise her if she were indicted.
Instead, she found out on her own—then fled.

After arriving at the courthouse in Framingham, Margaret appeared before District Judge Robert V. Greco.
Margaret wore street clothes. She had no wig. Her hair
was a blondish-red. The judge ordered her held without
bail as a fugitive and set a November 24 pre-trial hearing.
A governor's warrant would be prepared in Nevada and
sent to the governor of Massachusetts to send Margaret
back to Las Vegas. Horton said to reporters that Margaret
had told police she wanted to stay in Massachusetts because "she said she feels safer here." But he didn't think
she could avoid extradition. "It's a waste of time," he said.
"In 15 years, I've never seen one of these delays work."

In Las Vegas, the case was assigned to District Judge
Joseph Bonaventure, a blunt-talking, fair, but not overly
patient Queens-raised jurist who already had his hands full
with another big case: The Binion murder trial. Pre-trial
proceedings had begun in the case of a former topless
dancer named Sandy Murphy and her reported lover, Rick
Tabish, in the 1998 death of her boyfriend, gambling figure Ted Binion, of the Binion Casino family.

But Margaret wouldn't be coming to Las Vegas any
time soon. "She absolutely plans to defend herself. She

has told me she did not commit this crime and has no knowledge of it," Margaret's court-appointed lawyer told the press. By the end of November, Nevada Governor Kenny Guinn signed a warrant to return Margaret Rudin. It was delivered to Massachusetts authorities, but Margaret got a delay in her rendition, as extradition is called in Massachusetts. She had hired a new lawyer, Robert George, a well-known Boston attorney, who persuaded the judge to give him three weeks to file papers contesting the legality of the arrest. Echoing the statements of the court-appointed lawyer before him, George said, "We plan on fighting her [rendition] to Nevada every step of the way and when the time comes to litigate the legality of her current situation, we'll be prepared to produce evidence indicating she was illegally arrested and charged."

From jail, Margaret wrote a couple of letters to Paul Winthrop. He didn't reply. He had been warned by a police investigator to stay away from her, that she could get him into trouble. "It tore my heart out that she was in jail and in a lot of trouble, but I didn't go to her," he said. "She must hate my guts by now. She wanted me to come and see her, put me on her visitors' list. She wanted to talk with me, so on and so forth. As a clergyman, I don't have to tell anybody anything. I suppose I could have gone to the prison to see her without a problem. Then again—I didn't need any problems."

But Margaret did find somebody who would listen. On January 10, 2000, she gave her first media interview since fleeing Nevada, telling the *Boston Herald* that she was fighting rendition because she was innocent and feared she would be killed before standing trial. "I'm very concerned, that's the reason I left Las Vegas," she told reporter Tom Farmer in an hour-long interview at MCI–Framington.

She certainly didn't look like a cold, calculating killer and a sly fugitive. Farmer said she spoke in a "soft, grandmotherly voice, with her bright blue eyes occasionally tearing as she grasped her hands together on a visiting room table."

Outlining what would be her defense at trial, Margaret said her husband had lived a dangerous life, full of fraudulent real estate deals, illegal gun-running, drug trafficking and tax evasion, and that the list of people wanting him—or her—dead wasn't a short one. "There are a lot of people who can back up that Ron was doing a lot of fraudulent deals," she said. "There were a lot of things he must have been involved with that I didn't know about."

She complained about the trustees Harold Boscutti and Sharron Cooper, saying that they had her "disinherited" after his death so they could gobble up a larger share of Ron's estimated $11 million estate. Yehuda also was working against her. She said her one-time financial adviser had claimed to be an ex-agent of the Israeli Mossad who was now working with the trustees to ace Margaret out of Ron's money. (Yehuda denied that.)

Her attorney, Robert George, told the paper the defense would "lean in the direction" that Margaret "did not commit this crime."

"I don't think the facts hold together on their own," he said. "You cannot be tried on mere suspicion alone and the motives and underlying circumstances of the probate matter certainly should have led investigators down other paths rather than toward Margaret Rudin, who was an easy scapegoat for the trustees as well as the authorities."

Back in Vegas, prosecutor Chris Owens replied to Margaret's remarks: "If she wants to tell that story, we invite her to come back and tell it to a jury."

The extradition fight would grind on for the next two months. Margaret's claims were rejected first by a judge, then by an appellate judge, before she was finally ordered to return to Nevada. At 8 a.m., on March 15, Margaret—described by a local paper as "stylishly dressed and freshly coiffed"—boarded a prisoner transport van at the jail in Framingham for the 2,750-mile journey back to Las Vegas.

Las Vegas authorities had opted not to send out detectives to escort Margaret back by commercial airline travel. The official explanation was that it was cheaper to do it this way. This was untrue. Metro had already sent the detectives out to pick up the evidence from the apartment and the cobbler's shop. Instead, the detectives wanted to play it safe. They didn't want her accusing them of doing anything improper in the long hours during the flight back to Las Vegas. So, she would make the bulk of the slow trip aboard a van operated by a private prisoner transport company called TransCor America, Inc. Considered a high escape risk, Margaret was to be shackled with ankle and wrist chains. After a long day's driving, the van would stop for the night, with Margaret bunking in whatever local jail they were near.

As Margaret was carted off to Vegas, her former roommate, Joseph Lundergan, was arrested for investigation of being an accessory after the fact of harboring a fugitive. "He met her and harbored her at his apartment and we have probable cause to believe he knew she was wanted for murder in Las Vegas," Horton told the media. Lundergan pleaded innocent and was released on his own recognizance without commenting. Horton later acknowledged that it was unusual to arrest somebody on a harboring charge because it's so hard to prove. Lundergan, who was taking a number of medications, might easily not have known what he was doing. But Lundergan made a mistake. "He decided he wanted to put himself out all over the paper and television and make himself a hero," said Horton. "That's enough, mister." The charges against Lundergan were later dismissed.

28

BACK IN VEGAS

It normally takes TransCor as long as two weeks to deliver a prisoner cross-country. But because authorities in Las Vegas were eager to get Margaret back, the trip was expedited. On Sunday, March 19—after five days on the road—Margaret rolled into Las Vegas, where she was promptly issued a navy jail uniform that resembled surgical scrubs, and booked into her new home at the Clark County Detention Center. Her dormitory-style room was not much worse than her rooms in the Phoenix YMCA, or Joe Lundergan's apartment in Revere—only now she wasn't free to leave, with or without her wig.

The following Wednesday, she made her first court appearance before Bonaventure, telling him she didn't have enough money for a lawyer. Her hot-shot Boston lawyer stayed in Boston, and a public defender was assigned; he had spent all of 30 minutes talking to her before the hearing. On the last day of March, she returned to the court to enter her pleas of innocent on the three counts contained in the indictment that had been handed up almost three years earlier: murder, accessory to murder and unauthorized surreptitious intrusion of privacy by listening device. She waived her right to a speedy trial within 60 days and was given an October 30 trial date, even though her public defender, Will Ewing, asked for a date of January 2001.

Margaret was placed in a very special cell, one in which she wasn't the only famous inmate. In what was more of a small dorm room than a cell, with single beds instead of the usual bunks, and long windows overlooking the street, Margaret was housed with two ex-strippers in the headlines: Sandy Murphy, whose trial had begun in the Binion killing, and Jessica Williams, awaiting trial on charges that, while high on marijuana, she ran down and killed six teen-agers picking up trash on a freeway median. Although Margaret wasn't subjected to the same discomforts of other prisoners, she began feeling like she wasn't getting the treatment that a person accused in such a highly publicized case deserved. She complained that her court-appointed public defenders weren't of the caliber of her cellmate Sandy Murphy's counsel, Tom Pitaro and John Momot, both top-notch private counsel. Margaret, who had gone through a half-dozen lawyers or more—including Momot at one time—before she fled, wanted a new attorney.

She spelled out her complaints in a March 10 hand-written letter to Judge Bonaventure.

Dear Judge Bonaventure,

Last month you ruled my public defender must proceed to trial on 10-30-00. With only six months to prepare for a case the district attorney still classifies as 'Open Murder;' the Writ of Habeus Corpus is still being answered so the charges against me can be defined; the courtroom countdown clock is only 22 work weeks away from my trial. Also, I have been told the public defender assigned to my case is preparing three murder cases he must take to trial within these same 22 weeks (880 work hours)—and the team supervisor is even busier. This is not a "normal" case to prepare for trial as it will require extensive work hours because of the unusual complexities of my case.

The *combined* investigations targeting me have been ongoing, since 12-20-94, by LVMPD, the District Attorney's staff, the private attorneys and private investigators hired by the trustees of my husband's estate. These co-trustees are also beneficiaries and the court allowed them to use my husband's money to target me while Judge Lehman would not allow me to have a dime to defend myself. What no one realizes is *not* one attorney who represented me during the past five years has ever taken a deposition, written witness statement, subpoenaed any records (etc.) so absolutely nothing has ever been done. Whosoever must defend me at trial is up against impossible odds.

Within the past seven weeks, that's with public defenders in solitary confinement—protective custody; I feel as if my assistance in my own defense is discouraged although I have nothing but time to read and study the prosecutors' "discovery." So far the P.D.'s have provided me with little "evidence" to rebuttal: in the past two weeks I've only received 100 pages, in the past six weeks I've only received 2000 pages. If the public defender is so overworked he can't provide all discovery against me; if he can't read the 2000 pages I've returned and follow through on my suggestions prioritizing "evidence"; if he is having to divide his time, energy and budget to prepare for three murder trials at the same time—there is no way I can possibly receive a fair trial.

This is causing me extreme anxiety, worry and apprehension that a horrid high profile case, as my problems have turned out to be, should become at the most opposed end of Lady Justice's scale from Sandy Murphy's "dream team" defense. It appears as if justice is equal to whatever defense a client can buy.

The end result is the public defenders' staff is extremely overworked, unfortunately. Are there alternatives? Is there a middle ground?

I'm requesting a court appointed attorney of the caliber of proven defense excellence as a JoNell Thomas, Richard Wright, Tom Pitero or. . . . Whomever. Could your Honor consider my request please?

> Sincerely,
> Margaret Rudin

The judge held off on deciding whether to replace Margaret's lawyers for a couple of weeks. In the meantime, the defense attorneys whom she wanted fired appeared before Bonaventure on May 26 arguing that the charges should be thrown out for lack of evidence. But prosecutor Chris Owens rattled off the key parts of the state's case, from her allegedly suspicious demeanor after Ron's disappearance to the blood in the house. Four days later, Bonaventure ruled that Margaret's lawyers were fully competent and denied her request to replace Jordan Savage and Will Ewing with private attorneys. The judge, in a wry reply to Margaret's request for a Dream Team like that of Sandy Murphy's, noted that Murphy's attorneys were in fact excellent, but they hadn't kept her out of trouble. Murphy had been convicted just a week earlier in his court of murder and other charges.

Margaret's problems didn't end here. The next complication arose when she started getting visits from a jailhouse spiritual adviser named Joseph DeLeo. The visits were arranged through the jail's religious coordinator, who had contacted the Central Christian Church, which sent over DeLeo. Margaret would claim that DeLeo had represented himself as a pastor with the church, with doctorate degrees in philosophy and Christian counseling. Margaret was impressed with him.

Margaret says they struck a deal by which she would sell him all book and movie rights to her story for just $1. She gave him a bill. On the front, it read, "I Love You!! XXOO."

In exchange, Margaret said, he promised to use any money he got from reselling her story to Hollywood or to a publisher to help pay for her legal defense, to provide for her grandchildren, and to assist the Central Christian Church's jail ministry.

"I own her image. All proceeds would go to me and my Christian ministry," DeLeo told *Review-Journal* entertainment columnist Norm Clarke.

DeLeo helped her with public relations matters. He set up an interview for Margaret with the TV show *Extra!* Speaking to the camera through the Plexiglas at the Clark County Detention Center, Margaret told reporter Phil Shuman: "I do want to get it across emphatically, I'm innocent. I have absolutely no doubt that's going to be proven at court."

In a segment that aired June 12, 2000, she called the prosecution's proposed motive—that she'd killed for money—"ridiculous." She spoke of Ron, of his "drinking problem," which, she said, "I didn't know about before. He had financial problems which were severe."

Shuman asked: "Why did you flee? Why did you leave the area?"

"There's a lot of reasons that will be coming out at trial that I don't want to go into."

"That makes you look bad," the reporter suggested.

"But it won't when they know the reality."

She said associates in shady business deals may have wanted Ron Rudin dead. "Let's just leave it at what I said so far."

"Business associates?"

"I don't want to name names."

Phil asked: "Are you scared?"

"No, I'm not. I'm positive that when this comes to trial . . ."

"That . . . ?"

"That I'm going to be found innocent because things will be disclosed that have gone on."

Margaret also spoke at length to the *Review-Journal*'s Glenn Puit, who described her as a gentle, kind, courteous, soft-spoken, church-going grandmother. In short, not the kind of woman who would go around shooting, decapitating and burning people. "I am an extremely family-oriented individual," she said in the article, published June 25, 2000. "My children and grandchildren, they have always come first." Margaret was hopeful that justice would prevail in her case. "I am sure I will be acquitted," she said. "The most important witnesses in this case are going to be the people who have known me best, not the people who have professed to be close to Ron." Those testifying against her are liars, and "You have to consider where that information is coming from." Her sister Dona, for instance, "doesn't get along with the family. . . . She doesn't get along with anyone."

She pointed to "problems with the evidence," but would go no further to explain, for instance, why a handyman thought he'd found blood all over her carpet. She also said she had "no earthly idea" how the .22-caliber Ruger from Ron's house ended up in the killer's hand, then at the bottom of Lake Mead.

She spoke about her life on the run, wearing wigs and putting in brown contact lenses. She wouldn't say who helped her or why she ran, though hinted that the information would come out at some point. "There is an attorney who knows the answer to that question," she said cryptically. "He will be subpoenaed." She laughed at police for thinking she was in Chicago when she was really in Mexico, though police claimed they purposely floated the Chicago report to flush her out of Mexico. And she insisted that life on the run was actually pretty good.

"It was a liberating experience," she said. "I loved it. It was exciting. I had lots of adventures.

"It was the first time in my life I was alone."

By early July, she was alone no more. Her dorm-like cell was starting to feel a little too cramped for Margaret with the two younger women. She began to complain that Sandy Murphy, then 28, and Jessica Williams, then 21, had engaged in "inappropriate conduct." Jail officials conducted an investigation but could not substantiate the provocative, if vague allegations. "All three parties were interviewed, and both Williams and Murphy vehemently denied any kind of inappropriate conduct between the two of them," one jail official told the *Las Vegas Sun*.

Murphy's lawyer, John Momot, said, "There was no romantic relationship between them. Sandy was just comforting her." Williams' attorney John Watkins said that

Margaret "isn't playing with reality." He added: "As far as I know, Jessica likes guys."

Still, jail officials, who had placed the women together specifically to avoid aggravation, split them up immediately. The day she complained, July 7, Margaret got moved to another cell.

There was also a shakeup in the defense team. Gone were the public defenders. On board was a private attorney named Michael Amador, a former deputy district attorney who ran a small but successful private practice. Amador was never at a loss for self-promotion, telling reporters that he was a tough prosecutor, so tough he got the nickname "Slamador." In his full-page ad in the Las Vegas directory, he billed himself as "more experienced, better prepared & willing to fight against any prosecutor or lawyer in any courtroom, anytime you need a successful trial attorney to handle your case." The ad also said he took payment plans and: "*Se Habla Espanol.*"

He had handled murder cases as a prosecutor and as a defense attorney, but he would soon find out that he had never handled anyone quite like Margaret Rudin.

Amador took Margaret's case for free, though Judge Bonaventure would approve public funds for a private investigator and expert witnesses with the warning "this court is not about to give a blank check to Miss Rudin and Mr. Amador." Among Amador's first priorities was to put the wraps on this spiritual adviser seeking a gag order on Joseph DeLeo to keep him from talking about what Margaret had told him during their private talks in the jail. "DeLeo has breached the confidentiality of his relationship with Ms. Rudin as her clergyman and her counselor and . . . intends to use information received as a result of confidential and privileged communications for his own profit," said Amador's court papers. Information began to surface that DeLeo wasn't a pastor at all, of the Central Christian Church or any other church, just a member, and that he had something of a history.

Amador dug up documents showing that DeLeo was involved in horse racing. It turned out that the New York State Racing and Wagering Board had revoked DeLeo's racing license and prohibited him from participating in harness racing. Horses he'd owned had allegedly tested positive for drugs in 1998 and 1999. But he was never prosecuted for any crime, and DeLeo attributed the problem to a rogue employee of his.

DeLeo told the *Las Vegas Sun* that he did visit Margaret, every day in fact, and that she never seemed unhappy with him. As for his credentials, he claimed to have doctorates in both Christian counseling and philosophy of religion, and had been certified by the American Association of Christian Counselors. Whether he was a minister or not was a question of semantics, he said. "There are no qualifications to be a minister," he said. "If you crack open a Bible and minister, you're doing God's work. My motives are nothing but above board."

Still, the whole thing was a little embarrassing for both church and state. The Central Christian Church issued a press statement saying that it had asked DeLeo "to refrain from representing himself in any capacity affiliated with Central Christian Church or its ministries." A jail official said DeLeo was no longer eligible to minister to inmates.

Margaret filed a fraud complaint against DeLeo in civil court, alleging deceit and breach of contract. Amador brought all this before a somewhat impatient Judge Bonaventure, who said, "I'm here to conduct a criminal trial. What do I care if he's a pastor or not?" DeLeo got an attorney, who assured the judge that DeLeo would not talk about his jailhouse discussions with Margaret because it would breach clergyman/penitent ethics, even if DeLeo wasn't officially a pastor. DeLeo, in the end, wouldn't cause any more distractions for the defense. The defense would find plenty of them elsewhere.

With the DeLeo fire put out and Margaret's jail arrangements now settled, it was time to get down to the business of building a defense. As the civil trial showed, Amador had plenty of ammunition for a reasonable doubt case. There was no witness and no confession, just evidence that Margaret had hired a guy to clean up a crime scene—and then acted suspiciously unconcerned about her dead husband.

But Amador decided to go a step further. He believed that buried in the thousands of pages of Ron Rudin's business documents was another defense, one that showed that Ron was engaged in dangerously unscrupulous business dealings that could have gotten him killed. The likely alternative suspects would be the trustees, Boscutti and Cooper, who stood the most to gain both by the death of Ron and the framing of Margaret, because she would be aced out of her 60 percent inheritance.

So Amador's pre-trial motions dealt heavily with Ron's business and the official investigation. His motions, filled with typographical errors, made bold accusations and audacious statements, but offered little evidence to back them up. Amador quickly painted himself as a crusader for justice who would use his special inside knowledge of the workings of the DA's office to outsmart his adversaries.

"Because of the intensity of my particular style of practice, ineffective assistance of counsel is never a viable legal issue," he wrote in a November 11, 2000, letter to prosecutors in which he not only asked them for some documents of evidence, but also put them on notice that he had hatched a strategy, one that "I employ in every defense case of any magnitude, but which I make every attempt to keep hidden from the prosecution.

"Out of respect for you gentlemen and for the lead detectives on this case I will make this purpose perfectly clear: I am setting a trap for you and Detectives Vaccaro and Ramos," Amador wrote. This trap involved Amador's knowledge of evidence that "has been hidden from the defense because of the fear that it [could] lead to Margaret Rudin's acquittal.

"It has been kept from you gentlemen because of your ethical responsibilities to turn it over to the defense," he wrote. ". . . This you see is the nature of the trap, and I rely upon your integrity for it to work. What irony then, that it has the very fact of my trust in you gentlemen, and my distrust of the motives and means of others over which you have no control, that guarantee the success of this endeavor."

He concluded by calling himself "nothing more, nor less, than a gentleman and a man of honor committed to a sacred task. I know both of you gentlemen to be of the same ilk."

When perplexed prosecutors showed the letter to the judge, Bonaventure told Amador to stop talking about traps and just ask for what he wanted.

Amador's legal motions were equally unorthodox. In one, he argued that the murder charges should be dismissed on the grounds that the police and prosecutors had entered into an "unholy alliance" with the trustees—a motion that in and of itself is actually not uncommon in such a case. But then Amador went on. The motion said that Ron and his then–business partners Boscutti and Cooper were "far from being honest business people," cheating the IRS, falsifying signatures and engaging in a "long criminal association." Amador cryptically made note of "something very important" that happened in 1994, setting in motion events in Ron's life, "each of which was serious enough to have resulted in the murder of Ronald Rudin." He didn't say what this was. But he suggested that police had some ideas of what was going on.

"The Homicide Detectives were well aware of other potential suspects, but failed to Investigate [sic] and chose to take the lies of Cooper and Boscuitti [sic] as gospel," the motion said. Amador said there was a mob angle in the case. Quoting his own knowledge of the police department from his days as a prosecutor, he noted Crazy Horse Too night man Blasko's mob past, but didn't say how this related to Rudin.

Rather than independently and fairly investigating the case, Amador claimed, police had proceeded to cooperate with the trustees in the effort to deny Margaret her inheritance. The cops became "the slaves to the financial interests of the beneficiaries/trustees of the Rudin Estate." Amador declared: "This conduct is perhaps the most egregious and outrageous government conduct ever perpetrated by the prosecution in the history of the State of Nevada."

Amador concluded with even more rhetorical punch, "I do not care by whose hand this Indictment will fall, but let there be no confusion or doubt, defense counsel will give no quarter, heed no threat, nor be overcome by as many as who may oppose me. Margaret Rudin will prevail, and as she does so to [sic] will Justice be served."

Another Amador motion, this one to suppress all evidence obtained by the pen register and wiretaps, began by ripping the credibility of bookkeeper Sharon Melton and her story about hearing what Amador called "machine gun fire" the morning Ron didn't show up for work. He noted, correctly, that Melton never mentioned the gunshots when she first talked to police, but went out of her way to accuse Margaret of being insensitive. Then, in a highly unusual use of street slang in a legal brief, Amador asserted: "Sharon Melton's most consistent asset to Ronald Rudin Realty had been that she blew the boss (the, deceased herein) on a regular basis." He offered no proof of an intimate relationship.

In the hearings to consider the motions, Margaret was led into the courtroom in her jail scrubs and shackles. She had lost a bid to wear street clothes, but the judge did let her wear a white sweater. She would sit at the counsel table next to Amador's paralegal and wife, Lisa Nowak.

The judge listened to testimony from witnesses including a former prosecutor who had overseen the grand jury and from Detective Vaccaro, but even before his ruling, the judge made no secret of what he thought of Amador and his motions. After berating him one day for showing up late, Bonaventure chided Amador for his use of "blew the boss" in legal papers. As Amador questioned Vaccaro, Bonaventure observed in the middle of questioning, "I really don't see the relevance." Prosecutor Chris Owens called the claim of a conspiracy "woefully lacking with regards to a factual predicate." Oddly, Amador didn't present an oral argument in support of his own motion, saying he would do it in court papers to be filed in the next month.

Then Amador didn't file the court papers.

The judge rejected both the electronic surveillance motion and the conspiracy motion.

Amador tried another tactic, filing papers calling for the district attorney's office to be disqualified from the case and replaced by the state attorney general's office on the grounds that the head of the DA's office, Stewart Bell, had once worked for Margaret Rudin as her divorce lawyer. The fact that the man now trying to put Margaret away for murder was once fired by her, screamed "conflict of interest," Amador argued, and to prove it, he put Bell on the stand.

The situation spoke to just how incestuous the Las Vegas legal community is. Not only had Bell been Margaret's lawyer, but he was also once a colleague of Judge Bonaventure; the two started work at the public defender's office on the same day in 1971. Amador, himself, had once been a deputy DA, working with many of the people on the other side of the courtroom trying to convict Margaret. In a rocky round of questioning, Bell professed to have absolutely no memory of the case of *Krafve* vs. *Krafve*. (Prosecutors' records, including the grand jury transcript and the wanted poster, misspelled Margaret's maiden name as *Krafbe*.) He said he'd handled thousands of divorces while in private practice from 1977 to 1994. Amador kept challenging that claim. Bell said it rang no bell.

Bonaventure grew restless. "We've been here a long time and I haven't heard anything yet. I don't see the point here."

The judge would deny that motion, too.

The defense then waged the fight which stood the best chance of success: trying to keep the jury from hearing anything about the 1988 fight between Margaret and Ron which resulted in the gun going off in the bedroom. To prove that the shooting actually happened, prosecutors had tracked down the painting that had been hit by the bullet and found that a small hole had been patched over. The prosecution argued that the incident bolstered the state's claim that jealousy was one of the motives in the murder case. If she had pulled a gun on him once, she may have done it again.

Amador convincingly argued that this prior bad act, particularly since it was so far in the past, would tend to inflame the jury without adding anything to the case at hand. The judge agreed, and ruled that accounts of the shooting would not be told to the jury.

It would be a rare—and short-lived—victory for the defense, overshadowed by a much more sensational development. Prosecutors, in filing their motion to introduce the 1988 shooting, attached documents that gave an intimate look into the lives of Margaret and Ron, and offered a revealing glimpse into Margaret's psyche.

According to the prosecution, Margaret didn't just listen to Ron's private conversations in his office. She wrote down what she heard. The prosecution released 25 pages of Margaret's musings, penned as she had her earphones on, overhearing everything picked up by the little ivory-colored bugs planted in the offices of her husband and bookkeeper Sharon Melton. The logs had been in the hands of the lawyers for Ron's trust, but fell through the cracks, and didn't get to prosecutors until late in the year 2000.

The entries cover a critical time, from July 1994 to

November 1994, just weeks before Ron's disappearance. How much of what Margaret wrote down actually happened and how much was skewed by her isn't clear— Sharon Melton, an antagonist of Margaret who pops up in many entries would later claim that some of the log notes were exaggerated versions of actual events.

Either way, the logs showed the extent of Margaret's desire to know every single thing that went on in Ron's life. She listened to the most tedious of details of Ron's real estate business, from his discussions with business colleagues about interest rates and regulatory matters, to Ron's perpetual problems finding employees with whom he could work. Ron was shown complaining constantly about his many secretaries and, in particular, about the late Ron Danner, who was always borrowing money from Ron and scamming him on expenses. In one entry, in October 1994, Margaret wrote that Ron "goes on and on about how Danner won't be paid for months if he doesn't get his ass in gear." Ron also complained about Harold Boscutti, the man who would end up with more than $1 million of Ron's estate.

Overall, Ron was portrayed as a real piece of work, moody, foul-mouthed, harsh on women. He was quoted as calling Margaret a "tramp" and another woman a "cunt." He once joked about putting a machine gun on his desk and killing "the next fuckin' woman that walks in."

As Margaret saw it, Ron also had a complicated relationship with Sharon Melton, confiding in her at times, but then complaining about her, too. But that was nothing compared with Margaret's observations of what Sharon was saying about Margaret. Lengthy passages have Sharon going crazy over Ron's decision to let Margaret open an antique shop in the mall—and Ron doing everything he can to ignore his strong-willed bookkeeper. Margaret quotes Ron as saying, "Fuck her, it's none of her business what either one of us does."

Sharon also was overheard warning Ron that Margaret

was out to kill him. According to a November log entry, "Last week, Sharon told Ron, 'Don't eat anything at the house. She is poisoning you.'"

But what proved most important to the murder case against Margaret were her entries about Ron's extra-curricular activities with women. One entry, in October 1994, had Ron calling an anonymous woman at National Title. According to the entry, Ron told her "he wishes he could make her day better by just talking to her and that he wishes he was in a hotel room with someone special." Margaret overheard several calls between Ron and Sue Lyles, including one in November in which she said that Ron's co-workers had spoken of her as Ron's girlfriend.

"She asked to see him," Margaret's log said, "and he made plans to meet her at above address." In the margins, Margaret wrote the address of a condominium that Ron had recently purchased on Pecos Way. According to prosecutors, Margaret then hired private detective Tony Desio, who had one of his operatives watch Ron and Lyles go into the condominium on November 15, 1994.

A letter to Margaret from Desio spelled out the operation in detail. Written on the letterhead of Colt Protective Security on East Flamingo Road, the letter was dated November 21, 1994.

Dear Miss Rudin:

　　As per your instructions, Colt Protective Security, Incorporated conducted a surveillance of one Ron Rudin.

　　It was the understanding of Colt Protective Security, Incorporated that the purpose of this surveillance was to attempt to document the activities of Mr. Rudin in or about the vicinity of 327 Pecos Way, Las Vegas, Nevada on November 16th, 1994.

　　The surveillance was to commence about 11:45 a.m. Operative JF of Colt Protective Security was assigned, and about 11:30 a.m., operative took position with a clear view of 327 Pecos Way. The building appears to be a townhouse with security bars on the windows. There was a sign on one of the windows advertising "House for sale." A yellow light is on in front of the house.

At about 11:50 a.m., Mr. Rudin was observed operating a black Cadillac bearing Nevada license plate RRR-1. Immediately following was a white female with reddish brown hair, shoulder length. She appeared to be in her late 40s or early 50s, medium build, wearing blue denim skirt, denim jacket and white blouse. She was operating a brown Ford Taurus bearing Nevada license plate 575 ECW.

Mr. Rudin walked to her and both entered 327 Pecos Way. Both, apparently, remained therein for about 30 minutes.

At about 12:20 p.m., both Mr. Rudin and the unidentified female exited the building, entered their respective cars and departed the area. Mr. Rudin headed west on Desert Inn Road and the unidentified female went in the opposite direction.

It should be noted in the brief time Mr. Rudin and unidentified female were observed together, there were no signs of affection displayed between the two.

Department of Motor Vehicles records check of Nevada license plate 575 ECW was conducted with the following results: 575 ECW, 1989 Ford four door sedan vehicle identification number 1FABP52U7KG281649, registered owner, Sue R. Lyles, Las Vegas, Nevada, 89119. Last registered 9/6/94; due to expire 9/6/95.

This report is to confirm the verbal report given to you via telephone. The information contained in this report is for your exclusive use and furnished at your request. Department of Motor Vehicle information should be considered accurate but not guaranteed.

If you have any questions, don't hesitate to contact us.

                              Respectfully submitted,
                              Anthony Desio, president.

Within days, Sue would get the anonymous letters accusing her of having sex with Ron on dirty carpets. Ron and Sue would meet at that same condominium on Saturday, December 17, to discuss the letters—the last time Sue would ever see Ron.

29

THE TRIAL

It's an unlikely place for so many dreams to begin. A block south of Fremont Street's Four Queens Hotel and Casino, on the first floor of a turquoise-colored county building, couples line up to apply for licenses to get married in the state of Nevada. The only romance here, though, is in the minds of the soon-to-be betrothed, for this building also houses the Clark County criminal courts, where so many dreams die.

Two lines snake through the ground-floor lobby of the courthouse. The one on the right heads to the six windows at the Las Vegas Marriage License Bureau, a DMV-looking office where friendly clerks type up the names, dates of birth, addresses and other vital information for the purposes of getting the necessary paperwork for a wedding, which could take place within minutes if the couple so wishes. Outside, on Second Street, taxis and limousines wait to take couples to any of the city's more than 80 wedding chapels, where a ceremony can start at around $150.

This is a high-volume operation, Las Vegas being such a popular place for weddings because of the speed and lack of blood test. In 1999, more than 114,000 marriages were recorded. People arriving at the line at the courthouse encounter a sign telling them that only the bride and groom may enter the office because of the large number of applicants. The office is open 8 a.m. to midnight, Monday through Thursday, and then 24 hours a day Friday through midnight Sunday. The line moves swiftly, though on big days—like Valentine's Day—the wait can be an hour or more.

Both the bride- and groom-to-be fill out separate applications, showing a driver's license or passport as proof of ID and age. People aged 18 or older can get a license with relative ease; people 16 to 18 need a notarized permission letter from a parent or legal guardian. Once at the license bureau window, the couples pay $35, cash only, and head for the ceremony. Some are in such a hurry that they show up in full wedding formal wear to fill out the application. Outside the courthouse, where homeless people ask for change and court employees take their smoking breaks, wedding parties pose for pictures, before heading for the chapel. After the wedding, there's a $7 fee to record the marriage certificate.

To the left of the marriage license office is another line. Here, people enter the courthouse. The attorneys, the clients, the witnesses and the families must line up to go through a metal detector, ensuring that nobody tries to settle a dispute outside the courtroom with a gun or knife. It is not uncommon to see, from the wedding license line, a woman sobbing over the loss of a husband, father or child to the penal system. Men can be seen stamping out of the building in anger. Uniformed guards are posted to keep the peace.

Down the hall from the metal detector, then right down another hall at the end of the corridor, is a spacious courtroom that District Judge Joseph Bonaventure borrowed for the case of the *State of Nevada* vs. *Margaret Rudin*. Normally, he sits upstairs, in a smaller courtroom, but this one was used to accommodate the expected media crush. He brought his court staff downstairs, but left behind his sign, posted just below the bench, reading, "The truth takes few words." A judge in Las Vegas for 23 years, Bonaventure did have a reputation for expressing himself in words that were indeed few, and not infrequently quite loud, delivered in a strong New York accent. He was the youngest of eight children from a working-class Queens family. His parents were Italian immigrants: his mother a seamstress, his father a cab driver. He'd had to learn to be heard. It would serve him well in this case.

*   *   *

The pre-trial wrangling ended with a big victory for the prosecution and a big loss for the defense, and hard feelings that would continue throughout the trial. The prosecution scored when it persuaded the judge to let the jury hear Ron's directive to the trustees, telling them to use extraordinary means to investigate his death if it was violent. This would add a creepy element to the prosecution's case: the victim predicting his own death.

The defense, meanwhile, hit another wall.

Apparently no longer thinking his adversaries were of his same gentlemanly ilk, Amador accused prosecutor Gary Guymon of lying by disclosing to the public that a wallet found in those boxes sent by Margaret to her friend in Utah had been the one used by Ron at the time of the death. If true, this would look particularly bad for Margaret. Amador said the wallet was in fact an older one, with a long-expired driver's license. Amador also claimed that Guymon had been tardy in telling him that the critical witness Augustine Lovato had been promised a $25,000 reward for his cooperation in the case. Incensed, Amador said that Guymon's acts were so egregious, he should resign from the DA's office.

Prosecutors denounced the allegations as "garbage." The judge agreed. "Resign from the district attorney's office?" he said. "If that's not outrageous, I don't know what is." Bonaventure said Amador presented no evidence to support either charge; neither the newspaper clipping about the wallet nor the record in the case about Lovato backed him up. And on Monday, February 26—just before the first group of potential jurors were to come in for questioning—the judge unloaded on Amador.

"Mr. Amador, you tried to steal some of Mr. Guymon's reputation and it won't work in this court," he said. "It's outrageous, the motions you're filing." Amador responded, "I only know how to move forward and aggressively."

That's certainly how he handled the media. Amador, it

seemed, was everywhere the week before trial, giving interviews to *48 Hours* and *The Early Show* on CBS, as well as to local reporters. In an interview with Kim Smith of the *Las Vegas Sun*, Amador was all bravado, saying that the trial, to be televised live on Court TV, would be the "single- most complex and intriguing case in Las Vegas history." He added, "What I will present is the whole story, and not bits and pieces offered by paranoid prosecutors who are afraid of losing on national TV."

Opening statements were held on March 2, 2001, before a jury that had been selected in just two days. The judge told the panel the trial would last about four weeks. The courtroom was packed with media and spectators. Court TV had its robotic cameras mounted on the walls and a little mini-studio for reporter Mary Jane Stevenson set up under a canopy on the courthouse lawn. TV satellite trucks lined the street. Margaret was led into the courtroom by a bailiff. She wore a dark suit jacket over a white turtleneck, and her hair was pulled back in a simple ponytail.

There was a new face at the defense table. To help Amador with the work load, the judge had earlier assigned another defense lawyer, Bonaventure's old friend Tom Pitaro, to handle some of the witnesses. Though he had just lost the Binion case, Pitaro was considered one of the best trial attorneys in Las Vegas, one who could think quickly on his feet and come up to speed very fast—skills essential for this case, because he only had weeks to prepare.

Also added to the defense team were two investigators, also among the best in the state, Mike Wysocki and Tom Dillard. They too were fresh from the Binion trial, though they had been on opposing sides. Wysocki had worked for the defense of Sandy Murphy, while Dillard had been an investigator for Ted Binion's estate, gathering evidence used against Murphy at trial.

Amador was there too, of course, seated to Margaret's right.

But somebody else was not. Amador's wife and legal assistant, Lisa Nowak. Her absence would be explained later.

The prosecution, which has the burden of proof, went first. Deputy District Attorney Chris Owens walked up to the podium and, before introducing himself, read to jurors Margaret's diary entry of August 1987. This was the entry in which Margaret speaks of the "onetime stage production called Margaret's Life," and how she had learned that as director, producer and star, how much control she had.

"It may remind many of this Shakespeare quote from the play *As You Like It*—that all the world's a stage and that all men and women are merely players," Owens said. "Margaret at this point in her life, as she records in her diary, had decided that she was going to have her life, in this fifth marriage, as she liked it. And as she says in her diary, the way she was going to do that was through control."

And, oh, did she try to do this.

"Like an individual in the center of her own soap opera, she sat and manipulated, like a puppeteer pulling strings by use of wiretaps, recordings, information that she gave out, information that she didn't give out, the movement of evidence, the covering of evidence, the cleaning up of evidence," Owens said. "She tried to get the control that she wanted in her life."

The prosecution's opening was threatened to be drowned out by the clash of symbols, but the point was made. This was going to be an ambitious and potentially messy prosecution case. They were going to seek to portray Margaret as a grand manipulator, toying with Ron before killing him, then trying the same string-pulling after the murder. Approximately 70 witnesses would testify about events spanning 13 years in 2 dozen or more locations. There would be hundreds, if not a thousand pieces of evidence, and charts, graphs, photographs and a timeline to help keep everything straight.

Owens introduced Ron to the jury, describing him as a respected businessman. He said the last contact that Ron had had with anybody but the killer was a little after 8 p.m. the evening of December 18, 1994, when Dottie Flint called looking for Margaret, and Ron told the caller that Margaret was out and he was alone. Four days later, Ron's car was discovered by an "employee" at a "men's club." Owens didn't mention that the employee had once worked for the mob and that the club featured topless dancers. Ron's body—"such as it was"—was discovered January 21, 1995, by fishermen at Nelson's Landing, the prosecutor told the panel.

Owens described what the fishermen found as "basically a handful of charred human remains," with a skull that had ended up downhill. As he spoke, a picture of Ron's skull, lying on what would have been his left cheek, came up on the courtroom's computerized evidence presentation system, the image displayed on a screen in front of Margaret at the defense table. Margaret put her head down and closed her eyes.

That was about all the emotion Margaret showed during the prosecution's presentation. She mostly wrote on her legal pad or whispered to her attorneys. At some points, particularly when Owens discussed statements that Boscutti and Sharron Cooper had attributed to Margaret, she shook her head with a disgusted smile.

Owens discussed the physical evidence and the motive—"simple greed"—and previewed for the jury the testimony of Yehuda Sharon, whom the prosecution was going to tap one more time. Owens spoke of Augustine Lovato, of the blood in the bedroom, the gun in the lake and Margaret's flight and subsequent capture. "We will be asking you to return a verdict of murder," he said. "We will be asking you to write the final scene in the play, stage play or production that Margaret calls it, of her life."

Owens then read Ron's directive in the trust that calls for the investigation if Ron were to die violently, and the demand that if any heir were involved, that heir was to be axed out of the inheritance. "Mr. Guymon and I will be back up here asking you to write the final scene in this play, and that will be the final scene that finds Margaret accountable, accountable for the death of her husband, Ron Rudin. That is the verdict that will not only bring accountability to Margaret, but will bring justice to this case, and will bring some measure of vindication to Ron Rudin for what happened to him."

Michael Amador gave the defense opening, and it would be a doozy: "I reviewed again this morning most of my opening statement and threw it away. I don't know, maybe it's just something I do." Or maybe he shouldn't have. Long, rambling and at times just plain weird, the defense opening focused as much on Amador as it did on the facts of the case. "If you want to know an opinion about me—I guarantee you'll find some. It's different for different people. Not too many people know me. I have few close friends," he said, then made this link to the murder case: "Like Ron Rudin had few close friends." He talked about how he, Amador, would go to his son's soccer games and how he knew many of the cops involved in the case and how he would sometimes get frustrated and yell at his office staff.

The judge would interrupt Amador several times. With his eye on the clock, Bonaventure said he didn't mind 10 or 15 minutes of Amador's philosophical musings in front of the jury, but, "I wish in all respect that you would just get to what the evidence in your opinion tends to show. And then move on. I hate to interrupt you. I'm obligated as the judge to do that."

Amador, it seemed, ran into problems everywhere. He couldn't figure out how to use the courtroom electronic system in which pictures can be flashed on a big-screen TV in front of the jury and on monitors set up in front of the witness stand and the counsel tables. The prosecutors had to come over and help. Margaret had her head down, her eyes closed during this episode. Finally, a picture of

Ron's skull popped up on the monitor, and Amador made the vague remark: "What was left reveals some things that happened."

Amador then showed a picture of the Cadillac parked at the Crazy Horse Too and told jurors, for the first time in about an hour of talking, exactly what he thought the evidence would show. He said that four people, probably men, were inside that car, and that the mud that came off their boots onto the floorboards did not match the mud at Nelson's Landing, where Ron's remains were found.

He started to establish a key defense claim: that the body was not burned at Nelson's Landing. But he took a side trip into refuting the prosecution's claims of what Margaret's motives may have been. Amador made one of his stronger points, suggesting that jealousy over Ron's affair with Sue Lyles couldn't have been a good motive because "Sue Lyles wasn't the first." He also contended that money couldn't have motivated Margaret to kill. "She would have been better off in a divorce," he said, though he didn't elaborate.

He then leaped back in time to 1978, telling the jurors to take a close look at the circumstances surrounding Peggy Rudin's supposed suicide in the master bedroom. Amador hinted that Ron may have gotten a break in this case, telling jurors that Ron had friends in the homicide division of Metro. These ties may also have blinded investigators looking into Ron's case. "Ron Rudin was such a close friend to many of them, it helps understand why they were so zealous and did the things they did," he said.

Amador linked Peggy's death to the Ron Rudin case. He suggested that the evidence of the luminol test that supposedly showed lots of blood from Ron's slaying was flawed. "Their entire case rests on certain things," he said. "If they don't provide you with evidence as to these certain specific things, they have no case, because it's a circumstantial case. The circumstances must all fit, one after the other, collectively, and if one piece of it is pulled out, the whole thing falls."

Amador began bouncing around some more. In one breath he went back to the prosecution's claim that money was a motive. He told the jury to take one look at the Rudins' modest house and they could see why money may not have motivated Margaret. "You know why he lived there?" he asked. Then, in a whisper, he answered his own question: "He couldn't afford to live anywhere else. That's the truth."

Amador then went back to the crime scene. "I anticipate that the evidence will show in this case that Ron Rudin was not shot in his bedroom, that no murder took place in that bedroom and that there is actually no physical evidence of any kind that you can rely upon to believe that," he said.

It was getting to be too much for the judge. During a break, he told the attorney, "I keep saying: I let you get away with a lot, Mr. Amador," he said. "The purpose of an opening statement is just to indicate what the evidence is going to show, and not going into your personal beliefs and your passion and your soccer dad and your yelling at staff and when you were a green lawyer and you knew all the cops and you used to be DA and you communicate differently." The judge had apparently written all these things down as he looked to be reading them off. "I never heard that in an opening statement in my life."

30

LOVERS AND OTHER WITNESSES

The prosecution began the presentation of evidence with visions of a dark and stormy night. Two of the fishermen at Nelson's Landing recalled finding the skull, and later criminalist Sheree Norman described the scene as she found it the next day.

The autopsy results were given by Dr. Robert Jordan. Antiques picker Bruce Hornabach told the jury about warning Ron that his life might be in danger. Richard Aker of the Spy Factory testified about the listening devices that Margaret had used. Dottie Flint came in to talk about that final phone call to Ron shortly after 8 p.m., on December 18, 1994.

The testimony by all these witnesses was for the most part straightforward, interesting, and important to the prosecution's case. The defense scored a few points, getting Jordan to express doubts about the prosecution's theory of how the body was dumped, but otherwise no major advances with cross-examination. The first drama of the trial—outside of the growing animosity between Amador and the judge—came when the prosecution began calling the women in Ron's life, starting with his mistress Sue Lyles.

It was late afternoon on the second day of trial. It had already been a long day of testimony and jurors were getting fidgety. Michael Amador's cross-examination of a peripheral witness—a lawyer from the civil trial who was needed to get some documents into evidence for the prosecution—went nowhere; jurors' eyes were wandering.

Sue Lyles was called into the courtroom from the hallway outside, where she had been waiting on a bench during the other witnesses' testimony. After taking the oath, she sat in the witness chair, looking like she wanted to be anywhere on Earth but in that courtroom. She was a middle-aged woman in a smart blue jacket and white blouse, and she carried a black handbag. She wore glasses. The corners of her mouth dipped down, in a perpetual frown. Her voice was quiet and raspy, as though she had to force the words out. Several times she had to be reminded to speak up or to pull the microphone toward her.

Her testimony began outside the presence of the jury. It was a *voir dire*, in court terminology, a limited amount of testimony, so the judge could decide whether to allow the letters into evidence, as well as statements from Ron Rudin that he suspected that Margaret had sent them.

Prosecutor Gary Guymon gingerly questioned Sue about the anonymous letters she'd received at her home and how she and Ron had discussed them. "I told him I didn't know whether or not he should confront her. He knew better than I," said Sue. "I don't know whether or not he was going to confront her. He was very angry."

Through it all, Margaret stared at Sue from across the courtroom. Sue generally looked only at Guymon, though occasionally she would dart her eyes in Margaret's direction.

Guymon's gentle questioning gave way to blistering cross-examination from Tom Pitaro, who showed no mercy for Sue. In a loud, sometimes sarcastic voice, he pounded Sue on inconsistencies between her testimony and her previous statements to police or in court.

"I was extremely upset when I gave that statement," she tried to explain. "Ron was missing."

But his questions kept coming fast and furious, sometimes overlapping her answers, resulting in warnings from the judge. Why didn't she mention the Melissa/Natalie issue in her police statement? Why did she describe Ron as "upset" in 1994 but then called him "angry" in that day's testimony? Why did she lie to police by failing to mention that her relationship with Ron was intimate? On it went, and each time Sue responded that she wasn't thinking straight in the days after Ron's disappearance.

"I wasn't thinking about the prior times and was only thinking: Ron is missing. What's happened to him?" she said. "I was thinking about current things that had happened."

After 25 minutes of this, the first part of her testimony was finished. Over strong defense objections, Bonaventure would allow the jury to see the anonymous letter and hear Sue's testimony about Ron's comments that he believed Margaret had sent the letters.

After a brief break, Sue returned to court, looking even more haggard than before. Now she would face the actual jury. Jurors perked up in their chairs and leaned forward, anticipating day-ending fireworks. Sue spoke of her life, her affair with Ron, her marriage that had ended after 29 years. She explained why she didn't tell her husband about the affair until after the civil trial.

And she told the jury about the letters.

Pitaro then launched his cross-examination, portraying Sue as a woman who'd built an elaborate deception—against her husband, her children, Margaret Rudin and police. He said she was cheating on her husband. She responded quietly, "It's not a word I would use."

He asked her repeatedly about inconsistencies between her trial testimony and her original statement to police. Each time, she said she had made her comments to police when she was upset.

"You were upset, not because of what you did, but because you got caught?" he asked. "Isn't that right?"

She didn't answer.

"Isn't that right?" he said more loudly.

Again no answer.

"Isn't that right?!"

Finally, she said, "I was upset. I didn't want my children to know."

By now, it was nearing 6 p.m. The rest of the courthouse had closed for the day and the building ventilation had apparently been shut down. Though it was cold and drizzly outside, the windowless courtroom was hot and stuffy. Jurors started sipping water and fanning themselves with their notebooks.

"Isn't it true you were upset because you got caught, not because of what you did?" Pitaro repeated.

"Yes," she said softly.

"No . . . further . . . questions," Pitaro said with dramatic pauses between the words.

Guymon re-questioned her briefly. When finished, Sue Lyles wiped her brow with her hand. Her face was flushed. She got off the witness stand and walked straight for the back door, looking at neither the jury to her left, nor the attorneys—and Margaret—to her right.

She walked through the lobby and exited the courthouse through the glass doors, past the line of couples getting marriage licenses, into the damp desert air.

The trial temporarily lost its emotional edge with the March 7 testimony of Harold Boscutti, Ron's business associate and trustee of his estate, who described what he called Margaret's bizarre activities after Ron's disappearance. Boscutti said that Margaret seemed more worried about Ron's money than about Ron. Amador was able to use Boscutti in cross-examination to bring out details of Ron's allegedly shady business dealings and tried to portray Boscutti and co-trustee Sharron Cooper as cruel toward Margaret by taking away her house and car. Boscutti admitted that when all was said and done he was more than $1 million richer because of Ron's death.

The trial quickly returned to a higher intensity on March 8, when the prosecution called bookkeeper Sharon Melton. As with Sue Lyles, the prosecution treated Sharon gently, taking her through her work with Ron, the frantic morning that he disappeared and the confusion with the trustees afterwards. Sharon also told how Margaret entered the office and claimed that Ron had been found, just days before he actually was.

The cross-examination by Amador was, as expected,

tough—though not as much as the one that Sue Lyles underwent. For one, Amador's courtroom style was considerably different from that of his co-counsel Tom Pitaro. While Pitaro came out guns a'blazin', Amador picked his moments, at times being nice to Sharon, at times grilling her. He elicited evidence about the promissory notes in the names of people who apparently didn't exist. Amador asked if these promissory notes were "executed to give the impression that Mr. Rudin was borrowing money and carrying debt when in fact he was not?"

"Correct," said Sharon, also confirming that she had confronted Ron about what appeared to be a scheme to avoid paying some taxes. She said Ron stopped his ways and started declaring the proper income to the IRS.

"Did you help him cover up these phony notes?" Amador asked.

"No, I didn't," she said. "As long as someone was claiming it as income, I didn't have a problem."

"You can say all sorts of things," Amador snapped.

After a prosecution objection that Amador was admonishing a witness, the judge reprimanded Amador—one of many times during the trial. "Don't make any comments. Just ask questions," Bonaventure said.

At another point, Amador tried to undermine Sharon's credibility, taking her to task on her claim that she'd heard gunshots the morning Ron didn't show up for work. He noted that the murder weapon had a silencer. The lawyer suggested that Sharon made up the gunshot story so the trust could deny money for Margaret.

"I'm not saying that was the time he was murdered," she said. "All I'm telling you is what I thought I heard."

Amador also questioned Melton as to why, if she was so worried about Ron, she had gone to a donut shop rather than the police station. "Is that a local substation for the police?" he asked.

"Do you want an answer for that?" she said in a calm voice.

Amador also went after Sharon for her media appearances.

"You've been waiting for this trial for a long time, haven't you?" Amador asked.

"I've been waiting for justice for a long time," she said.

When he asked her if she'd gotten paid to go on *Hard Copy*, *Inside Edition* and *America's Most Wanted*, she leaned into the microphone and said, "I got paid by nobody."

"You don't have to get mad at me," Amador said.

"I want to make the record clear."

"We're going to make the record clear about a lot of things," Amador said.

"Good," Sharon said, "we're on the same side."

31

WE WON BY LOSING

Since Amador's strange opening statement, there had been rumors of trouble in the defense camp. The Monday after the opening, the judge—normally a stickler for starting on time—kept the jury waiting for hours during the morning while he held a secret meeting with defense attorneys and prosecutors. The rumor sweeping the courthouse was that the case was on the brink of a mistrial, that Margaret was so unhappy with her defense that she wanted the plug pulled and the case started over with new counsel. But no one would comment and the trial chugged along.

Prosecutors presented more evidence of Margaret's actions after Ron's disappearance, calling the police clerks who took the missing persons reports. They also called legal attorney Patricia Brown to talk about Ron's fears that his wife would kill him—and the terms of the directive. They also introduced the tape of Margaret's statement to the missing persons detectives.

For the defense, Pitaro continued to play pit bull. Sometimes he went overboard—he got particularly rough with tax preparer Carol Kawazoe, who seemed to have no agenda but did tend to give rambling answers to straightforward questions. But other times, his style worked. He elicited vital information from missing persons detective Frank Janise: that he had gotten on his hands and knees on Ron Rudin's bedroom and didn't see any blood.

Amador, however, stumbled. Though he had skillfully cross-examined Sharon Melton, he tried to use the cross-examination of Patricia Brown to introduce a series of documents related to Ron's real estate business. But the documents were poorly organized and Brown often appeared to be the wrong witness to talk about them. The judge barked at Amador, "I'm confused and I imagine the jury is confused with all these documents. This doesn't seem like a murder trial to me. It seems like a civil or tax trial." He also chided Amador for his continued tardiness to court, noting that on this particular morning he was out doing a TV interview.

Things would get even worse for Amador. On Wednesday, March 14, nine days into the trial, the prosecution called one of the most damaging—and, for Margaret, emotionally hurtful—witnesses, her sister Dona, now remarried and going by the name Dona Cantrell-Robinson. While the jury had seemed restless during other testimony, and particularly during Amador's tedious, document-filled cross-examination of Brown, the appearance of the 49-year-old younger sister of Margaret re-energized the panel. Jurors immediately started taking copious notes as Dona—who bore a striking resemblance to Margaret—unloaded on her sister.

Dona discussed Margaret's tumultuous relationship with Ron, including her talk of divorce; the purchase of the listening device; her seeming lack of concern for anything but money; and covering her tracks after Ron disappeared. She spoke of Margaret totaling her husband's assets before his remains were even found and how she had destroyed the cassette tape the day police searched the house. She recalled how when she told Margaret, "I hope you don't know something," that Margaret had slowly replied, "I . . . don't . . . give . . . a . . . shit."

In the cross-examination, Amador questioned Dona about upheavals in her own past, including marital strife and a history of mental illness that had her taking medication for depression. The judge didn't want this line of questioning to continue without a hearing, so he sent the jury home. Bonaventure said he found the questions distasteful. "It's sounding like a Jerry Springer show here on this case," he said. But Amador insisted that the issues were relevant: for instance, the medication may have interfered with Dona's memory.

Through it all, Margaret never looked up, never

showed emotion. But that night after her sister's first day on the stand, she met with her lawyers and investigators at the Clark County Detention Center for three hours. The next day, Thursday, court was delayed for two and a half hours while Margaret huddled with her attorneys. Finally, at 11:30 a.m., Bonaventure convened court and asked Margaret what was going on.

In a soft voice, she said, "I would like to ask for a mistrial because I don't believe Mr. Amador is prepared enough."

The judge ordered the lawyers and Margaret to see him in his chambers, where Margaret again said she thought Amador wasn't ready. In chamber she said he was particularly ill-prepared to question her sister Dona "because I knew the things she was going to try to say." When she had heard the judge complain, once again, about Amador in court, she had made up her mind. "That's when I decided I have to follow my instincts at this point, and my instincts say you can't just go on saying things are going to get better," she said. She said that Pitaro had done everything he could, but "I was just so frustrated and so upset after we left court yesterday."

The judge noted that Amador hadn't really done much of anything the previous day, that much of the session consisted of Dona's direct testimony, and that Amador only got out a few questions about her mental health when the judge sent the jury home for the hearing. But Margaret insisted the problems ran deeper. She said that the investigation of other witnesses still was lacking—or hadn't been done at all.

"It scares me so that I get panicky thinking, how can we go forward when this is my life?" she said.

Pitaro then laid out the defense's problems in more detail.

"For whatever reason it's not ready, it's not ready," he said. "That's obvious to any observer of this case, that for the first two weeks this is not the way you try cases, and this is not the way you try murder cases."

The problems were many: Witnesses who hadn't been interviewed, documents that hadn't been read or properly filed, experts who hadn't been retained. Pitaro said he would open a witness file and there would be nothing in it.

"What we are putting on in front of the world is a farce, and that disturbs me as an attorney because I'm a participant in it and I do the best I can and everyone does the best they can, but this has become a sham, a farce and a mockery," he said.

Pitaro said he felt "terrible" bringing these things up and that he was not trying to assign any blame. "It is extremely personally distasteful to me to be in these chambers making these representations because I like this guy. I like Mike and I think he's to be complimented, not criticized for the burden he took on," said Pitaro. "But he took on a burden that he should not have taken on."

Pitaro asked: "So is this case ripe for a mistrial? Yeah. That's the court's choice, not mine. But I don't know how we get out of this bind. I don't know how the state gets out of it, I don't know how the defense gets out of it. I leave it with you."

The judge thanked Pitaro and asked Margaret if she had any problems with what he'd just said.

"Nothing," she said. "He's perfect."

With his co-counsel now having fully eviscerated Amador's efforts in front of the judge, prosecutors and the client, it was left to Amador to speak for himself.

"I've spent, I guess, the last hour making notes and writing down my thoughts regarding certain problems and issues involved in this case," he said. "I don't believe in allowing someone else to describe my inadequacies or unpreparedness when the proper person to discuss it is me."

"You know," the judge reminded him, "we are going to go in open court at 2 o'clock to put these same representations on the record."

"I do. I do, Judge," he said. "In fact, I'll be more— I'm not going to read through my notes for you right now. I'll just give you an idea of the things I'll talk about, but I'll ask permission from the court—I know you always allow me to make a record—that you allow me the time to read through it and make a complete record."

And so, then, before going public with it all, Amador spelled out the situation in chambers—the defense attorney now defending himself, his reputation.

"I don't think the problem with the trial has been lack of diligence or lack of effort or time spent on the case," Amador said. "When I spoke to Margaret initially and reviewed the grand jury transcript and a second grand jury transcript, I could tell from the case that it was complicated and involved a lot of witnesses, but it wasn't so complicated that I thought for a minute that even I alone with a lot of staff would be able to prepare adequately for trial.

"But there were additional issues that I wasn't completely aware of until after I already became attorney of record, when I received a lot of additional information from the public defender's office, and it was far more complex than any case I've ever seen. And I mentioned it in court before and most people couldn't believe it could be more complicated than the Binion case that you had. And few people other than myself and Margaret know that it is far more complicated. And the defense that she had asked me to investigate and that I spent a great deal of time investigating were the areas where it took too much of my time to the detriment of other areas of the case. Witnesses who didn't cooperate and who wouldn't talk to us, and that's just a part of the way the game is played.

"However, there were witnesses that we needed to talk to that were on Margaret's witness list, certainly many of the witnesses that Margaret may have suggested would not have been witnesses that we could actually call. And the issues presented yesterday with Dona Cantrell I think would be a good example. There were issues that I think we could properly go into and other issues of other bad acts that were simply remote or not relevant to the issues that you would have to make a decision on. But, nevertheless, it would have been incumbent upon me to present my case to have investigated each of those concerns prior to trial to the extent that she would feel comfortable that we were prepared with each of the witnesses."

Amador spoke of problems he'd had with the private investigator he had used before Wysocki and Dillard were assigned. He said he was hit with a load of documents at the eleventh hour.

Then he explained why his wife wasn't at the defense table. There was "an abrupt end of my relationship with her." He lost not only a wife, but a legal assistant. He also lost his receptionist, who was his mother-in-law.

"The court noticed that weekend a month before Super Bowl weekend, a month before trial that I had some difficulty in getting motions in by the deadline," said Amador. "I would be hitting the deadline and trying to get an extension an hour here or perhaps the next morning. It wasn't through a lack of diligence. I would spend every day at the office and work on motions oftentimes until two, three o'clock in the morning because even our motion practice was extensive. And it interfered with my preparation in other areas."

He said he spent a lot of time on the scientific evidence—and wasted a lot of time with an expert witness who flaked out on him.

"I can't say the blame is on someone else, it's my fault because it's my responsibility," said Amador. "The lack of time and other efforts that we had to spend time on required me to ask him to do this and it wasn't done. I shut down the ordinary daily active part of my practice . . . and I took the court at its word when you said I would not get another continuance, that it wasn't going to happen."

It all came to a head with the testimony of Dona Cantrell-Robinson.

"Margaret had occasion to see her sister on the witness stand, a very damaging witness," he said. "Would I be prepared to cross-examine her? I think experience and a certain degree of talent would allow me to examine her and discredit her. There are issues and other statements I think that would also do so, but you know what's missing? What's missing is the time that we would have needed to follow up on issues that Margaret had raised and asked us to look into. Other witnesses, as to events and circumstances that would have been helpful for impeachment purposes. And we didn't do it. It's not that I didn't want to do it, it's that in terms of the priorities of time and efforts I spent upon two other portions of the case to the detriment of this part of the case."

Finally, he admitted what everybody else had known: the opening statement was a mess.

"The week before trial I saw what was before us, I saw the intense need for additional witness preparation and I spent an enormous amount of time in doing everything I could to prepare as many as possible. I prioritized the most important witnesses—Melton, the other witnesses called the first week," he said. "But those efforts left me absolutely exhausted by the time I gave my opening statement. I had slept little just trying to make up for lost time to get ready for the witnesses I knew that would be called. . . . By the time I was ready to give my opening statement, I was overwhelmed and I could hardly think. And my efforts in the opening statement were inadequate."

He concluded by saying, "I don't like, like I said, having to admit fault nor mistakes; nobody does. Criticism of attorneys comes without limitation from the press and from others. But that's a part of getting a degree of an attorney and that's a part of what we do in our practice. If I'm criticized, if I'm used to blame a mistrial, then so be it. Because again, it's not me, it's Margaret's rights to a fair trial that are paramount and the only thing that's really important."

The judge asked if he thought his performance had

perfect, Mr. Amador, and you indicated, thus far, you feel you were effective. Is that correct, thus far?"

"Judge," Amador said, the swagger returning, "I said I thought we won every witness."

After having a weekend to mull it over, Bonaventure made his ruling. Late in the morning of Monday, March 19, he read it from the bench, the longest and most detailed ruling of the case. He began by waxing philosophical. "A trial lives and breathes, with each one having a life of its own, its own unique personality with all its ebbs and flows," he said. "At any point in time during a trial, its participants can describe its status, with each side having directly opposing views as to how it is progressing. Those same views can be 180 degrees divergent from the day before. An attorney can describe the appearance of a trial in such grand hyperbole as his vocabulary allows and another, in good faith, can offer to fall on his sword on behalf of his client.

"But," the judge said, "to declare an abrupt halt to an ongoing murder trial, the sword must be one of tempered steel and not silicone rubber."

Amador and Pitaro watched, expressionless, as did the prosecutors, Owens and Guymon. Margaret had a slight smile on her face. She knew what was coming. The judge had gathered defense lawyers into his chambers before reading the ruling.

In his ruling, which quoted from a number of cases, Bonaventure said that to declare a mistrial was a step of great magnitude—and one fraught with some risk for the prosecution. A misstep by the judge, and jeopardy could attach to the case: Margaret could get a mistrial and, because a person can't be tried twice for the same crime—double jeopardy—she could walk away free.

The judge traced the rocky history of the case since Amador took over seven months earlier, on July 27, 2000, making note of the continuances, the appointment of Pitaro and Amador's tardy filing of motions. He also noted meetings in which Margaret had voiced her concerns but was later satisfied with her defense. The judge went over that final day in chambers and in court in which the lawyers outlined the shortcomings of the defense.

Bonaventure then fed Amador's words back to him. "Mr. Amador, on behalf of Mrs. Rudin, asks this court to declare a mistrial due to not being prepared, although he feels they have won every witness so far in the case," he said. "And although he feels his opening statement fell below the standard (required by law), he is not willing to say his entire performance has—nor is Mr. Pitaro willing to comment on such."

Quoting from another decision, the judge said: "A defendant is entitled to a fair trial but not a perfect one."

Noting that Margaret "has made it a habit of changing and removing her civil and criminal attorneys at will," the judge said it would be a "dangerous precedent" to declare a mistrial under these circumstances. "There is no room in a court system already clogged up to grant attorneys the ability to stop a trial due to his or her perception of possible future performance," he said. "There is a need for a finality in a system that is already second-guessing itself."

With that, the judge found against Margaret. Any screw-ups by Amador amounted to "harmless error." The judge did, however, give the defense more money for investigation and an expert witness, and more time to prepare for their case in chief.

The cross-examination of Margaret's sister, Dona Cantrell-Robinson, was to continue.

Outside of court, Amador spun the decision as a victory for the defense. "I won the motion by having it denied," he said. "Her only chance of an acquittal is with us, with this trial."

32

CIRCUS-CIRCUS

Whether he thought he had something to prove—or whether he just had a little more time to prepare—Amador seemed re-invigorated after the ruling, as he launched into a cross-examination of Margaret's sister.

"Isn't it true that you are so jealous of your sister that you would do almost anything to hurt her?" he asked.

She replied, "I think just the opposite is true."

Amador elicited some damaging information, including Dona's acknowledgment that she had taken anti-depressants and the fact that she had accepted $2,000 for an interview with the TV show *Hard Copy*.

The judge, also, was a little different. He toned down his usual impatience for Amador, at least in front of the jury, though Bonaventure could only take so much. Amador tested the judge again when he asked Dona whether she'd had an intimate relationship with Detective Vaccaro. Dona had denied ever saying such a thing and the judge cut Amador short.

And there was a new Margaret in court. Gone was the simple ponytail. After Dona came to court, made-up, styled and accessorized, Margaret let her hair down and gave it a little wave. She started wearing more makeup.

So for an afternoon, at least, it was a new defense—far from the farce that Pitaro had called it. The questions were: Would it continue—and could the prosecution respond?

The aggressive defense continued when Augustine Lovato testified on March 20. Wearing a blue shirt and tie, Augustine—no longer the skinny kid of seven years earlier, but a man with thinning hair—recounted his tale of blood stains and the heebie-jeebies. He told the jury about cleaning up the stain in the laundry area, of ripping

up the stained carpet, of gazing uneasily at the portrait of
Margaret speckled with what he thought were blood
drops, of dumping the box spring and mattress in the alley
near the freeway.

The cross-examination was handled by Pitaro, and he
used his usual tough tactics. He established Augustine's
criminal record and drew out that Augustine had earlier
downplayed the nature of the fight—failing to mention to
police and the grand jury that the fight did in fact involve
a baseball bat. The lawyer established some inconsistencies in Augustine's various statements—the date he found
the gurgling blood in the bathtub had changed, the date
the new carpet was installed may have been in error—
and he tried to paint Augustine as a snoop who had no
business poking around the house the way he did.

But the thrust of the cross-examination was the con-
tention that Augustine couldn't be trusted because he was
in search of the $25,000 reward that had been posted be-
fore he went to police. Pitaro suggested that Augustine,
after working those days for Margaret in December, got
wind of the reward, then went out searching for her.

"If anyone needed a reward back in 1995, it was you
and your mother?" Pitaro asked.

"It didn't matter," Augustine said.

Pitaro replied sarcastically, "It didn't matter?"

"This was never about rewards," Augustine said, raising his voice. "This was about a man that was dead."

Later, Pitaro suggested that Augustine was an ingrate.
"This lady treated you decent?" he said.

Augustine agreed. "That's why I have a hard time be-
lieving this," he said.

Dripping with sarcasm again, the lawyer snapped,
"Thank you for repaying her in this way."

Pitaro tried beating up on Augustine's mother, Terry Hall,
who was called to corroborate some of her son's testimony. "Lock and load," the attorney said as the woman
was brought to the stand. But she was more than willing

to return fire, shouting, "That's not true!" when Pitaro suggested that her son was lying to get the $25,000 in reward money. She never backed down.

By now clearly the lead attorney in the case, Pitaro had even less luck rattling a key police witness, Detective Ramos, who on March 26 calmly denied every one of the lawyer's insinuations that police had railroaded Margaret and inadequately followed other leads. Never getting defensive and never raising his voice, Ramos said that police had kept their minds open and "I thought we were being pretty damn thorough."

The defense team, meanwhile, got a mid-trial boost when John Momot joined for free, saying he was doing it as a favor for Pitaro. That brought more firepower to the defense table with Momot handling the complicated scientific evidence, and giving Margaret her wish of months earlier: to have the Sandy Murphy Dream Team of lawyers from the Binion trial, albeit a little late in the game.

Momot's arrival came in the nick of time. The prosecution unveiled its most powerful physical evidence, eliciting testimony about the blood drops found in the bedroom of the Rudin home, with police lab man Michael Perkins opining that Ron was shot in the head there, and testimony about the discovery of the murder weapon at the bottom of Lake Mead.

The jury also heard about Margaret's activities the night the search warrant was served, including her trip to the Dumpster at the Circle K convenience store and her drive to Los Angeles International Airport with Yehuda. Jurors saw a surveillance picture at the airport, with Yehuda pulling a luggage cart and Margaret behind him.

DNA experts wrapped up the physical evidence portion of the case by saying that much of the blood found in the bedroom had the same genetic profile as the blood found on the handkerchief. Only one piece of biological evidence in the bedroom didn't fit: the white material scraped off the ceiling.

That, an expert reported, was probably brain material from a woman. The inference was clear and chilling: it belonged to Peggy Rudin.

The blood, the experts said, came from a man. Prosecutors would argue it was Ronald Rudin's blood, splattered on the same ceiling as his former wife's brains.

The prosecution then called Yehuda Sharon. Still enjoying immunity from prosecution as long as he didn't lie on the stand, Sharon didn't say anything bad about Margaret. Indeed, it seemed the only purpose in calling him was for the prosecution to suggest an accomplice. Ramos had acknowledged earlier in his testimony that Margaret couldn't have done all this without some help.

From the first question, he raised eyebrows in his April 4 testimony. Asked his name, Yehuda said, "Eugene Warner." After explaining that he went by two names, he gave long rambling answers in a heavy accent and used his favorite disclaimer—"Put it this way"—before answering simple questions. He repeated his account of renting the car, then the van, then going down to either Barstow or Victorville, turning around and coming back to Las Vegas, never using the van to transport an antique trunk.

Only this time, he brought something new: a photocopy of a receipt from an AM/PM gas station near Barstow showing that he had in fact stopped there early the morning of 12/22/94.

But prosecutor Gary Guymon, who was questioning Yehuda, suggested that the "4" in "94" was not as clearly printed as the other numbers, alleging that Yehuda had brought in an altered copy of the receipt. Yehuda denied this, but that wasn't the end of it.

In the midst of a very friendly cross-examination of Yehuda by Amador, the defense called for a mistrial, the basis this time not its own incompetence but dirty dealing by the prosecution. Pitaro argued that the prosecution only called Yehuda to discredit him with a "little stunt tactic," a legal no-no. Bonaventure denied the mistrial motion, but refused to let the prosecution beat up on Yehuda any more by calling a person from the gas station to testify that the price of gas and other information on the receipt was inconsistent with what would have been shown in 1994.

After losing the mistrial motion, the defense began to stumble, with Amador's problems returning with the cross-examination of Ron's second wife, Caralynne Rudin, who had told the jury that Ron was a "delightful man" despite his one problem—the drinking. She also spelled out some of the details of the Lee Canyon property sale she had helped broker. Amador attempted to use his cross-examination to elicit testimony to bolster the defense theory that some of Ron's shady business dealings may have gotten him killed.

Once again, Amador found himself drowning in documents. The judge became irritated when the documents weren't properly marked, weren't notarized as required for entry into evidence, and were just generally disorganized. It didn't help Amador's case that he agreed to meet with the prosecutor one morning before the jury arrived to sort things out, only to fail to show up.

"Why didn't you meet Mr. Guymon like you were supposed to?" Judge Bonaventure shouted.

"That was my fault," Amador said. Amador had been living in a downtown hotel during the trial. "I arise because of a wake-up call. The hotel didn't call me. . . . I apologize. I simply didn't get a wake-up call from the hotel and couldn't meet with him."

He said he hadn't gotten up until his son called him later that morning—he didn't say why he didn't use an alarm clock.

"I don't have wake-up calls!" the judge shouted. "I just get up."

By the end of the day the judge was so fed up with

Amador that he stormed off the bench and released the jury early.

After this, the trial plodded along with testimony about Margaret's near-capture in Phoenix and her actual capture in Revere, Massachusetts, and an appearance by trustee Sharron Cooper, whom Amador tried to use to again bring out more convoluted evidence about Ron's business dealings.

Finally, on April 10, after calling 66 witnesses over 23 tumultuous days, the prosecution rested.

"Hopefully," the judge told the jury, "the case will be submitted to you soon."

After all that had gone on, the defense of Margaret Rudin began quietly enough. The judge had given Margaret's camp an extra week to prepare, and the case started on April 16, 2001, with an expert witness, John DeHaan, who testified he didn't believe that the entire body of Ron Rudin could have been burned at Nelson's Landing the way prosecutors said it was. He estimated it would have taken 55 gallons of gasoline to burn Ron's 6-foot, 220-pound body—and even then it would have had to have been burned for four hours. The defense also called a general manager from US Rent-A-Car to say that Yehuda had returned a clean van. But under cross-examination, the witness noted that Yehuda also had said he had used the van to move a piece of furniture, mentioning nothing about the thwarted holy oil bottle trip.

The defense then put on a couple of friends of Margaret, including Jeanne Nakashima, who testified that she had attended the grand opening of Margaret's Antique Merchants on December 18, 1994, then returned to the shop that night, staying with Margaret until nearly 1 a.m. on December 19—the day Ron disappeared. In these hours leading up to Margaret's nocturnal visit to the tax preparer, they sat in the antique shop and talked. Jeanne's boyfriend was seriously ill and she was feeling down. It was a visit, prosecutors would point out later, that Margaret made no mention of in her statement to the missing persons detectives.

According to Jeanne, the next evening, Margaret went to Jeanne's house to hear her play the piano—she said she was an accomplished musician—and have some dinner. Ron hadn't shown up that day and Margaret "appeared very quiet, a little upset." Jeanne said that she'd told Margaret, "I hope he's not a wanderer like my ex-husband was. I fixed dinner for him. I waited for him to come home." She had told Margaret that they were living in Hawaii and that her husband wouldn't even leave the islands without telling her. Eventually, he always came home. She said she had also told Margaret how her grown son once disappeared in Las Vegas and that Metro police had told Jeanne she had to wait 48 hours before making a report.

Jeanne testified that Margaret later invited her over to Christmas at the Rudin house. Margaret, according to her friend, appeared "pale and tired and worried about her husband," though she admitted on cross-examination that in a photo from that day a smiling Margaret didn't look that way. Jeanne also noted that she'd never talked to prosecutors and that she was still a friend of Margaret's, visiting her in jail.

Another acquaintance whose actions were left out of Margaret's statement to police was Barbara Orcutt, who ran a lodge and restaurant on Mount Charleston that Ron and Margaret had frequented. The day that Ron disappeared, Barbara Orcutt said, she spoke to Margaret on the phone and then sent a wrangler out to search the snowy mountain for any traces of the Realtor. The wrangler didn't find him.

Later, in the spring of 1995, Margaret asked for—and then got—a job as a hostess in the cabin office, greeting guests, answering questions at the front desk, doing clerk work. Orcutt and her husband had some reservations about hiring Margaret because of the publicity linking her to Ron's murder, but they did anyway, and had no regrets. Since Margaret didn't have a car at the time—the trustees had taken away the leased Lincoln—she had to hitch rides up the mountain from other employees living in Las Vegas. Her employment didn't last long; in the fall, she gave two weeks' notice and quit.

It was on the third day of the defense case, April 18, that things began to heat up. The trouble started with what should have been another bland witness, an expert named John Thornton who was called to say that an analysis of the blood specks in the bedroom showed that Ron couldn't have been shot in there. The specks, he would say, were the wrong shape and size to have come from blood shooting out of Ron's head while he was in bed. He wouldn't say where he thought the blood had come from—"I don't have a clue"—though the defense had suggested nosebleeds.

To illustrate these points, the defense erected an elaborate display: a close replica of the south end of the Rudin bedroom. Looking like a stage set, the replica featured the back wall, two side walls, the sloping ceiling and a bed. The defense then colored in the places where the blood spots were found. It was all set up at one end of the courtroom, and jurors were allowed to leave the box for the audience seats to get a better look.

All was well and good until Pitaro and Momot decided to illustrate the defense's points with a demonstration in front of the jury.

"Bang! Bang! Bang! Bang! Bang!" Pitaro boomed, pointing his finger like a gun. Momot flopped dead in the courtroom. The demonstration was designed to show the jury that the blood specks couldn't have landed the way they did if Ron was shot where he was.

Prosecutor Chris Owens immediately asked to approach the bench, and the jury was sent out. Owens complained that Pitaro and Momot were acting as their own witnesses, which is against trial rules, by staging the shooting re-enactment.

"It's unprofessional, unethical," Owens said. "I've never seen anything like that. . . . It was not an ethical thing to do. It's just in line with the same kind of sandbagging stuff going on throughout the case."

Owens was so angry, he asked that sanctions be levied against the defense.

Pitaro replied, "This is my case and my defense of this lady. I didn't think it was outrageous. I thought it was good advocacy."

Judge Bonaventure, whose patience was in tatters because of all the problems—many on the defense side—that caused the trial to drag on, begged to differ.

"What it is, you keep saying that lady has a right to a trial. The state has a right to a fair trial too," he snapped.

"I think they are getting it," Pitaro snapped back.

Growing increasingly angry, the judge said, "The state has a right to a fair trial too. What you did, you asked the doctor a question, and all of a sudden, you and John Momot had that charade of going through something which, in effect, you're testifying and Mr. Momot is testifying. That's not the way the state gets a fair trial. You ask the doctor a question; let the doctor say a scenario; and he'll say: Well, a possible scenario would be this, this or this. Don't you and Mr. Momot have that charade. That's all I'm saying. Now, I'm not going to sanction you, but I'm going to caution the jury to disregard what you and Mr. Momot did when—"

Pitaro interrupted the judge, saying, "I think that's unfair to Mrs. Rudin."

"It's unfair to the state, too!"

"It isn't. It's—"

"Listen to me!" the judge said. "You better not start yelling, Mr. Pitaro. I made a ruling and it sticks. You understand that?"

"That's fine, Judge."

"Don't start yelling at me. I'm telling you, I'm sick of your yelling."

"I don't appreciate your yelling at me, Judge."

"That's too bad. I'm going to caution the jury that you were wrong doing that. And if you want to ask that doctor a question, let him testify."

When the jury returned, the judge told the panel: "What Mr. Pitaro did with Mr. Momot was highly improper, as far as this court was concerned. An attorney is not supposed to testify. It's up to a witness to testify. So I strongly urge you to disregard what Mr. Momot and Mr. Pitaro did."

The defense later called one of Ron's former employees, Susan Reasbeck, an attractive blonde who portrayed Ron as something of a creepy boss. When he wasn't hitting on her when she worked there in the late 1980s, he was having nosebleeds that made him sneeze, she said. Outside of court, she told Court TV that Ron once told her he'd been questioned about Peggy's death, but no charges were filed. "I just joked and said, 'Did you?' and he looked me right in the eye and said, 'Susan, no one will ever know,'" said Reasbeck, who added that she was so upset she'd wanted to run, not walk, away. She admitted to having some hard feelings toward Ron; one of his dogs had seriously injured her son. She also had nothing but kind words about Margaret, calling her "the ultimate lady."

After her, more witnesses friendly with Margaret took the stand. An uncle from Tennessee, Curtis Lynch, recalled that Ron and Margaret had visited Margaret's mother in Henderson, Tennessee, over Thanksgiving 1994—just weeks before Ron's disappearance—and everything had seemed fine between the two of them.

"They were conversing, they were holding hands and just being like a married couple should be," said Lynch.

Prosecutor Chris Owens tried to ask the uncle during cross-examination whether he knew that Margaret was bugging Ron's office at the time that she was acting as a married woman should, but the judge wouldn't let him.

Another person close to Margaret, Illinois lawyer Robert Will, said he'd spoken to Margaret on January 29, 1995, after she had flown to Illinois the night her house was searched. A couple days later, he met with her in his office. "She was very distraught, she was scared," he said. "I could observe that, her manner of talking. I know Margaret. She was very, very worried and very, very scared." Concerned that she might get arrested in Illinois, he advised her to return to Las Vegas and get a lawyer there.

Much of the rest of the day was consumed by the testimony of real estate expert Terrance Cluretie, who went through Ron's many transactions and determined that some were in fact shady, saying that it wasn't proper to use fictitious names as Ron did. The expert didn't say what this might have to do with Ron's murder, and the judge was perturbed that he'd even allowed the testimony. "The jury is fed up with hearing about these deeds, in this court's humble opinion," Bonaventure said.

And on that sour note, the defense rested.

Margaret was not called to the stand.

But it wouldn't end there. The prosecution began its rebuttal case the next day with more blood splatter testimony from their own expert, Michael Perkins, but this testimony was merely a side show. The main attraction now was the fight between the two loudest men in the courtroom: Judge Bonaventure and defense attorney Pitaro.

Things didn't begin all at once. They had gotten through the final day of the defense's case with just one minor flare-up. When they tangled over a procedural issue, Bonaventure griped: "I guess whatever Mr. Pitaro says goes. I guess he's running this courtroom."

The situation then deteriorated when Pitaro said he would have to call additional witnesses if the judge allowed prosecutors to call a rebuttal witness the defense didn't like. Bonaventure blew his top, apparently seeing this as a defense threat to prolong the trial.

"I don't care if this case goes on another month!" the judge stormed. "Don't threaten me!"

The judge called a recess, and as he marched off the bench, Pitaro asked to speak some more. "No, not now," the judge replied.

But after a break, Pitaro did get to speak his mind. He came into the courtroom to launch a formal complaint against the judge.

"I believe the conduct of the court has crossed the line," Pitaro said. "The court has continually, during the examination by defense attorneys, belittled, made snide comments, made comments on the questioning we are doing. You do it in front of the jury. . . . I do not believe that you are treating the attorneys with courtesy and dignity; and I think, unfortunately, it is reflecting on this jury with the way it is unfair towards the defendant, Mrs. Rudin. It's her trial."

Pitaro complained that the judge had made remarks in front of the jury suggesting that it was the defense's fault that the trial was lasting so long.

"We've known each other a lot of years," said Pitaro. "But you charged me with the responsibility to represent this woman. Maybe you don't mean it, and I'm sure, in the bottom of your heart, you don't, but Judge, it's got to the point—you can't say it in front of the jury every day, every witness, to make comments—and they are snide remarks."

He added: "I don't mind getting yelled at. That doesn't bother me. I've been yelled at all my life, and I can yell as loud as I get yelled at. And I don't mean any disrespect to you as the court or as an individual, but you can't do that with every witness to us."

Pitaro said the problem has gone on so long "it's now becoming a joke, and I don't like being the recipient of that joke because of her. I can take care of myself. My problem is in this courtroom, Judge, I have to take care of her.

"I say it with all the respect and humility and love I have for you: Don't do it."

The judge asked if a prosecutor wanted to say anything. Owens did.

"I've been here the whole time as well," he said. "I haven't—I don't share his opinion of the court's comments. I think a lot of what the court has done has been responding to yelling that's come from the defendant's attorneys in this case. Mr. Pitaro talks about snide comments. I think the person that's injected more snide comments and personal attacks in this record than anyone has been Mr. Pitaro. He has treated the court like some kind of a playground and kind of like a bully strutting around baiting everybody. That's my personal opinion. It's been a long trial. I think it's been uncomfortable personally for many of us here. I don't agree with what he's saying about the court."

"All right," the judge said. "I don't want to belabor this. . . . I have a responsibility as you do, Mr. Pitaro. You have a responsibility to your client. I have a responsibility to keep this case going along. I think any time I did raise my voice, it was always outside the presence of the jury. I don't want this case to disintegrate."

He paused, then made a thinly veiled reference to the O. J. Simpson trial. "There was a famous case in California that I think the judge took a back seat, like you would like me to take a back seat, and that case went on for nine months, and it was a travesty of justice in this court's opinion," he said. "I'm not going to take a back seat to defense counsels or to the state. I'm going to exercise my discretion as a judge.

"I've been a judge for twenty-two years and I'm not going to stop now."

He ordered that the trial resume. The testimony never quite measured up to what was going on between the courtroom players. The defense would call for yet another mistrial, this time on the grounds that the prosecution had withheld evidence that witness Bruce Hornabach, the antiques picker, may have lied when he said he sold Margaret an antique trunk similar to the one whose parts were found out at Nelson's Landing. Rather than grant the mistrial, the judge allowed the defense to call more witnesses to try to discredit Hornabach. Dealer Donald Schaupeter, whom Hornabach identified as his trunk supplier, said that he never sold it to him.

It was a small victory for the defense, but the final day of testimony was more important for that side of the courtroom because of a special visitor. Over the course of the trial, few people came to support Margaret. Some who otherwise would have, including sister Barbara LePome, were on the witness list and barred from attending (though Barbara was never called). On the final day, though, Margaret's daughter Kristina Mason was on hand. They exchanged smiles. As her daughter walked out of the court, Margaret said, "See you later, love you."

On April 24, both sides had called their final witnesses. It would soon be time for summations, then deliberations. The circus was about to fold its tent. Margaret was feeling good about things. She told a reporter that she was already planning her victory party.

33

DISHONOR IN THE COURT

On April 25, 2001, the longest day of the trial, attorneys gave their closing arguments. It began with the prosecution's presentation. Gary Guymon got the honors. Over three hours, he carefully led jurors through the prosecution's case, from the day Ron disappeared to Margaret's capture in Revere, Massachusetts, and everything in between, including Margaret's bugging of Ron's office. Guymon argued that the prosecution had easily proven the wiretapping count; the question was the murder charge. He said it was a question that Ron himself had answered. "Ron Rudin believed Margaret Rudin may kill him some day," said Guymon. "Ron Rudin was right."

Guymon concluded that Margaret Rudin did willfully and with premeditation kill her husband. "I submit to you when a person willfully aims the gun at a person's head, within a foot or feet from their head and deliberately pull the trigger, figure the fact this man dies they might inherit 60 percent of $11 million, and they premeditatedly and deliberately pull that trigger boom, boom, boom, boom, and take Ron Rudin's life and then stuff him in a box and burn him, that they too will be held accountable for their actions," he said. "The facts and circumstances in this case mandates a guilty verdict of first-degree murder with use of a deadly weapon. I thank you for your time."

After lunch break, the jury returned at 2:15 p.m. for Amador's remarks.

It should have been a tip-off that bad things were going to happen when Amador couldn't figure out how to operate the computerized evidence presentation system, the same problem he'd had with his opening statement. "I apologize," he said, mumbling something about how he had practiced it earlier and how his "computer guy" just got there and was trying to get it to work.

"The miracle of modern technology," Amador said. "Thank you, Your Honor, I appreciate the time that you provided. If it pleases the court, ladies and gentlemen of the jury, counsel, Margaret, John: The truth, ladies and gentlemen of the jury, the truth is that Margaret Rudin is innocent. It is also the truth that the state, as in every area of this case, failed to present any credible, relevant evidence that could lead any juror to believe that she committed any of the crimes alleged by the state of Nevada."

Amador then gave a highly detailed explanation of Ron Rudin's real estate transactions, so detailed that the summation went beyond the allotted 30 minutes, to an hour, then nearly two hours. Amador veered into other areas, talking about the evidence at the crime scene, about Sue Lyles, about the shortcomings of the police investigation, about the character of the prosecution witnesses. "If you looked into their eyes as they testified, these people had no souls," he said.

And on it went, history repeating itself, the summation dancing around from one topic to another the way the opening statement had. Jurors finally stopped taking notes. Amador ended by saying, "We do what we have to do, don't we? We do what we have to do sometimes to finish a cause, no matter what it takes. Never give up, no matter what. I always used to say that, never give up no matter what."

Then, his voice breaking, he pointed to Margaret.

"I'm humbled, I'm humbled by Margaret Rudin," he said. "Look at her. She's never given up. She fought the biggest, most powerful people in this county by herself. She had everything taken from her, stolen from her, from life, her grandchildren, her family, her home, everything she had and she never gave up. And I'm humbled by her strength."

The jury was sent out. The judge went bananas.

"This court feels you sandbagged the court, Mr. Amador," Bonaventure said. "You sandbagged me, you lied to me, you lied to the D.A."

The judge said Amador had promised to go only 30 minutes and only focus on the financial material, but instead strayed into other arguments. "Am I to limit now Mr. Pitaro from not going into these arguments?"

"Can I make a record on it, Judge?" Amador asked.

"Did you or did you not tell me you were going to limit the arguments to about 30 minutes and just to the trustees?"

"No, I didn't say that."

"You never told me that?"

"No, I didn't say that."

"I don't want to bother with you," the judge said. "I don't even want to bother with you."

The judge would later show Amador a transcript of a meeting in which the attorney did in fact agree to limit his remarks to 30 minutes.

"Regardless of the outcome of this case, and I don't care how it ends up, you, Mr. Amador, have lost this court's respect and believability," Bonaventure said, "and, most important, due to your constant misstatements of facts you have lost all honor before this court."

As angry as he was, the judge didn't take it out on Pitaro, giving him all the time he needed. Pitaro presented a thorough, well-structured summation that hit all the defense notes. The police honed in on Margaret at the exclusion of other good leads. Key prosecution witnesses shaded their testimony to get the reward money. How, he asked, could Augustine Lovato find blood in a room that had already been inspected by a missing persons detective? The physical evidence didn't add up to Ron being murdered in the bedroom. Margaret's demeanor after Ron's disappearance was misinterpreted by strangers. Margaret, he said, was under siege, deprived of money, car, home, doing what she had to do. "She is a woman now surrounded by vultures," he said. "She was trying to survive." That, he said, helped explain why she fled.

His summation neared its close with a nod to Margaret. While he wasn't humbled by Margaret, Pitaro did call her a "good and decent woman."

"She's a nice lady. She loved her husband and in his way he loved her," he said.

He reminded jurors of their serious undertaking, saying, "The decision you make is one that Margaret Rudin has to carry with her the rest of her life." He said that after nine weeks of trial, "the state did not meet its burden under the laws of the state of Nevada.

"The state of Nevada did not prove Margaret Rudin guilty of the offenses of which she's charged, they did not prove each and every element beyond a reasonable doubt. Because of that, you must enter verdicts of not guilty."

It was left to Owens to have the last word, rebutting the arguments by Amador and Pitaro. He lashed out at "smoke and mirrors" tactics by the defense and asserted that the defense proved nothing with all its evidence about land deals. Mocking Amador, Owens said he was not humbled by Margaret Rudin. Far from it. "Margaret Rudin won't take any responsibility. It's just everybody else's fault. And this defines her life and everything that we've learned about her in this case," he said. "This is a woman that has ice water in her veins."

It was nearly 10 p.m. when the bleary-eyed jurors and alternates who had listened to 10 hours of gabbing lawyers were sent home. They were told to return the next day to choose a foreman and begin deliberations.

But before they left, there was one little matter to clear up. Nobody gave it much thought at the time. One of the jurors, a woman identified only as Juror November 11, had caused a bit of a disturbance at the Golden Nugget Hotel, where jurors had their meal breaks, when she apparently started yelling because she couldn't smoke. The judge asked her if she still wanted to serve on the jury, and she said, "Absolutely." He also elicited a promise that there would be "no more dissension" at the Golden Nugget.

Neither the state nor the defense wanted to be heard on the issue. But that wouldn't be the last time they would hear about Juror Number 11.

34

LUCK BE A LADY JUROR?

Deliberations began Thursday, April 26, with jurors selecting a foreman, a retired Navy man who taught special education. He almost didn't survive the trial, having asked the judge to be excused in the third week because his students were going through too many substitute teachers. "They're eating them up and spitting them out," he said. But the juror agreed to stay on the panel out of civic duty.

Almost immediately, Margaret got good news. Late the first day of deliberations the jury sent a note to the judge asking if the panel had to follow the law on the wiretapping count, or if they could engage in what the note called "jury negation." A hearing was set for the next day, but then canceled after jurors said they had resolved the issue. The panel put in a full day's worth of deliberations before retiring for the weekend.

The following Monday, the trial that couldn't get any stranger just did. It turned out that on Saturday, Juror Number 11, the same one who'd caused a stir over her smoking, called an alternate juror and said, "I don't believe the state has proven its case," according to the alternate. Prosecutors called for the ouster of the middle-aged nurse, contending that she'd committed misconduct by violating the judge's admonition and discussed the case outside the jury room. The defense called for yet another mistrial, suggesting that the smoking incident was the reason for the phone call. Pitaro said the juror likely felt wrongly accused, then intimidated by the other jurors. But the judge denied both the mistrial request and the removal of the juror, saying, "this court is satisfied that this incident will not contaminate either the verdict or the jury deliberations." Deliberations were ordered to continue.

But while the judge didn't see any potential for contamination in the jury room, the courtroom was another story. In the hearing to discuss the juror, the judge, still angry over Amador's summation, refused to let Amador talk to him directly, forcing him to relay his comments through Pitaro. "I don't want him addressing me. I don't trust him," the judge said. Amador, also still stinging over the rebuke during summations, fought back against the judge, filing an affidavit saying he had warned the judge that he might exceed his 30-minute limit. "The court's lack of candor in this regard was yet another attempt by this court to ridicule the defense," the lawyer wrote, including a threat to take the matter to the state's judicial disciplinary commission. Margaret sided with her attorney, writing a note about the judge's comments during the trial. "These opinions, often expressed in anger, with loud, explosive tones in his voice, could not help taint the jurors," she wrote. "I expressed this at our defense team's prior request for a mistrial."

The judge's hopes for harmony in the jury room proved as overly optimistic as his prediction that the trial would last four weeks.

Day Four of deliberations brought the case to the brink of chaos. The foreman had sent two notes to the judge regarding the smoking juror:

At 8:15 this morning in the parking garage, Juror #11 informed me that she is changing her mind concerning her vote from yesterday. On 4-30-01 we voted and decided that, as to Count III of the indictment, Margaret Rudin was guilty of accessory to murder. Today she has recanted, and refused to change her mind. She has told us that she will vote not guilty from here on out.

P.S. Last week Juror #11 became very emotional

when she recalled a time when her police husband held a gun to her head. He was found not guilty in a court, and she remains bitter. It is unclear if she divulged this information in her 2-07-01 questionnaire.

In a second note, the foreman wrote:

Your Honor, I feel as though it is my obligation and duty as Jury Foreman to inform the court of my observations. Juror #11, I feel, is under severe distress due to the fact that:

1) She has lost her job because of this trial's length;
2) She has had an altercation with our bailiff, Hank;
3) There was a time, when attempting to discuss the evidence of this case, Juror #11 refused to listen or read the jury instructions that apply;
4) When trying to extract her thoughts, at one point she refused to answer and glared at me;
5) She admitted to all of us that she had preconceived expectations as to what the prosecution needed to prove to convince her of Margaret's guilt (this is inconsistent with the court's desire to keep an open mind);
6) She openly wept after we reached a minimum verdict on Count Two of the indictment. We're working our way up the ladder.

I believe that the above facts CLEARLY show why Juror #11 needs to be excused from her duties as a juror in this case.

Respectfully.

P.S. We have reached a verdict on Count One of the indictment.

P.S.S. At one point, Juror #11 said that "this could cost Margaret her life." Once again, Juror #11 has ignored the courts' instructions. We were supposed to only be concerned with innocence or guilt; not the penalty phase. Juror #11 isn't thinking clearly, rationally or logically. Please help!

To defend herself, Juror Number 11 also sent her own note to the judge:

It is my understanding that the jury foreman in this case felt both obligated and justified to question my ability to reach a fair and impartial verdict in this case.

With that in mind, I must go on record as saying that despite the fact that my decision was not an easy one, it was one I did NOT take lightly. The fact that my decision is not in alliance with my fellow jurors should never compromise my right as a juror.

I assure the court and your Honor that I have reviewed ALL of the evidence and read and re-read the court's instructions as given to the jury. My decision is based solely on the evidence presented and the instructions set forth by the court.

Sincerely,
Juror #11

There was now as much discontent among jurors as there was among the judge and defense lawyers. Deliberations were suspended, and the lawyers and judge tried to hash out a solution in a hearing. Tempers flared. At one point, prosecutor Owens called Pitaro a "jerk."

Juror number 11 was brought into court and questioned by the judge, who seemed most concerned about the fact that she'd failed to bring up the gun incident during jury selection, when she said she had never been the victim of a crime. But in the courtroom, she said she hadn't lied because her estranged husband had actually held the gun to his own head, not hers, and that she therefore didn't consider herself the victim of a crime.

For the defense, this was the dream juror. Margaret was looking at the mistrial she had sought so many times—or a hung jury, or even a conviction on the lesser charge of accessory, with a minimum term of a year in prison—a term Margaret had already served in jail. In the hearing, Pitaro said that tense deliberations were common and that "this foreman is out of line. He should be removed." Owens countered that the juror was unstable and had to go.

In the end, the judge again agreed to keep her on the panel, and deliberations resumed the following day, which would bring an even bigger surprise.

The panel had reached a verdict.

35

THE VERDICT

On Wednesday, May 2, 2001—six-and-a-half years after Ron Rudin failed to show up for work that Monday morning—many of the people who had played such a significant role in his life and death gathered in Judge Joseph Bonaventure's chambers. Among those on hand were Detective Ramos and Ron's ex-wife Caralynne. Ron's relatives would be watching the proceedings on Court TV. Also in the courtroom was Margaret's daughter, Kristina. With so much going on in the jury room, nobody knew just what to expect. But the fact that this jury, so fractured, could resolve its difference so quickly seemed nothing short of amazing.

For the reading of the verdict, Margaret stood at the defense table. She was smartly dressed in a dark blazer and burgundy turtleneck. Her ash-blond hair was neatly styled. To her right was Amador, to her left were John Momot and Pitaro. She looked directly at the foreman, a burly man. Her lips were pursed tightly.

The foreman read the verdict. For count one, unauthorized surreptitious intrusion of privacy by listening device—guilty.

Margaret blinked a couple of times, but otherwise didn't move.

For count two, murder—guilty.

This time she didn't even blink. She didn't flinch. She showed no emotion whatsoever.

Ramos would later remark that this was exactly how she'd looked when he first informed her that her husband had been murdered.

The clerk polled the jury. Tensions rose. Juror number 11 was crying.

"Juror Number 11, is this your verdict as read?" the clerk asked.

There was a pause.

After swallowing, the juror said, "Yes."

In tears, she mouthed to Margaret, "I'm sorry."

36

THE DOOR SLAMS

Leave it to the Rudin case, so strange before and during trial, to remain so afterwards. To the surprise of almost nobody, Juror number 11 said in an interview afterwards that she had been bullied into her vote. "They called me an idiot and irrational," the juror, who identified herself as Coreen Crovacs, told KLAS-TV.

But the jury foreman, who would reveal his name as Ronald Vest, insisted that no undue pressure was placed on her. "We didn't bribe her or threaten her. She came to this on her own." Calling the evidence against Margaret "overwhelming," Vest told reporters that the panel found 97 reasons pointing toward her guilt, and that they would have voted to convict on the first day of deliberations had it not been for the one holdout. Jurors were particularly swayed by the murder weapon being traced back to Ron's collection. The jury's list of possible people with access to that gun included only Margaret and Yehuda. The directive that Ron wrote also played into their decision, the foreman said. As for the defense case, he called it a waste. "I didn't buy any of it. I don't think any of us bought any of the defense case," he said. Amador, he said, "was bordering on incompetence."

Amador, meanwhile, showed no grace in defeat. Outside court, he said of the prosecutors, "They make me sick." Of the judge, he said, "I don't have much respect for Judge Bonaventure, nor do I have much respect for his opinion." He even blasted Pitaro and Momot, saying, "I would've put on a whole different defense instead of the *Reader's Digest* version that my co-counsel did when they were pressured to end the trial by the judge."

But it was Bonaventure who said it best. In his final remarks as he dismissed the jury, the judge thanked prosecutors Owens and Guymon and defense attorneys Pitaro and Momot. He pointedly left out Amador's name. "As to perceived problems with counsel," the judge said, "I find that well-timed silence has more eloquence than speech." He did offer this quotation: "Watch your thoughts. They become words. Watch your words. They become actions. Watch your actions. They become habits. Watch your habits. They become character. Watch your character. It becomes your destiny."

Amador would quickly find out what his destiny was. The woman who so humbled him with her strength would humble him anew. Always the writer, Margaret gave him the news in a letter:

Dear Michael Amador,

This is to inform you I no longer wish for you to represent me in a court of law, as a spokesperson to the media or to contact me personally. Please relay any messages to me through my friends Debby and Judy or thru Misters Pitaro, Momot, Wysocki; or Dillard.

Twice during the past two weeks I told them your actions and behavior greatly concerned me, I had reason to believe you are using drugs. They advised me that our priority should be getting through my trial with a united front. Once again I was greatly concerned but optimistic, I followed their advise but wrote you a long letter expressing all my concerns and requesting the return of my legal and personal possessions which I've been requesting since the first of the year. You ignored both my letter and my request.

You received notice that juror misconduct was present again and should have notified the judge immediately on 5-1 so he could confirm the report. You did not present it to the judge until late in the morning of 5-2; by that time it was too late, the jury had reached a verdict and Judge Bonaventure did not address the issue of juror #11 which could have finally resulted in his calling for a mistrial.

Your treatment toward my daughter during the past two days is inexcusable. At my request she asked for all my things; held by you in your office and residence to be given to her, but once again my wishes were ignored by you.

There are many more complaints I will address through the proper channels because your defiant personality and continuance of pursuing media attention is noted but will no longer be ignored by me.

Sincerely
Margaret Rudin

This was among several letters Margaret released to the judge. In another, written during the trial to Amador, she raised concerns that he had plans to sign a deal to write a book, which would be made into a movie with either Richard Gere or Andy Garcia playing him. She said she had signed three contracts with him, the third featuring a promise by her to pay Amador $250,000 if she ever got the money. She didn't know if she had voided the first two contracts.

In a surreal post-trial hearing, Margaret appeared before Bonaventure on May 9, 2001. This was no longer the steely Margaret of verdict day a week earlier. She burst into tears and made nearly incoherent remarks about how Amador wouldn't reveal to the jury that mobsters had killed Ron. Amador seemed taken aback. Under questioning by the judge—who was now speaking to him—Amador defended himself against a list of allegations. Among his claims were that unspecified people were out to get him.

"Mr. Amador, nobody's trying to get you. I think you're paranoid," the judge said. "Don't blame the state. Don't blame me. Miss Rudin made these allegations. That's why we're here."

Amador denied that he was planning to strike a book

or movie deal. The judge said that if he did, the county
should be reimbursed for some of the costs of the defense.

The judge also took up Margaret's allegations that
Amador was taking drugs.

"I don't use drugs," the attorney said.

"Are you under any prescription medication?" Bonaventure asked.

Just for allergies, said Amador.

Amador filed papers removing himself from the case,
but Margaret had beaten him to it by firing him. The lawyer then blamed the media for the bad things said about
him. He would claim he was "baited" into criticizing his
co-counsel. And he insisted that the trial would not hurt
his career.

"In six months," he said, "nobody will remember anything but my name."

In the shopping mall where Ron had spent so many years,
the drama that had surrounded his life and death was gone
and the place became a lot quieter—though not for long.
Margaret's shop, Antique Merchants, was converted to an
adult bookstore called Hot Stuff video, which drew the
ire of city officials who wanted it shut down. The store's
owners went to federal court, and on April 26, 2001—the
first day of deliberations in the Rudin trial—the owners
lost their appeal.

The offices of Ron Rudin Realty and Construction,
meanwhile, became a check-cashing company called
Payday-N-Advance. Across the hall, Jerry Stump still cut
hair in his cozy three-chair barbershop. He had been interviewed by a defense investigator and for a time there
was talk that he would be called as a witness for Margaret,
which made no sense to him. "I would have hung her,"
he said.

On verdict day, Jerry and two other barbers, along with
four or five customers, watched the local news on the
shop's TV set and saw Margaret getting convicted. A
cheer went up in the West Hill Barber Shop, a cheer they

hoped that Ron could hear. The conviction at last fulfilled the wishes of his directive. But otherwise he would've been uncomfortable with how the whole thing played out. "Ron," Jerry noted, "never did like the publicity."

Margaret Rudin, who had gone through so many husbands and so many lawyers, was assigned yet another new lawyer, this one from the public defender's office, to handle her post-trial matters, including a motion for a new trial.

The motion was 64 pages long with three affidavits from people who once were in Amador's inner circle. It was the legal equivalent of a public stoning. While the motion did cite judicial error and prosecution misconduct as among the grounds for a new trial, it was the performance of Amador that got the fiercest pummeling. "Mr. Amador's representation in this matter was constitutionally, legally, and ethically ineffective," the motion said— and watch it count the ways. An affidavit filed by his former assistant, Annie Jackson, presented a devastating portrait of the workings of his law offices. She alleged that he barely paid any attention to the case before trial, spending one entire month in France and Italy with his then-wife when he could have been preparing. He only got interested when the news program *48 Hours* got interested. And even then, TV, and not casework, took precedent. When the jail let Margaret out for special supervised visits to Amador's office, ostensibly to provide a better work environment, Amador instead used the occasions for interviews. Once, the show's crew knocked out the office's electricity by mistake, and Jackson's computer lost an entire motion she was helping Amador prepare. "It was," she said, "a nightmare."

Shortly before the trial began, Amador's love life went to pot and suddenly he was without his wife/paralegal Lisa Nowak and her mother, the receptionist. Now, Jackson was running the office herself and helping Amador with the paperwork. She said he wrote his opening statement the night before he delivered it, then, with Jackson's help, re-wrote the whole thing in an hour-and-a-half during a lunch break right before he stood in front of the jury. "The product of this time speaks for itself," she said. But then the grunt work had never seemed to interest Amador, Jackson claimed. Motions would be prepared an hour before they were due. "The office staff started calling Mr. Amador 'the last-minute man,' " the affidavit said.

Then there were the strippers. "Mr. Amador informed me, and this was during much of the trial itself, that he spent most of his evenings at strip bars, and in the company of strippers," she said. "In fact, on many occasions, Mr. Amador was bragging about the many strippers he was dating." The strippers started calling the office and even stopping by during business hours. Jackson saw Amador allow one stripper to go through the Margaret Rudin file.

At one point, he abruptly moved into the Four Queens Hotel on Fremont Street, and brought all his files with him, creating a filing fiasco. The other lawyers went through hell trying to find stuff, and eventually all the non–real estate files were transferred to Pitaro's office.

Finally, Jackson said, Amador lied about not having any book or movie deals in the works. She said that when the issue arose after the trial, he grabbed all the media contracts so he could put them in a little safe in the back closet. He also kept a number of files and some of Margaret's personal belongings—so, Jackson claimed, "Mr. Amador could use [them] in a movie or a book. He told Margaret Rudin he lost them because he did not want to return them."

In separate affidavits, Pitaro and private investigator Tim Dillard also rattled off Amador's alleged shortcomings, repeating many of the claims made during the mistrial conference early in the trial. The main one was lack of preparation: witnesses were poorly interviewed or not interviewed at all. What's more, Pitaro said, the defense opening statement was a mess. "It presented no cohesive theory of the defense save that and except that Ron Rudin committed real estate fraud," it said. Pitaro blasted Amador's professional behavior, saying he was often late to court. Pitaro didn't opine on why Amador did this, and Pitaro made no reference to possible drug use—though Jackson's affidavit said that after the mistrial motion was denied, "Rumors then started to surface about Mr. Amador's drug use, and Mr. Amador denied any such problem." She noted that he would regularly ask her every Friday for a $500 check or $500 in cash. A month into the trial, "the amounts Mr. Amador was requesting in cash increased dramatically," she said. What she suspected he did with this cash she didn't say.

Amador denied all of this. He called himself incredibly well prepared. He questioned the motives of his former colleagues, suggesting that they would say anything to get Margaret a new trial and he wouldn't be part of that. He noted that Margaret had a history of going through lawyers and trashing them afterwards: Amador himself had tried to make an issue of Margaret's relationship with her former divorce lawyer—now District Attorney—Stewart Bell. And as for the allegations of drug use, Amador didn't just deny it, he provided what he called proof that he was drug-free, releasing to the public the results of a lab test showing that in May of 2001 the urine of Michael J. Amador, Esq., was devoid of amphetamines, barbiturates, cocaine, opiates, PCP, marijuana and alcohol.

Margaret, meanwhile, bided her time in her cell in the Clark County Detention Center, awaiting sentencing of a term of up to 20 years to life, which raised the very real possibility that she would die in prison. She filed her own affidavit in support of a new trial, complaining, "My defense team was not prepared for trial." She told anybody who would listen that many of the problems in her case were Amador's fault, this split between them as bitter as any of her divorces.

One of Margaret's many post-trial interviews was with Court TV, both on camera and with the network's Internet audience. On May 31, 2001, Margaret engaged in an on-line chat with Court TV, which introduced her as "a very special guest, convicted murderer Margaret Rudin." One exchange would have been peculiar in any other case, but was par for the course in this one. The comments came from a man claiming to be one of Margaret's four living ex-husbands. He got on-line and wished her a happy birth-day; she had turned 58 that day. "Oh my God," Margaret replied, "I'm so touched. Thank you with all my heart. I'm going to cry." The man identified himself as "Walt Z.," a name that doesn't pop up in the many divorce pa-pers. Could this be the mysterious husband No. 3, or a pseudonym for one of the other living ex-husbands? Nei-ther he nor Margaret would say. Margaret felt he was legit. He did, after all, know it was her birthday.

Margaret chatted some more, but—as with other media interviews—she steered clear of the specifics. No expla-nation for the blood in the bedroom. No comments on who she thought really killed her fifth husband. She ac-knowledged that there was still much left unsaid about her side of the case, but she wouldn't say it until the next trial. She was certain there would be a next trial. And the tumultuous events from her first trial offered ample op-portunity for a new day in court—another scene in the production that is Margaret's life.

AFTERWORD

On Friday, Aug. 31, 2001, Judge Bonaventure denied a new trial for Margaret Rudin and sentenced her to a minimum of 20 years in prison for killing her husband. Attorneys said they would appeal.

That same day, in the same courthouse, Michael Amador filled out an application for a license to marry Maggie Mabie, a California woman who fell in love with him when she saw him on Court TV.

APPENDIX: LISTENING LOGS

Here are excerpts from what prosecutors said were Margaret's listening logs, from June to November of 1994, ending just weeks before Ron's disappearance.

The logs began with Ron talking tough to one of his friends and tenants, Gene DeFlorentis, a gun dealer, now deceased. Margaret used her own little abbreviations—"R" for Ron, "@" for about, "M" for Margaret.

> 6-8-94
>   R. and Gene D. talking @ criminal back on street and shooting to kill, @ them breaking into Gene's store.

The next few days, Margaret wrote about Ron calling a travel agent for a trip to the Mayo Clinic the following month. There were also notes about Ron's schedule—he planned to spend Father's Day up at Cold Creek, along with conversations about the mundane business of buying and selling fixer-upper real estate.

By mid-June, Margaret expressed surprise that Ron was talking about installing another security system at the office and house without telling her.

> They came over for preinspection when I wasn't home and will do the installation while I'm @ work I guess.

Then, Margaret jotted down two entries about Ron sweet-talking ladies. Margaret first thought one of them was a Sue, but then reconsidered, crossing out Sue's name.

6-17-94 Noon.

Ron was his flirty "up" self—rec'd call from Sue [line through name]. One hour ahead time zone they said—so it was probably New Mexico (the woman there calls periodically).

7-7-94

R. is talking to a woman at National Title and he says, "I'll take you to Europe w/ me next time I go. Are you married?" and he goes on and on about how great Europe is, yet when we were there he complained constantly @ *everything!*

But Ron could turn on women, Margaret observed a week later in recounting a conversation between Ron and Ollie Grinfelds, and another between Ron and bookkeeper Sharon Melton. Ron used a favorite term, *dissident*, which Margaret spelled "dissadent."

7-14-94 (Thur.)

R. told Oli, "M is a tramp, just a tramp, what more can I tell you about her that's nice. She doesn't care about that car.

Yesterday, he told Sharon I was always running out of gas in my car and that Danner is "nothing, nothing but a disadent." He acts like Dr. Jeckly [sic] and Mr. Hyde to everyone's face and their worst enemy to their back.)

In early August, Margaret recorded a conversation showing the foul-mouthed side of Ron, as he denigrates somebody named Peter in a conversation with a man named Ed. He also had it in for an insurance agent named Sara.

8-3-94

He made fun of Peter (R. said, "He's a whiner, a bitcher and a negative son of a bitch. Can you imagine him slobbering all over you, that would be a turn off against sex for any woman? He doesn't have any brains, he'll not call, he doesn't want to work! I'll take 4 For Sale signs up. Fuck that guy who wants to pay 9% interest on my lot, let him keep pickin his fuckin nose, there's no more fuckin' lots in this county. Lot 156 is $17,500 and it should move right away.

8-4-94
   Sara @ 9:30. Insur. Agent
   Sharon and Ron talk terrible @ Sara, she's old and incompetent.

That Saturday, Ron was back to sweet-talking a woman in a discussion about his Cold Creek properties.

Sat. 8-6-94
   R. talking to *a woman*? tell a long, sad story to her @ C.C. costing him millions and he said he would rather die than go back up there to sell the lots but he can't get anyone to sell all they are interested in is the $. He puts on his sexy voice and says "it's been nice talking to you."

September brought office turnover, with a new "girl"— a secretary, as Margaret saw Ron's lousy personality alienated people.

9-13-94
   I wonder how long this new girl will last because in 1988–89 he had 24 girls coming and going constantly, quitting or being fired in one year. He's so difficult and moody and phoney and a perfectionist and unrealistically critical of everyone that he's impossible to work for in the office. He just bought _____ Pecos Way, a condo off D.I.

Margaret didn't have the address for that condo, but noted in the margins that it was off Desert Inn. This was

apparently the same condo where Ron and Sue Lyles
would meet that Saturday before his disappearance.

A few days after this September log entry, Margaret
was still thinking about Ron's moods, finding parallels
between her life and that of the victim of a murder case
that had been gripping the nation that year.

9-14-94
    A TV program w/ Nicole Simpson's therapist said
the hard side of men who abuse their partner does not
show up until they are in a relationship then their *dark*
side comes out. The hot beginning changes and they
blame their partner for the change and take it out, emotionally and/or physically on the woman in their life if
and when she dares to disappoint them. (It really
touched me as I walk on egg shells all the time).

Ron spent September 18 at Cold Creek with his secretary and another man . . .

    . . . even though he says this is the last week he'll
advertise this year and he has had no results from his
needed ego-boosting ads that cost several thousand
dollars a month. He won't be up there alone because
he's so afraid of the "hardcore dissidents" as he calls
all the owners up there.

The next month, Ron has it in for women again. This
log was made from a conversation between Ron and Harold Boscutti, according to Margaret's notes.

10-13-94
10:20 AM
    R. tells him to put a machine gun on his desk with
the plate filled on his desktop pointed at the entrance
and shoot the next fuckin' woman that walks in.

A couple of days later, Margaret recorded this conversation between Ron and Sharon, in which Ron complained

about his Hispanic housecleaner, then things switched to Sharon getting mad again about Margaret's antique store, which Sharon called a mini-mall.

10-15-94

R. goes in to Sharon and tells her I let that fuckin' Mexican use his T-shirts as rags and it's all my fault. I should watch her better. He said it's just like Stella I do everything to upset him.

Again, five days later, the antique shop grated on Sharon. Ron made reference to the bar he once owned in the shopping center—and an ill-fated effort to bring in topless dancers as entertainment.

Thur
9:30 AM
10-20-94

R. and Sharon discuss my minimall. Sh. Asks all kinds of questions and he answers evasivelly. Thank goodness he walks out of his office and into Vicky's office to end their conversation. Sh. Returns to her office to see if she closed out the McIlanine Act. already. Sh. Told him he should put in the topless bar instead of my minimall and he said, "I've already done that. It was so rank. Nothing but fights and drugs."

That same day, Margaret recorded a conversation between Ron and a woman at National Title whose name Margaret apparently didn't know, because she left it blank on the page. Sue Lyles would later tell authorities that she used to say she was from National Title in phone calls to Ron.

10-25
12:15 PM

R. called national Title and said to _____ that he wishes he could make her day better by just talking to her and that he wishes he was in a hotel room with someone special and his day would be going much better than it is.

R. called national Title back and said are you closed Mon. for Admissions Day (yes) He said, "I need to work, I don't have anything to do on a day off so I'll be here working even though it's a holiday."

By the end of the week, Ron was in a terrible mood.

10:50 AM
Fri
10-29-94
R. is down on the world *again* today. He's miserable and nothing is right.

By early November, though, Ron's spirits had improved, thanks to a woman at National Title—only to have to face the now-routine problems with Sharon over the antique store and Danner over his poor work habits.

11-2
9 AM
R. calls Nat. Title and says, "Hi sweetheart do you miss me? Good. I gues I'd better talk to Donna." To whom ever answered the phone.

Margaret sensed trouble between Ron and Sue, only to see a rebound later that day.

11-4
4:10 p.m.
Sue Lyles *called* R. and he was cool with her and complained @ his bad week of dealing w/ contractors for my shop and he put her on hold quite a long time while he talked w/ Suzanne @ L.C. and then his apt. with glass contractor came in and he cut her real short and said, "If your'e out and about tomorrow—you

dind't work today, did you, then give me a call." And
he cut her real short and no affection at all in his voice.
No flirty tone means she is on her way out . . .

4:45
R. called Nat. Title and told the girl answ. Phone,
"Hi, traveling companion, you sure looked sexy today"
and then did his sexy voice with Andrea too. I know
the difference in his methods, intent and voices.

On Saturday, Ron was in the office, talking again to
Sue, when Margaret picked up the phone and called him.

Sat. 11-5-94
3:40 PM
Sue calls Ron, he talks again like a distant friend
to her—R. asks where her husband is this afternoon
and he says tell him you have a husband to support.
R. tells her he's had a lot of women in his life who
put their families first and it's not unusual in the real
world—I've been thru this—it happens a lot. It's fan-
tasy to think otherwise.
I called him. He put her on hold and told me he
was interviewing a carpenter on the phone and said let
him wait while I talked to him then after a long talk
said to me let me, let him go and went back to her and
said, "I've got to go, the other call is Margaret. Call
me sometime." He again was not flirty nor friendly.

By the following Tuesday, Ron was a regular grump:

8:15 AM
11-8-94
R. calls Dave and said, "Do you want me to send
overnight mail this offsite agreement, they don't want
it what about the thousands of people who need recreation land in NV.?
Then he went off on his tangent moods and com-

plained constantly @ "liberal son-of-a-bitch Democrats
and the incompetent women of Dept. of Water Re-
sources and how he tries to be nice to them but he gets
nowhere." He's down on the world and so dismal that
Dave even knew to cut the conversation short. R. said,
"I'll call you back later if I hear from Yam."

R. complained, "I'm not getting anywhere with National Title. I called down there to call me, they aren't
following up. They won't last long as a Gunfighter."

The last entry in the log, for later that morning, November 8, 1994, concerned Sue Lyles, who had just
learned that her relationship with Ron had been discovered and suggested how they could handle things when
she called the office and got the secretary.

11:40 AM
   Sue called Ron—he told her . . . not to give Jill her
right name but any time she calls to say she's Sue from
National Title, can you remember that he says. She
asked to see him and he made plans to meet her at
above address at that address and time.

Margaret wrote in the margins:

11-15-94
   11:45 AM, quarter to 12
   DI and Pecos, 327, R side.